CAE

Gold PLUS

exam maximiser

PEARSON
Longman

Elaine Boyd

Contents

Introduction to the CAE Gold Plus exam maximiser

The *CAE Gold Plus exam maximiser* is specially designed to maximise your chances of success in the Cambridge Advanced English Certificate.

The exam maximiser will help you prepare for the Cambridge Advanced exam by offering you:

- **further practice and revision** of all the important vocabulary, grammar and skills (reading, writing, listening and speaking) that you study in the *CAE Gold Plus Coursebook*

- **more information** about the kinds of questions you will have to answer in the CAE exam

- **guidance** with strategies and techniques you should use to tackle exam tasks

- **exam-style exercises** so that you can practise using the techniques

- **a complete sample exam** which you can use for practice just before you sit the exam. This means that you will know exactly what to expect in each paper and that there are no unpleasant surprises.

How can I use the *CAE Gold Plus exam maximiser?*

The **exam maximiser** is very flexible and can be used by students in a variety of situations and in a variety of ways. Here are some typical situations:

1

You are doing a CAE course with other students probably over an academic year. You are all planning to take the exam at the same time.

You are using the *CAE Gold Plus Coursebook* in class. Sometimes you will also do the related exercises or even a whole unit from the **exam maximiser** in class, though your teacher will ask you to do exercises from it at home as well. You will use the entire **exam maximiser** or you will use it selectively, depending on your needs and the time available.

2

You have already done a CAE course and you are now doing an intensive course to prepare for the exam.

Since you have already worked through the *CAE Gold Plus Coursebook* or perhaps another CAE coursebook, you will use the **exam maximiser** in class. This, together with the *CAE Practice Tests Plus New Edition*, will give you a concentrated and highly focused short exam course.

3

You have a very short period in which to prepare for the CAE exam.

Your level of English is already nearing CAE exam standard, though you have not been following a CAE coursebook. You now need exam skills. You will use the **exam maximiser** independently, because you need practice in the exam tasks and how to approach them.

4

> You are retaking the CAE exam as unfortunately you were not successful in your first attempt.

You may be having to retake the exam because you were not sufficiently familiar with the exam requirements. You will not need to follow a coursebook, but you will use the **exam maximiser** to develop your exam techniques and build up your confidence.

5

> You are preparing for the exam on your own.

Maybe you are not attending a CAE class but wish to take the exam and prepare for it independently. You will get the practice and preparation by using the **exam maximiser** by itself. You can give yourself extra practice by using the *CAE Practice Tests Plus New Edition* just before taking the exam.

What is in each unit?

Each unit in the **exam maximiser** contains **Vocabulary** sections. These practise the words and expressions which you studied in the *CAE Gold Plus Coursebook* and introduce you to some new words and expressions as well. There are plenty of exercises to do, including exam-style tasks from Paper 3 (English in Use) and crossword and wordsearch grids for a bit of fun. There are also opportunities to practise the vocabulary through Paper 5 (Speaking) tasks.

You will find two **Grammar** sections in each unit. By doing the exercises in these sections, you can practise and revise the grammar points you have studied in the *CAE Gold Plus Coursebook*. Some of the exam-style tasks focus on a particular grammar point to give you plenty of practice but in the exam each task will test a variety of structures. Once again, there are always exam-style tasks from Paper 3 (English in Use), together with **Tips** to help you complete the tasks. There are also opportunities to practise the grammar points through Paper 5 (Speaking) tasks. In these tasks, you can hear example answers by listening to the recordings of good CAE candidates performing the speaking tasks.

Every unit has a **Listening** section. These sections help you train for each of the four parts in Paper 4 (Listening). First, you read some information **about the exam** and then you are given some advice on the **strategy** you should use in that particular part. You do an exercise to help you practise the strategy and then an exam-style listening task. There is a vocabulary activity at the end of most listening sections as well, so that you can practise dealing with unfamiliar words and phrases. The tasks get more difficult as you move through the units in the **exam maximiser**, so that by the end of the book they are at the same level as the exam.

There is also a **Reading** section in each unit. Like the Listening sections, these provide you with information **about the exam** and **strategies** to use in each of the four parts of Paper 1 (Reading). You do some exercises to help you with the strategy and then you do an exam-style task. There is a vocabulary activity at the end of most reading sections as well, so that you can practise dealing with unfamiliar words and phrases. There are also some exercises asking you to think about the audience and the genre to help you identify different styles of writing. Like the listening sections, the reading sections are easier at the beginning of the book but at the level of the exam at the end.

At the end of each unit there is a **Writing** section. Once again, you are given information **about the exam** and the kinds of writing tasks you have to do in Parts 1 and 2 of Paper 2 (Writing). You are also given a **strategy** to follow and then have an opportunity to put it into practice by reading an exam-style task and doing some exercises, often using sample answers. You write your answers to these exercises in the **exam maximiser**. Finally, you write your own answer to the writing task. There is also an **Improve!** section in each unit to show you how to improve your answer and maximise your marks.

In Papers 1, 3 and 4 of the exam you have to transfer your answers to an answer sheet. Unit 14 gives you practice in filling in these answer sheets.

Once you have worked through all the units, you will be ready to try the **Practice exam** at the back of the book.

Then you'll be really well prepared for the CAE exam.

Good luck!

Exam overview

There are five papers in the CAE exam. The papers are:

Paper 1 Reading (1 hour 15 minutes)
Paper 2 Writing (1 hour 30 minutes)
Paper 3 Use of English (1 hour)
Paper 4 Listening (40 minutes)
Paper 5 Speaking (15 minutes)

Each paper receives an equal weighting of 20 percent of the marks. Your overall grade is based on the total score for all five papers. There are three passing grades, A, B and C. To pass with a grade C, you need about 60 percent of the marks.

For Papers 1, 3 and 4 you have to write your answers on a separate sheet. For Paper 2 you write your answers in the answer book.

Paper	Formats	Task focus
Reading four texts, 34 reading comprehension questions	**Part 1:** answering multiple-choice questions on three themed texts **Part 2:** choosing which paragraph fits into gaps in a text **Part 3:** answering multiple-choice questions **Part 4:** deciding which section of a single text or which text out of several contains given information or ideas	**Part 1:** reading for detail, opinion, tone, main idea, attitude, etc. **Part 2:** reading to understand text structure, cohesion and coherence **Part 3:** reading for detail, opinion, tone, main idea, attitude, etc. **Part 4:** reading for specific information, detail, opinion and attitude
Writing **Part 1:** one compulsory task **Part 2:** one task from a choice of four	**Part 1:** using given information to write an article, report, proposal or letter of 180–220 words **Part 2:** producing one piece of writing of 220–260 words from a choice of article, competition entry, contribution to a longer piece, essay, information sheet, letter, proposal, report, review	**Part 1:** selecting from and developing given information to produce a persuasive piece of writing **Part 2:** writing for a specific reader, using appropriate layout and register, using a variety of functions
Use of English five tasks, 50 questions	**Part 1:** multiple-choice cloze: choosing which word from a choice of four fits in each of 12 gaps **Part 2:** open cloze: writing the missing word in each of 15 gaps in a text **Part 3:** word formation: changing the form of the word given so that it fits into the gaps in the text **Part 4:** gapped sentences: choosing a word to fit into gaps in three different sentences **Part 5:** key word transformations: using the given key word to complete a new sentence which means the same as the given one	**Part 1:** vocabulary and lexico-grammar **Part 2:** grammar and lexico-grammar **Part 3:** vocabulary and lexico-grammar **Part 4:** vocabulary **Part 5:** vocabulary and grammar
Listening four tasks, 30 questions	**Part 1:** three short extracts, each with two multiple-choice questions **Part 2:** long text with eight gap-fill sentences **Part 3:** long text with six multiple-choice questions **Part 4:** five short texts to match to one of eight options	**Part 1:** understanding feeling, attitude, opinion, purpose, etc. **Part 2:** understanding specific information and stated opinion **Part 3:** understanding attitude and opinion **Part 4:** understanding gist, attitude, main points and context
Speaking four parts	**Part 1:** interview: the examiner asks each student questions on basic personal information **Part 2:** comparing and contrasting three pictures: each student has to speak for one minute **Part 3:** interactive task: students discuss a task together using a visual prompt **Part 4:** discussion: the examiner asks questions related to the theme of Part 3	**Part 1:** giving personal information **Part 2:** giving information and expressing opinions **Part 3:** sustaining an interaction, exchanging ideas and reaching a decision through negotiation **Part 4:** expressing and justifying opinions and ideas

Exam tips

General

- Do what you can first, then go back and do the more difficult questions.
- If you don't know an answer, guess. You don't lose marks for wrong answers.
- Remember to check your answers carefully. Check especially that you have filled in any mark sheets correctly.

Reading

- Time yourself carefully. Work out how long you have for each task and don't spend too long on one task. If you get stuck, go on and come back to the tricky questions later if you have time.
- Always read the texts through quickly first to get an idea of the organisation and topic. This will only take you a couple of minutes and will help you find the information you need to answer the questions.
- Don't read every word in a task if you don't need to. Remember, scanning is a reading skill and you will need to do this to get everything done in time.
- In Part 1 and Part 3 tasks, read the stems (the first part of the questions) very carefully. Make sure the answer you choose is correct when you match it with the stem.
- Don't be misled by 'wordspots' – where you see the same word in the text as in the questions. It may not be the answer.

Writing

- Make sure you complete all the functions you are asked for in a Part 1 task (e.g. explain, describe and recommend).
- Balance your answer so that you don't write too much on one function and not enough on another.
- Choose your Part 2 task carefully so that you can show a range of structures and vocabulary. Don't just pick the genre you are most familiar with.
- Don't write too many or too few words. Plan your writing to avoid this.
- Remember to use paragraphs and to organise your points clearly.

Listening

- Use the context you are given in the instructions and the questions to predict the outline of what you will hear.
- Use the few seconds you have before each task to scan the questions quickly so you know how what you will hear develops.
- Don't panic if you miss one answer. Listen carefully until you hear words that connect you to the next question. Remember, you hear everything twice.
- Don't be misled by 'wordspots', i.e. when you hear the same word as a word in the question. It may not be the answer.
- Don't choose an answer just because it seems right. Remember, the answer must reflect what the speaker says.

Use of English

- Read each instruction very carefully to make sure you know what you have to do. This is especially important in tasks where you need to change a word or where you must use the word you are given.
- Read any texts through quickly before you start so that you get a general idea of what they are about. This will help you choose your answers.
- Remember that collocations and fixed phrases are very important at CAE, so think carefully about where you may need to consider these, e.g. in Part 1 and Part 5.
- Check your spellings, tenses and singular/plural agreements very carefully.
- Be aware of what problems may be caused by your first language, e.g. you may find articles or prepositions difficult. Check these particularly carefully.

Speaking

- Remember normal speaking behaviour, i.e. take turns with your partner. Ask the examiner if you need him or her to repeat something.
- Always give reasons for what you say and try to use a range of language.
- Don't worry if you and your partner do not agree in Part 3 of the exam, but try to reach a conclusion, even if it is only that you disagree.

Vocabulary 1: music 1

1 Find out what these types of music are. Use your dictionary or the Internet. Match each type of music to the pictures below.

rock	pop	hip hop	heavy metal	indie
punk	rap			

2 Match the music words on the left with their meanings on the right.

1 album   a) a recording made or sold illegally

2 track   b) a professional performer

3 bootleg   c) a CD which consists of different songs or music by different people

4 artist   d) a group of songs or pieces of music on a CD

5 compilation   e) the words of a song

6 lyrics   f) a single song or piece of music on a CD

3 Put the following words into the correct gaps. Make sure the word is in the correct form.

label	plug	sign	charts	gig
distribution				

We played some really awful .... on our way up the ladder. Eventually we managed to get .... to a really good record ...., who also said they would pay for the .... of our records. Anyway, they were as good as their word and our record got heavily .... on the radio and so we managed to get to number 18 in the ....

4 Choose the correct phrasal verb in each sentence. Check the meaning of both phrasal verbs in each sentence in a good dictionary, such as *The Longman Phrasal Verbs Dictionary*.

1 I managed to *set up* / *gear up* a deal with a good distribution company.

2 Our record *got up* / *shot up* the charts as soon as it was released.

3 We've been *gearing up* / *driving up* to the release of our first record next month.

4 We've already *geared up* / *lined up* some dates for live gigs.

5 They're hoping to *put out* / *put up* a record in the spring.

rock   pop   hip hop   heavy metal   indie   punk   rap

Grammar 1: overview
▶ CB page 7

1 Correct the grammatical mistakes in these sentences. Sometimes there is more than one mistake. One sentence is correct.

1 As a singer, I was forced doing awful jobs before to hit the big time.

2 Rock bands' wealth means that the people are very jealous of them.

3 I suggested him to knock at producers' doors to get a record deal.

4 He wants that we practise the song again at the weekend.

5 I've been desperate in breaking into singing for years – now's my chance.

6 I think bands today are too similar and they all look the same as well.

7 They're very boring because, such as most boy bands, they only sing in one style.

8 He was paid millions for the copyright so he can have loads of money by now.

2 These sentences all have a mistake in word order. Correct the mistake.

1 Bigger profits will mean definitely more companies taking risks.

2 The group quite felt pleased with their success.

3 Is that the group which was voted last year the best?

4 You can be even a success without being able to sing!

5 We never must download music without paying for it.

6 The chance to be an overnight success is hardly ever offered.

3 Match the sentence beginnings with their endings.

1 I would have gone to the concert if

2 If I had a recording deal

3 I'll be going to the concert on Friday unless

4 I wish I

5 I wish he wouldn't

a) I would be in the charts by now!

b) had seen them play live.

c) get tickets without asking me.

d) I had managed to get tickets.

e) I have to work.

Listening: sentence completion (Part 2)

About the exam: In Paper 4, Part 2, you have to complete the gaps in eight sentences. The sentences always come in the same order on the recording. You may need to write one or two words. You must write ONLY the words you hear.

Strategy

1 Read through the questions. Think about what kind of words you are listening for.

2 On the second listening, check your answers.

3 Make sure your answers are grammatically correct and that there are no spelling mistakes.

1 Look through the sentences and decide which type of word (e.g. noun, adjective, etc.) should go in each gap.

2 You will hear a talk on the radio about the rise of urban music. Listen and complete the sentences.

THE MUSIC OF THE CITY

The urban scene has become a powerful **(1)** ……….. in modern music around the world.

Urban music now outsells **(2)** ……….. and has a quarter of the market.

In October 2003, the top-selling records in the **(3)** ……….. chart in the USA were all made by black artists.

In Britain a member of the royal family has presented a **(4)** ……….. of urban music.

Urban music has been popularised by major artists working with leading **(5)** ……….. and rap artists.

Hip hop came about through a mix of music styles and **(6)** ………..

Urban music has spread quickly due to the fact that its **(7)** ……….. matches our modern lifestyle.

Urban music is more dynamic than pop because it is developing and willing to **(8)** ………..

3 Listen again and check your answers.

4 Complete these sentences with the correct form of these phrasal verbs from the talk above.

move on	get in on	filter down
grow out of	catch on	

1 The money generated by artists never seems to .... to those at the bottom.
2 His new style .... his work with musicians in South America.
3 The music business .... very quickly because there's always something new to consider.
4 I think their music will .... because it's very different from what's around at the moment.
5 The success of rap has made many artists think, 'OK, let's .... this!'

Reading: multiple matching (Part 4)
▶ *CB page 8*

About the exam: In Paper 1, Part 2, you match questions or statements to several short texts.

Strategy
1 Read the text quickly to find out what it is about.
2 Underline key words in the questions.
3 Find phrases or words in the texts that have a similar meaning to key words in the questions.

WHEN WILL I BE FAMOUS?

Conventional wisdom has it that the path to pop fame is instant and easy, thanks to the explosion of reality TV shows such as *Pop Idol*. In fact, it's more difficult now than ever before.

A

In Colchester, teenage girls stand shivering beside the roadshow truck of local radio station SGR. It's a Saturday afternoon and an unsigned boy band by the name of D-Rail are performing a bizarre version of 'Maniac', from *Flashdance*. They follow with what will be their first, <u>self-released</u> single – a charity ballad called 'How Do I Say Goodbye?'. Afterwards, D-Rail hang around to sign autographs, all part of trying to promote themselves, and so it seems as if Chris, Robert and Matt are famous. But hardly anyone here today knows or cares who D-Rail are. D-Rail won't even be paid for their efforts. It will be a miracle if they sell one extra record as a result. Three months on from this date and D-Rail have released 'How Do I Say Goodbye?' <u>under their own steam</u>, but it has sold only 1,300 copies, hitting No 63 in the charts. Despite this indication that their music is simply not good enough, they have left their manager and are ploughing ahead[1] with a new single, whose video <u>they shot</u> in March <u>for £3,000 after Chris negotiated the production company down</u> from their quote of £25,000.

B

There's also 27-year-old Baz, who has been in the pop game for six years now. In Baz's experience, record companies can be unforgivably cruel. A few years back he approached one label whose records he had collected in childhood. When his former manager called to ask their thoughts, he was told: 'No, we're not interested in him at all.' Baz is looking now for a P&D (production and distribution) deal, to pay for his releases. 'If it hasn't happened by the age of 29, I'll look into[2] doing something else,' he says, unconvincingly. If being a pop star doesn't work for him, he might manage other artists – lofty ambitions for a man who has put together several singles but not yet released one, let alone got one inside the Top 40. Baz, meanwhile, is gearing up for the release of his first single, 'Positive Reaction'. He's signed a P&D deal covering the manufacturing of 1000 CDs, distribution and plugging. 'I'd like the single to go Top 10,' Baz says, 'but I'd be happy with Top 20.'

C

Making more progress is 24-year-old Sneha Mistri, known as Mistri. She's looked into[2] P&D deals, but when she wanted to release her first single herself last year, she realised that if she paid for the manufacturing and distribution, she wouldn't be able to afford a video, or a publicist. Instead, she contacted OD2, a download operator, who agreed to sell her track online, which freed up[3] cash for advertising. To pay for 'Intoxicating', Mistri took out an £11,000 loan, £5,000 of which went on a video. 'I hate to think how much it's cost over the last five years,' she says, 'but it has been an investment. You see people on *Pop Idol* shooting into the charts having only been trying for six months but they disappear just as quickly. By doing it this way I know that if – when – I make a success of this, I'll be able to keep going.' Mistri has now signed to a management company and has live dates lined up throughout the summer.

D

Then there's Bloke – aka Sophie, Abbe, Faith and Gina – whose prospects seem rosy because after the success of teen boy bands Busted and McFly, lots of record companies are hovering around[4] girl groups who can play their instruments. But their manager, Jeremy Nargi, is realistic, knowing that landing a deal with a label is just the first rung on a very shaky ladder and doesn't necessarily mean that a single will get made. One of his other acts signed to Sony a couple of years ago, had £800,000 spent on them before their first single and parted company with the label not long after that single got to No 12. So the recording companies are cautious. Keeping costs down, getting Bloke above the radar will, he reckons, cost £100,000. 'It's good that there is a perceived market for this type of group, but it's become like the space race,' Nargi says. 'It's "first man on the moon" stuff. People are signing acts like this now – so we've got to make sure we get attention and that people know we're here, even if we don't have a deal.'

E

Also there's an unsigned girl trio, Genie Queen, in Liverpool. They first came to light 12 months ago, when one of their songs popped into people's inboxes as an MP3. 'Just One Of Them Days' sounded like a hit, the rest of the songs turned out[5] to be amazing, but even they had been dismissed by almost every major label. The band is managed by Andy McCluskey. 'We've seen some unsigned local pop groups,' says Anna from the band, 'and the more we see them being messed around by their managers, the more we realise how lucky we are to have Andy.' One of them, Lauren, has now quit, but the band have just recorded a techno epic and there's a chance they'll make it to the bigtime. Last year, McCluskey took a holiday. Standing on a beach in California, 'It hit me that if I stood on that beach for the next two years, rather than continuing with Genie Queen, I'd be £250,000 better off. I thought to myself, "Why am I doing this?"'

1   Underline the key words in the questions. The first one has been done for you, together with the answers in the text.

2   For each of the questions, choose from extracts A–E.

Which pop act ......

is <u>funding</u> their <u>own career</u>	A	1	C	2
was disillusioned by a record company		3		
has not yet made a record		4		
has formed a business deal outside the industry		5		
recognises the importance of publicity		6		7
has used the Internet to further their pop career		8		9
mentions putting a time limit on their pop career		10		
is likened to other acts		11		
feels they are in a better situation than some other acts		12		
has not been signed despite making good records		13		
has been doing publicity that is ineffective		14		
has lost a member		15		

3   Look at the numbered verbs in the texts and decide which definition is best in the context.

1   A   to continue doing something when it is difficult
    B   to do something which takes a long time

2   A   to be happy about something that is going to happen
    B   to find out more by getting the necessary information

3   A   to make a system work more easily
    B   to make something available by not using it for something else

4   A   to stay close to something because you are waiting for something to happen
    B   to stay in one place

5   A   to make or produce something
    B   to have a particular result

Vocabulary 2: music 2

1   Complete the crossword with words related to the music business.

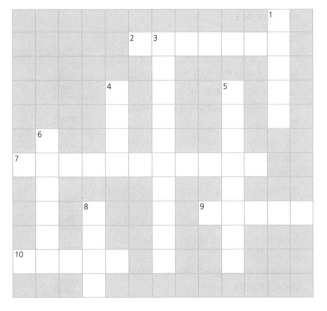

Across

2   They went on a lot of TV shows to .... their new album.

7   .... lets you forward songs to your friends and has changed the music business.

9   They don't do original songs – they only do .... versions.

10   The .... was really small but a lot of people were squashed in there!

Down

1   Their .... album showed a lot of promise and we hope they record more.

3   The band has got a bad .... for being rude to journalists.

4   The singer signed an autograph for one of his ....

5   It's illegal to .... commercially produced songs without paying.

6   They released a very good .... so I hope their first album will be as good.

8   The band went on .... in 2007 and sang all over Europe.

2a   The columns below show very common suffixes. Change these words by using an appropriate suffix and put the words into the correct columns. One word can be used in two columns.

prominence	critic	resign	similar
demonstrate	pure	depend	politics
confidence	able	centre	alter	inform

-ity (noun)	-ation (noun)	-al (adjective)	-ent (adjective)

2b   Which words change the syllable which is stressed when they have a suffix?

Use of English: word formation (Part 3)

1   Read the text below. Use the word given in capitals to form a word that fits the space. There is an example at the beginning (0). In this text all the words require suffixes. In the exam, you will be required to use prefixes and suffixes.

TIP! Decide what type of word is missing from each gap.

DRIVE CAREFULLY!

Researchers have discovered that the speed at which people drive can be **(0)** *dramatically* (DRAMA) affected by the speed of the music that they are listening to in their cars. The latest research was a **(1)** .... (COMPARE) study showing that drivers who listen to fast music have twice as many accidents, **(2)** .... (REGARD) of the genre of that music, as those who listen to slower music. The research is **(3)** .... (SCIENCE) proof of something many have long suspected and, worryingly, the car is where an **(4)** .... (INCREASE) number of people listen to music nowadays. The study showed that listening to fast music was **(5)** .... (INFLUENCE) in people taking more risks, such as going through red lights. In the **(6)** .... (TRY), the drivers' heart rate fluctuated less when they were listening to no music than when they listened to any kind of music. That music is a **(7)** .... (DISTRACT) shown by this lack of variation in the heart rate of the non-music subjects. **(8)** .... (FORTUNATE), the problem can be resolved – drivers should apparently choose music with a slower tempo or turn down the volume to a **(9)** .... (REASON) pitch. But there are other problems in the car. There is now an enormous amount of **(10)** .... (TECHNOLOGY) equipment for cars, with hands-free mobiles, navigation systems and screens for DVDs. Soon we will all need drivers.

From BBC News at bbc.co.uk/news

Speaking: (Part 1)

About the exam: In Paper 5, Part 1, your partner and the examiner will ask you some questions about yourself and your opinions.

Strategy
1 Try to expand your responses – don't just answer 'yes' or 'no'.

1 Look at these questions. How would you answer them? Write responses, then compare your answers to the examples in the answer key. Listen to the answers on the CD.

Do you prefer staying at home to watch a DVD or going to the cinema?

Do you listen to American music or do you prefer music from your country?

Which film that you've seen has made the biggest impact on you?

Grammar 2: verb tenses (perfect aspect)
▶ *CB pages 13–15*

1 Write sentences using the words given. You will have to put the verbs into their correct form. Each sentence contains at least one perfect tense.

1 If / you / meet / me / at 6pm, / I / get / the tickets / by then.
2 In / my film career, / I / have / a variety of roles / and / enjoy / them all.
3 I / get / home / that evening / and / discover / that / my DVD recorder / steal.
4 He / be / finally / hanging up / his guitar. Next month / he / sing / and / record / for 20 years.
5 I / try / to get / a recording contract / for months / now.
6 They / only / build / the film set / for ten minutes / when / the rain / start.

2 Put these state and event verbs into the following categories:

like, smell, believe, possess, understand, love, have, hate, hear, know, want, dislike, own, taste, prefer, belong, care

1 Verbs of feeling:
2 Verbs of thinking or knowledge:
3 Verbs of possession:
4 Verbs of sensation:

Use of English: open cloze (Part 2)
▶ *CB page 12*

1 Read the text below and write in the word which best fits each space. Use only one word in each space. There is an example at the beginning (0).

TIP! Read the whole sentence to help you decide which word is missing.

FLYING HIGH

You no longer have to run **(0)** ..*away*.. to the circus to learn the skills of the big top. If you **(1)** .... ever dreamed about flying on a trapeze, taming lions or making people laugh then you can go along to **(2)** .... of several schools around Britain to learn how. I tried it for a day to see how I would **(3)** .... on. It comes as a shock when you find out **(4)** .... difficult it is to master even basic circus skills. Complete concentration is important because **(5)** .... it you can hurt yourself. The classes are absorbing and the experience of being told **(6)** .... to do is relaxing, especially if you are one of those people who spends much of the day **(7)** .... to make decisions. I enjoyed what I did on my day there and have **(8)** .... surprised at how much I remembered. **(9)** .... you don't need to be particularly fit to start learning some of the disciplines, you'll need a high level of fitness to take **(10)** .... in the trapeze work. Those already **(11)** .... shape and who have a good sense of balance, like skiers, are **(12)** .... an advantage. All equipment is **(13)** .... but you need to bring your own trainers with ankle support and tights to protect the skin on your legs. It's really **(14)** .... giving it a shot – you may surprise **(15)** .... and then you'll be able to impress and entertain your friends.

Writing: formal letter (Part 1)

About the exam: In Paper 2, Part 1, you may have to write a formal letter to someone. Your letter will have to be between 180 and 220 words.

Strategy
1 Read the question and underline the functions that you are asked to fulfil.
2 Decide what information from the question will support each of these functions.
3 Remember to use your own words and expand the information in your points.

1 Read this task.

You are studying in Canada and recently attended a concert by the group Fairplay. However, you were disappointed by the concert and decide to write to the organisers.

Read the advertisement for the concert and the email below from your friend. Then, using the information appropriately, write a letter to the organiser, Mr Wilden, saying what you were dissatisfied with and why and asking for appropriate action.

2 Underline the three functions your answer must cover.

3 Tick what you need to include in your letter of complaint.
1 why you bought the tickets
2 why you are writing
3 the problems you had at the concert
4 what your friends think of the problems
5 what you want Mr Wilden to do
6 what you enjoyed about the concert
7 what you were expecting

Put the points you need to include in an appropriate order.

4 Which of these is 'appropriate action'?
1 asking for a refund and some extra money as compensation
2 asking for a refund
3 asking for a free ticket to another concert
4 telling him you will be contacting a lawyer
5 asking him to do the concert again

5 Read this sample answer. Rewrite the underlined parts in more formal language.

Dear Mr Wilden

I am writing about the Fairplay concert on Saturday night. I went to the concert and I was very disappointed by several things. I tried to speak to someone at the concert but they told me to write to you.

First of all, when we got there ¹we couldn't sit so we stood up, which meant we couldn't see the group very well at all. The tickets ²cost a lot so we expected seating, especially as your ad had implied this. Secondly we had to listen to a support act for over an hour and a half and ³they were rubbish and then Fairplay were only on stage for an hour. I don't think we got our money's worth at all. Finally, during the interval there were no refreshments so we were forced to go outside to get something and then had to stand even further back when we returned.

I think the seats were overpriced and ⁴you didn't do what you said you would do in your ad. Therefore, ⁵I want you to give me part of the ticket cost or at least send me a voucher for a free ticket to the next concert you promote.

⁶I expect to hear from you quickly.

Yours sincerely

6 The table below shows what your writing is assessed on in the exam. Complete the table with what you need to do in the previous question in order to fulfil each point.

task	
organisation	
range	
accuracy	
register	
effect on target reader	

use formal language and a polite tone
balance the functions appropriately
persuade the audience of your argument
order the functions appropriately
use paragraphing and linking words
use a variety of vocabulary
make sure the audience has enough information to respond
use advanced level structures and vocabulary in places
check that structures, vocabulary and spelling are correct
cover all the functions required
use a variety of structures

Improve!

Expand your answer by explaining your reasons fully.

7 Write your own answer to the task in Exercise 1. Use your plan from Exercise 3 to help you and remember to use formal language. Write your answer in 180–220 words.

UNIT
2 Spend it or save it

Reading: multiple choice (Part 1)
▶ *CB page 20*

1 You are going to read three short texts on the topic of money. Read the texts quickly and decide which of the titles below best suits each text.

Text 1 a) THE CREDIT CARD BURDEN
       b) CONSIDER YOUR OPTIONS!

Text 2 a) HOW TO GIVE A BRAND IMPACT
       b) STARS STILL TOP SELLERS

Text 3 a) A LOTTERY WINNER'S STORY
       b) SPEND, SPEND, SPEND

Put the titles in the boxes below.

2 Read the texts and answer the questions.

1	Title:

The most expensive way to buy anything is on credit. If you don't already have a credit card – don't get one! Because you have to pay interest on any outstanding balance, it only makes things cost more unless you pay off the balance each month. If you already have an outstanding balance on a credit card which has been running for a while, it is a very good idea to transfer this debt to another card with low interest rates so that more of your monthly repayment actually goes towards repaying the debt. And the sooner the better – if you are paying 20 percent interest or more, you are really being ripped off. Many companies offer 0 percent interest on balance transfers for six months and then a fairly good rate after that – applying online is pretty painless too.

The quickest way to get rid of credit card debt is to first arrange the lowest interest deals possible. (Remember it is worth asking your current lenders if they would give you a lower rate. Tell them you're thinking of changing cards and they might be persuaded!) Then pay the minimum monthly repayment on all but the most expensive card – pay as much extra into that as you can manage until it has gone, then move on to the next most expensive. It takes staying power to do this as it may take years, but it is possible – the more frugally you live, the quicker you can do it – and YOU CAN DO IT!

1 The writer suggests you should transfer your debt promptly if
  A you have reached the limit on your current card.
  B you want to pay off your outstanding balance.
  C you have had a credit card debt over a long period.
  D you can find a card offering a 0 percent interest rate.

2 What is the overall purpose of the piece?
  A to encourage readers to negotiate the best deal for their credit cards
  B to tell readers how they can avoid credit card debt
  C to reassure readers that interest payments can be reduced
  D to help readers free themselves of credit cards

2	Title:

Spend any evening watching TV and it is inevitable that you will see celebrities featured in commercials. The same thing happens with newspapers and posters – the celebs are there smiling at you. There is no doubt that advertisers everywhere continue to queue for the services of personalities, hoping that some of their magic will rub off on the brand persona and thus boost sales.

Exploiting the public's admiration, even worship, of well-known stars is a trick that has been employed by advertisers for as long as can be remembered – even Marilyn Monroe advertised shampoo. It can be argued that this bygone era was undoubtedly one in which stars were often adored as untouchable and immensely glamorous. The logic therefore went like this: associate Brand X with a star and some of their glamour or kudos would be associated with the product. This, in turn, increased sales because the public wished to emulate the habits of the rich and famous.

Given our modern preoccupation with celebrity, most brands see it as even more important that they capture a star for their ad campaign. And indeed most customers today are persuaded into a purchase if they think that having the product will make them more like the star they emulate.

3 What point is exemplified by the reference to Monroe?

A The more famous the star, the higher the sales of the advertised product.

B Well-known stars can be used as a brand name on some products.

C Film stars used to be used in advertising in a different way from today.

D No one is so famous that they won't appear in an ad.

4 What does the writer think about using celebrities in advertising?

A It is an advertising strategy that is used too often nowadays.

B It is becoming an increasingly effective method of selling.

C Consumers are confused by so many celebrity commercials.

D It is impossible to avoid advertisements which use celebrities.

---

3 | Title: _____

Elaine and Derek Thompson won £2.7 million on the National Lottery in December 1995. With over 40 fellow lottery winners the Thompsons have formed a network so that they can swap their often alarming experiences and avoid the pitfalls of instant wealth.

Mrs Thompson, 42, feels that others could benefit from talking to a winner. 'It would have been nice on the night of the win to speak to another winner. We had a winner's advisor but they do not know what it is like to be told you are getting a cheque for £2.7 million. We wanted someone to tell us why we were feeling sick, why we couldn't sleep and all the things flashing in our minds. Ninety percent of the people I have spoken to feel the same.'

The win for the Thompsons was easier than for most because Derek was an accountant. Apart from investing in race horses and taking their family on luxury holidays, the couple have remained very much as before. Mrs Thompson said, 'If I meet anyone who is being negative and nervous about the money I say, "There's nothing to be nervous about, spend some time getting used to it."' She also tells them they will have to develop a thick skin and get to know who is genuine and honest.

5 Why were the Thompsons able to cope with their win?

A because they had a winner's advisor

B because of Mr Thompson's job

C because they already had some investments

D because they spoke to other lottery winners

6 What is the purpose of the text?

A to get lottery winners to form a support group

B to offer Mrs Thompson's services as an advisor

C to outline the problems associated with a lottery win

D to describe the problems the Thompsons encountered

---

3 Match each text to the most likely people it was written for:

a) people in the same business

b) other people in the same situation

c) ordinary consumers

4 Read the texts again and find words or phrases that mean the following. Use a good dictionary, such as *The Longman Exams Dictionary*, to help you.

Text 1

a) money you owe

   debt or ....

b) amount of money paid regularly to pay back money you have borrowed

   ....

c) to be charged too much for something

   ....

d) an agreement or arrangement

   ....

e) the ability to continue doing something difficult until it is finished

   ....

f) economically, living simply

   ....

Text 2

g) when a quality or feeling another person has transfers to you

   ....

h) to increase and make more successful

   ....

i) using something fully and effectively

   ....

j) period of time in the past

   ....

k) imitate

   ....

Text 3

l) a group of people who are connected

   ....

m) problems or difficulties that are likely to arise in a particular situation

   ....

n) appearing very quickly

   ....

o) to not care if people criticise you

   ....

17

Vocabulary 1: compound adjectives
▶ *CB page 24*

1 Find compound adjectives which mean the same as the following in the grid below. Words appear down, across or diagonally.

1 mentally exhausted from working too hard
2 happening only once
3 without much money
4 annoyed or bored
5 tired and unhealthy
6 with lots of buildings
7 having a lot of money
8 physically tired

P	O	N	E	H	A	R	U	P	O
E	R	W	O	R	N	O	U	T	N
H	A	R	D	U	P	T	W	H	E
A	L	L	H	A	L	N	E	O	O
F	L	R	U	I	T	S	L	W	F
E	O	G	U	P	H	K	L	N	F
D	U	B	U	R	N	T	O	U	T
U	T	F	R	E	E	O	F	T	B
P	W	O	R	D	O	F	F	S	U
F	R	U	N	D	O	W	N	S	P

2 Match the compound adjectives on the left with their typical collocations on the right.

1 last-minute   a) story / idea / theory
2 long-term   b) agreement / promise / contract
3 far-fetched   c) strategy / plan / investment
4 self-centred   d) decision / bargain / deal
5 water-tight   e) reply / humour / action
6 quick-witted   f) person / nature / generation

3 Use the words in the box to complete the compound adjectives in the sentences.

TIP! Underline the noun after each compound to remind you of typical collocations.

long	hard	short	one	air	old
level	mass	self	so		

1 He wrote a very ....-hitting report on the need for people to cut back on spending.
2 It was a rather ....-sided account of how they had got into debt.
3 We have a ....-term agreement to supply them, which will be reviewed after three months.
4 I don't like working in ....-conditioned offices – they're too cold.
5 He's a good man in a crisis – he's very ....-headed.
6 He doesn't think you need qualifications because he's a ....-made man.
7 If we focus on selling ....-produced items we can really cut our prices.
8 Traditional banks can be very ....-fashioned and conservative about who they will lend to.
9 Our ....-called financial advisor lost us loads of money by recommending bad investments!
10 They have a ....-standing problem of trying to keep costs down.

Listening: multiple choice (Part 3)
▶ CB pages 24–25

About the exam: In Paper 4, Part 3, you will hear someone being interviewed by another person. You will have to answer six multiple-choice questions.

Strategy

1 In the exam you have only one minute to read through the six questions, so use your time carefully.
2 Read through the first part (the stem) of each question, which is given before the options A, B, C or D. This will give you an overview of the conversation.
3 Then go back and read through the options for each question.

1 Read the first part (the stem) of the six questions in Exercise 2. When you have done this, tick the points below that you think are covered in the interview.

• whether students buy ethical brands
• a comment on anti-branding
• Channel 4's approach to students
• students' views on ethical brands
• how Channel 4 usually sells its products
• what type of products students buy
• what brands students like
• how to sell luxury brands to students
• students compared with older people

2 You will hear part of a radio interview in which a marketing consultant, Martin Laurell, is talking about marketing products to young people. For questions 1–6, choose the answer (A, B, C or D) which fits best according to what you hear.

1 According to Martin Laurell, how are students different from older people?
   A They spend more money on branded goods.
   B They are specifically targeted by big brands.
   C They are more willing to listen to messages from advertisers.
   D They are very critical of traditional advertisements.

2 What does Laurell say about anti-branding?
   A It has affected how young people look at advertisements.
   B It has become an effective way to market certain products.
   C It has shown how strong many brands are.
   D It has stopped us judging others by how they dress.

3 Laurell says that students choose a brand based on
   A intelligent advertising.
   B familiarity.
   C quality.
   D cost.

4 Laurell claims students select specific products based on
   A what their friends have chosen.
   B advertising.
   C the long-term benefits the brand can offer.
   D how fashionable the brand is.

5 What is students' attitude to brands which are seen as ethical?
   A They think the ethical companies charge too much.
   B They wish the products were more readily available.
   C They agree that these products are a good idea.
   D They would like to see a better range of products.

6 What marketing tool did Channel 4 use to attract students to its brand?
   A Access to a music celebrity.
   B Tickets to music festivals.
   C Reduced prices on music CDs.
   D Free specialist magazines.

3 Listen again and check your answers.

4 Many phrasal verbs have more than one meaning. Listen for these phrasal verbs in the talk above and choose the meaning the speaker uses.

1 settle down	a) to become calm and quiet
	b) to start living or working somewhere with the intention of staying there
2 be taken in	a) to be allowed to stay somewhere
	b) to be deceived by somebody
3 talk down to	a) to talk to someone as if they are less intelligent than you
	b) to persuade someone to reduce a price to a particular amount
4 weigh up	a) to spend time talking to someone in order to form an opinion about them
	b) to consider the advantages and disadvantages carefully
5 set (somebody/ something) apart	a) to make somebody seem different
	b) to save for a special purpose
6 give out	a) to tell people information, especially officially
	b) to give something to a lot of people

Grammar 1: relative clauses
▶ *CB pages 22–23*

1 Combine these sentences with a relative pronoun to form a single sentence.

1 He consulted his bank manager. The bank manager told him it would be unwise to take out a loan.

2 Australian dollars and cents were introduced in 1966. They are completely different from the US notes and coins.

3 Even young children can open bank accounts. They often maintain them for the rest of their lives.

4 Banks carry out extensive market research. The market research tends to show that students are attracted by special offers and free gifts.

5 Mortgages are offered by most banks. Mortgages are special loans for the purchase of a property.

6 There are several similarities between the old and new Australian currencies. One of them is the size of some of the coins.

7 I am very impressed with my bank manager. He is always very friendly and helpful.

8 One day I had to do my banking with a new teller. I had never spoken to her before.

2 Correct the errors in the relative pronouns in these sentences.

1 Something what worries me is the high interest rate on that loan.

2 She is part of a business group, among who she is the only woman.

3 I'm opening accounts at two banks which interest rates are good.

4 It's worth investing in people which businesses are doing well.

5 The advertising manager who's proposal I like is coming to see me tomorrow.

6 Companies use celebrities which have high profiles to sell their products.

Use of English: open cloze (Part 2)

1 Read the text below and write in the word which best fits each space. Use only one word in each space. There is an example at the beginning (0).

A NEW WAY TO MAKE MONEY

Not many people realise that **(0)** ....*the*.... digital age has brought new ways to make money. And these are ways which anybody **(1)** .... participate in – you don't have to be a businessman or have set **(2)** .... your own company. One very simple way to make extra cash has been brought **(3)** .... by the development of the digital camera. With **(4)** .... of these modern cameras, you **(5)** .... longer have to be a professional photographer as, **(6)** .... a digital camera, anybody can now take simple pictures **(7)** .... are high quality and sell them for a lot of money. As long as you know what kind of pictures to take, you can then send them to an agent, **(8)** .... will market them to thousands of publishers for you. The agent does all the work and takes **(9)** .... percentage from each sale. This usually costs you nothing to arrange and can make you hundreds of extra pounds per month. Millions of images are bought and sold online every month; **(10)** .... demand is increasing and, in fact, has **(11)** .... been as high. It's worth taking advice to find out the kind of pictures that are **(12)** .... high demand and also to look for a reputable agent to sell them on **(13)** .... behalf. So, **(14)** .... your lack of technical know-how, you may end up **(15)** .... able to give up your regular job and, in terms of earnings, the sky's the limit!

Vocabulary 2:
advertising and marketing
▶ *CB page 26*

1   Put the following words into the correct boxes. Some words may appear in more than one box.

pop-ups   classifieds   hoarding
target audience   jingle
mass-market   logo   full-page ad
flyers   consumer   slogan   media

types of ad
audience
features of an ad
location

2   Check the meaning of the underlined words in your dictionary. Then match the phrases in 1–6 with the phrases in a–f to create a sentence.

1 We need to increase <u>circulation</u>
2 We booked the ad for <u>prime time</u>
3 If we <u>pitch</u> the ad at the <u>luxury market,</u>
4 The location of the <u>billboards</u> is critical
5 The brand has gone <u>downmarket</u>
6 We need to highlight the <u>product features</u>

a) then we'll need to place it in magazines that are <u>upmarket</u>.
b) since we <u>plugged</u> ourselves on local radio.
c) to the way we <u>promote</u> ourselves.
d) if we want more <u>advertising revenue</u>.
e) so people are aware of the <u>innovations</u>.
f) to catch the maximum number of viewers.

Use of English: word formation (Part 3)
▶ *CB page 23*

1   Read the text below. Use the word given in capitals to form a word that fits the space. There is an example at the beginning (0).

TOO MUCH ADVERTISING?

Nowadays advertisers are prepared to do more and more to get their message across.

There are more and more magazines with an ever larger proportion of ads, where clearly a fortune has been spent on the **(0)** *production* (PRODUCE) of the ad. This may be because the advertisers have paid to use a famous celebrity or because of using an exotic **(1)** .... (LOCATE) as background or because the ad uses expensive photography and **(2)** .... (GRAPH). We are becoming **(3)** .... (INCREASE) sophisticated so it is also becoming more **(4)** .... (CHALLENGE) to catch our attention. At the same time, as more and more people are hooked into an ever-expanding range of TV channels, advertising on television is becoming **(5)** .... (PRICE). Because of this, some pundits say the TV companies may be losing their market as the Internet competes for our attention. It is becoming **(6)** .... (ECONOMIC) now for companies to use TV as they don't get the returns they demand on their **(7)** .... (INVEST). But advertising on the Internet has opened up a whole new ball game of **(8)** .... (POSSIBLE). In fact, consumers are getting very **(9)** .... (RESENT) as the mainly pop-up ads used on the Internet are seen as a gross **(10)** .... (INTRUDE) of privacy by most of us.

Speaking: Part 3

About the exam: In Part 3 of the Speaking test you have to complete a problem-solving task with your partner(s).

1 Look at the task below and read the discussion two candidates had. Underline the words or phrases they use to express an opinion.

W: Ok, we have to decide first what method we think is most effective, don't we? Personally I think television is because it's got colour, sound and the ads can be interesting.

M: I'm not sure I agree – I read magazines a lot and the ads do sink in even though I'm only reading the articles.

W: It seems a boring way to advertise, but I suppose a lot of people do read magazines, so I'm happy to go along with that.

M: Now, what's the best way to advertise a CD? Well, I'd say radio again cos it's music!

W: Hmm …… You may be right. But I'd go for instore promotions actually 'cos you've got the customers there.

M: Not sure I completely agree but I can see it might work well …… (*fade*)

2 Here are different ways of advertising. Explain which advertising you find most effective and say what you think the best way would be to advertise a new CD.

Grammar 2: articles
▶ *CB page 27*

1 Underline the correct alternative, *a*, *an*, *the* or *θ*, in each sentence.

1 We pay by direct debit three times *the* / *a* year.
2 I need to go to *the* / *θ* bank to close my account.
3 Apparently he's *an* / *the* excellent accountant and comes highly recommended.
4 Where's *the* / *a* cheque book that I gave you yesterday?
5 They said they would pay me for *an* / *a* hour's overtime.
6 When she went to *the* / *θ* university, the fees were very expensive.

2 Complete the sentences with *a*, *an*, *the* or *θ*.

1 I put .... money into my savings account every month.
2 I was thrown when he asked me .... question about my income.
3 Apparently it's very easy to get sponsorship for .... tennis.
4 At the meeting we discussed whether to introduce .... uniform for staff.
5 The government should do something to get .... unemployed working again.
6 She's been looking for .... job for ages.
7 We're going to go over the accounts in .... morning.
8 We bought the house from .... Browns, who were friends of ours.
9 I can honestly say it's .... cheapest credit card I've had.
10 Their son plays .... piano so they invested in an expensive one.

3 Complete these sentences with the nouns in the box, adding an article if necessary.

goods	information	news	politics	means
times	power	bank		

1 .... ordered via the Internet are subject to a delivery charge.
2 I gave him .... he needed to access my account details.
3 Did you hear .... last night about the rise in interest rates?
4 Whether they lower the tax is down to .... I'm afraid.
5 He's broke – he hasn't got .... to pay back the debt.
6 The rise in Internet advertising is a sign of ....
7 Celebrities are important in advertising as they have .... to make or break a brand.
8 Is there .... near here please?

Writing: informal letter (Part 2)
▶ *CB page 28*

About the exam: In Paper 2, Part 2, you may have to write an informal letter to someone. Your letter will have to be 220–260 words.

Strategy
1 Read the question and think about the points you need to include.
2 Decide how many paragraphs you need and the content of each paragraph. Make sure your plan is balanced.
3 Remember to use a variety of structure and vocabulary to show range.

1 Read this task.

You receive this letter from your penfriend, Sam.

> I've managed to save quite a bit of money now. What I'd really like to do is use the money to go on holiday as I haven't had a holiday for ages and I'm starting college in October. But I'll need a car when I go to college so I don't know whether to put the money towards the car. What do you think I should do? Write and let me know what you think.

2 This task asks you to give advice. What do you need to include in your answer?

• a question about why she is asking you to help
• reason why holidays cost a lot of money
• reasons for choosing a holiday
• what a friend of yours did
• reasons for choosing a car
• what you think she should do
• where she can buy a cheap car
• sympathy for your friend's problem

Put the things you need to include in the best order.

3 You need to write 220–260 words. Decide roughly how many words to include in each paragraph and how many points to include in each paragraph. Compare your ideas with the information in the Key.

4 Read this sample answer and underline all the informal expressions.

Dear Sam,

Lucky you! I wish I had some money saved. I think you've done very well to save some money. I can understand you're confused about what to do.

If you have a holiday, it'll be a good idea because you say you haven't had one for ages and it will make you nice and relaxed before you start your hard studies at college. You've been working hard and everybody needs a break. At the same time, your life at college may be much easier if you've got a car and you won't get the chance to save the money again so I can see why you want to use the money for a car.

If I were you, what I would do is have a short break somewhere cheap, such as camping with some friends, so you can relax, but then I'd save most of the money for a cheap car. Why don't you just buy something small and second-hand as you won't be driving long distances? Actually, you may want to think about whether or not you do really need a car. Isn't there a good bus or train service where you live? If you have a car at college, you'll always be giving your friends lifts and it could make you fed up.

I think a holiday is the most important thing and if you have enough for a car then that'll be good, but I don't think it's essential. Write and let me know what you decide to do!

Love
Mina

┌─ Improve! ◄

Make sure you use a variety of grammar for the functions in your writing, e.g. *I would ..., If I were you ..., Why don't you ...*, etc. for advice.

5 Write your own answer to the task in Exercise 1. Use the information on what to include in Exercise 2 to help you. Write your answer in 220–260 words.

UNIT
3 What makes us tick

Listening: multiple matching (Part 4)
▶ *CB page 33*

About the exam: In Paper 4, Part 4, you will hear five extracts of individuals talking on the same theme. You have to do two tasks as you listen and match the extracts to statements. There are three extra statements in each task that do not go with any of the extracts.

Strategy
1 Read through the statements in each task.
2 Underline the most important words in each option. These are usually the noun and either the subject, the verb or an adjective.
3 Remember you will not necessarily hear the key words but a synonym or paraphrase for them.

1a Underline the key words in the Task One options below.

1b Match these paraphrases to some of the key words from the options.

envious	cross	started to be	did the same
cash	job	took	went out with
made a problem	speaking	no longer	

Vocabulary 1: adjectives of character
▶ *CB pages 30–31*

1 Complete the crossword with adjectives used to describe personality.

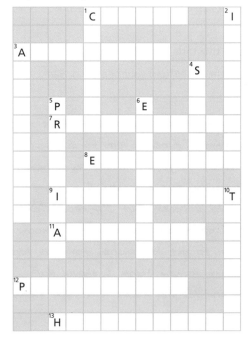

2 You will hear five short extracts in which different people talk about a problem they had with a friend. You will hear each extract twice. Use the second listening to check your answer.

TASK ONE

For questions **1–5**, match the extracts with the problems, listed **A–H**.

While you listen you must complete both tasks.

A My friend stopped talking to me.
B My friend stole my girlfriend.
C My friend became very jealous of me.
D My friend copied everything I did.
E My friend got very angry with me.
F My friend got me into trouble at work.
G My friend always asked me for money.
H My friend asked me to lie for her.

Speaker 1   **1**
Speaker 2   **2**
Speaker 3   **3**
Speaker 4   **4**
Speaker 5   **5**

TASK TWO

For questions **6–10**, match the extracts with the person who helped resolve the problem, listed **A–H**.

A my uncle
B my sister
C a colleague
D a friend's relative
E a teacher
F my mother
G another friend
H a professional advisor

Speaker 1   **6**
Speaker 2   **7**
Speaker 3   **8**
Speaker 4   **9**
Speaker 5   **10**

Across

1 thinking about what other people need or want and trying to help them (6)
3 behaving in a confident way, so that people notice you (9)
7 sensible and able to make good judgements so you can be trusted (11)
8 active and confident and enjoying spending time with other people (9)
9 confident and able to do things by yourself in your own way (11)
11 determined to be successful (9)
12 understanding situations and people's feelings well (10)
13 studying or doing a job with a lot of effort (11)

Down

1 wanting to know about things (7)
2 wanting to do things as soon as possible; not willing to wait (9)
3 very determined to succeed or behaving in an angry or threatening way (10)
4 having a healthy mental and emotional state (6)
5 good at making decisions based on what is possible and will work (9)
6 having the physical or mental strength to do things with determination (9)
10 willing to believe that other people are good and honest (8)

2 Underline the correct word in each of the sentences.

1 She never talks about all her successes – she's so *loyal / modest / charming*.
2 I like his direct honesty but some people find him too *tolerant / contrary / frank*.
3 She'll never change her mind no matter what you say – she's so *stubborn / persistent / spoilt*.
4 He won't go out with just anyone – he's very *competitive / discerning / tender*.
5 I like him because he doesn't judge people – he's very *calm / affectionate / open-minded*.
6 He refuses to change his ideas and he can't see that he's being unreasonable! He's very *narrow-minded / rebellious / obstinate*.

Now check any words you don't know in your dictionary.

Use of English: multiple choice cloze (Part 1)

1 Read the text below and decide which answer (A, B, C or D) best fits each space. There is an example at the beginning (0).

TIP! Think carefully about the words each option usually goes with. Make sure your choice collocates with the words before or after the gap.

THE TRUTH ABOUT LOVE

This week we celebrated Valentine's Day – or those of us who are **(0)** ....*C*........ romantics did. The 14th of February gives everyone who's anyone a chance to **(1)** .... what they have learned to their fellow sufferers about the **(2)** .... of that universal problem – love. Francis Farnsworth, the TV presenter, is a case in **(3)** .... He's a very gentle host and I'm sure has a **(4)** .... of gold, but he talks a **(5)** .... of rubbish sometimes! Last night he hosted a TV chat show called *What is Love?* and it was no **(6)** .... He started off badly by having a **(7)** .... of opinion with the author, Tania Monte. Ms Monte always expresses extraordinary views without any apparent **(8)** .... of contradiction. Last night she was setting **(9)** .... her rules for a perfect relationship when Farnsworth accidentally called her Tina. Tina is the name of her ex-husband's girlfriend and any **(10)** .... of him – or her – is like a red rag to a bull to Tania. Farnsworth apologised and said that it had been a slip of the tongue brought **(11)** .... by a momentary **(12)** .... of concentration, but it took the diplomatic skills of the other guests to **(13)** .... our Tania down again. But it was only a **(14)** .... of time before he upset her again by referring to her boyfriend, Nick. She had been vehemently **(15)** .... that there was even a grain of truth in the rumours about her engagement to football star Nick Perez. Love is never simple – even for the experts!

	A	B	C	D
0	A insufferable	B untreatable	C <u>incurable</u>	D unrecoverable
1	A give out	B come up	C show up	D pass on
2	A nature	B way	C character	D essence
3	A aspect	B point	C detail	D instance
4	A heart	B centre	C core	D nucleus
5	A mound	B stack	C load	D heap
6	A departure	B exclusion	C variation	D exception
7	A difference	B contrast	C disagreement	D conflict
8	A worry	B fear	C concern	D anxiety
9	A up	B about	C out	D with
10	A recognition	B reference	C communication	D mention
11	A about	B in	C over	D along
12	A pause	B lapse	C break	D gap
13	A relax	B soothe	C calm	D ease
14	A matter	B problem	C issue	D situation
15	A refusing	B denying	C opposing	D retracting

Reading: multiple choice (Part 3)
▶ *CB pages 34–35*

About the exam: In Paper 1, Part 3, you read a text and answer seven questions. You choose each answer from four alternatives. Only one of the alternatives is correct.

Strategy

1 Read the title, any subheadings and the text quickly to get the general idea.

2 Look at the questions and try to answer them without looking at the alternatives. Find support for your answer in the text.

3 Choose the alternative that is closest to your answer.

1   Read the text quickly and decide if Professor Aron has

a) a positive view of love.

b) a negative view of love.

c) an objective view of love.

2   Read the text on page 27 and answer the questions. Choose the answer (A, B, C or D) which you think fits best according to the text.

1 In the first paragraph, we learn that Professor Aron has been researching

A   the uniqueness of human motivation.

B   how humans achieve success.

C   the forces behind human relationships.

D   different ways in which humans are effective.

2 Professor Aron's theory explains that we fall in love when we find somebody who

A   we think is good-looking.

B   is the right kind of person for us.

C   gives us a chance to like them.

D   shows that they like us.

3 The Groucho Marx joke is mentioned in the fourth paragraph to show

A   how some people think when they lack self-esteem.

B   that we all want to be part of a group.

C   how people behave when they find someone unattractive.

D   that we can miss opportunities for falling in love.

4 According to Professor Aron, people easily fall in love when

A   they are engaged in doing something else.

B   they are affected by a particular situation.

C   they are frightened and need protection.

D   they share an experience with another person.

5 In the sixth paragraph, what does Professor Aron say is a mistaken belief?

A   that people fall in love with old friends

B   that many people fall in love at first sight

C   that love is the same in most countries

D   that there are different varieties of love

6 Professor Aron claims that being attractive

A   can cause problems in a relationship.

B   can hide other more important qualities.

C   is less of an advantage than other qualities.

D   makes other people think you are unintelligent.

7 Other research into the chemical response to love shows that

A   depression can be a normal part of falling in love.

B   love can cause unnecessary suffering and illness.

C   certain chemical levels are raised in the brain.

D   the response can vary depending on the time of year.

3   Look at the numbered words in the text and tick the best meaning in the context.

1 a) energy   b) forces

2 a) happiness   b) liveliness

3 a) rejected   b) confused

4 a) interesting   b) exciting

5 a) opposite   b) untrue

6 a) beliefs   b) qualities

7 a) start out   b) set off

Why do we fall in love?

Everyone does it at one time or another, but why? We're talking about falling in love. Professor Arthur Aron from State University of New York at Stonybrook has been exploring the [1]dynamics of what exactly happens when two people are falling in love.

He claims that our primary motivation as human beings is to expand the self and to increase our abilities and our effectiveness. One of the ways we accomplish this is through our relationships with other people. He says, 'We have learned in our research that it is important to feel that you have the ability to be an effective person, especially in relationships.'

But how does this theory of self-expansion explain the process of falling in love? Usually, we fall in love with a person who we not only find attractive and appropriate for us but is also someone who demonstrates that they are attracted to us. According to Professor Aron, this creates a situation with great scope for self-expansion. The fact that they are attracted to us offers a significant opportunity – when we perceive this, we feel a surge of [2]exhilaration!

However, his studies show that it does not always work this way. An interesting exception to this occurs if we feel badly about ourselves. The process gets [3]thrown off if we can't believe that another person is interested in us – like the Groucho Marx joke where we don't want to belong to a club that would have us for a member. We tend to miss out on opportunities for falling in love if we don't feel good about ourselves.

Professor Aron has also managed to define the conditions which are best for meeting someone and falling in love. He claims that when you meet someone under conditions that are highly [4]arousing – a political demonstration, turbulence on a plane, a stimulating performance – a time when the body is stirred up and excited, we tend to experience attraction at a heightened level. This effect is well documented, but the explanations for it are very controversial. Professor Aron believes that we come to associate the arousal of the situation with this person and our own self-expansion.

It's also interesting to look at when people fall in love. How long do you have to have known someone before you realise you are in love with them? '[5]Contrary to what most people think, the statistics show that most people fall in love with someone that they have known for a while. People only report falling in love quickly about 30 to 40 percent of the time,' says Professor Aron. He also points out that this varies from culture to culture – falling in love happens differently between cultures, but it does occur in most cultures.

I think most of us think that our appearance must factor into the equation of falling in love. Professor Aron says, 'This is interesting. We have found that if you are very unattractive, it can hurt you a lot in forming romantic relationships. However, being attractive doesn't help that much.' The professor has found that two important characteristics, kindness and intelligence, are vital to the process of falling in love. And attractiveness is not connected to these things. These two [6]attributes are things that people learn about someone from knowing them over time. Intelligence is critical in all aspects of life, especially in love. But kindness is the strongest indicator for a successful long-term relationship.

Other research confirms what we all know – that love can make you mad or sad. Some people suffer from a form of Obsessive Compulsive Disorder when they are in love, which means that they are, for example, constantly checking things. At the same time, this disorder can also make you depressed as it affects serotonin levels in the brain. Levels can drop so low that they [7]trigger anxiety and depression. But it doesn't last for ever – after a year levels usually return to normal. It may be that we need this chemical response for relationships to survive as some have suggested that you have to be mad to fall in love!

Grammar 1: modal verbs 1
▶ *CB pages 31–32*

1   Match the modals in these sentences to the functions a–i below.

1 I think I'll have to explain why I can't see him any more.

2 If you want me to listen, you need to calm down.

3 She can talk to strangers very easily.

4 I really couldn't help him with his problem.

5 You may find that she's not bothered about not being invited.

6 You mustn't be so aggressive at work, it won't do you any favours.

7 She doesn't need to tell everyone her plans – it's up to her.

8 I ought to go and see my Gran, but I haven't got time.

9 You don't have to go to her birthday party if you don't want to.

a) ability
b) inability
c) necessity
d) lack of necessity
e) possibility
f) strong internal obligation
g) weak obligation/external duty
h) lack of obligation
i) prohibition

2   Underline the correct modal + infinitive in each sentence.

1 You should remind him because he *might / should* forget.

2 He split up with her last year so I *wouldn't / mustn't* try to see her now.

3 He hasn't called but I suppose he *could / can't* call tomorrow.

4 He rushed out the door – he *must / should* be very keen to see her!

5 If she has another arrangement, she *should / must* call to let me know.

6 Oh, surely she *can't / mustn't* be late again – she's never on time!

7 He's seeing someone else; he *may / must* tell his ex-girlfriend, but I don't think he will.

8 I think she's going to finish with me anyway so I *needn't / can't* worry about how to end it.

3   Fill in the gaps in this letter using one of the modal verbs in the box. You may need to use them more than once.

can	might / may	can't	should	must

Dear Alison

I have just opened your letter. You said you sent one before but it (1) .... have got lost in the post! The garage also delivered your little present. You (2) .... not have spent so much money on me. It's absolutely ridiculous. In fact, you (3) .... not have bothered as I already have a Porsche! I (4) .... possibly accept it and have asked them to return it to you. You (5) .... try to be reasonable, Alison. You (6) .... possibly be as much in love with me as you claim to be. You don't know me at all and (7) .... possibly have any idea what I'm like. If you got to know me, you (8) .... even find you didn't like me at all. I (9) .... be quite irritating sometimes, I promise you.

I'm afraid I (10) .... ask you not to write to me again. This (11) .... seem harsh but that's the way it (12) .... be.

Regards

Rodney

Vocabulary 2: relationships

1   Match these phrasal verbs to their meanings.

1 get on with someone	a) start to like someone
2 fall out with someone	b) become annoyed or bored with someone
3 get fed up with someone	c) refuse to accept unfair treatment from someone
4 go for someone	d) have a friendly relationship
5 take to someone	e) start to love someone
6 break up with someone	f) have a quarrel with someone
7 stand up to someone	g) separate from someone
8 fall for someone	h) tend to like a particular type of person

2   Complete these sentences using the phrasal verbs in Exercise 1. Remember to put them into the correct tense.

1 Last summer I met a wonderful bloke and I really .... him. It hurt so much when we broke up.

2 Has Sam really .... Lucy? They were going out for ages!

3 I don't want to speak to him but he keeps phoning me – I'm .... him.

4 She tends to .... tall men with dark hair.

5 Alice is always arguing and .... people.

6 He'll respect you more if you .... him.

7 Sam was an odd character who she had never really .... though she got on with him well enough.

8 My sister and I are good friends and .... each other most of the time.

Speaking: (Part 2)

About the exam: In Part 2 of the Speaking test you have to speak about some photographs for one minute.

Look at this task. The pictures below show people in relationships. I'd like you to compare the situations and say what relationship the people in the pictures may have and how you think relationships might change over time.

Read and listen to what one candidate said. Complete the gaps in the conversation with the phrases in the box. The first one has been done as an example.

a) it looks as if	b) they must feel	c) I imagine
d) I suppose	e) maybe	f) I would think
g) it seems	h) I guess	i) it's possible that

In the first picture ....*(a)*.... the couple are very much in love. .... that they've only just met as .... they are quite fascinated with each other. .... they are thinking of getting married and of their life in front of them. The older couple also look happy – .... very comfortable with each other. .... they've been married a very long time and .... that must make them fond of each other. .... it's normal that in the early days of a relationship people are very happy and excited, but then, as time goes on, if they stay together .... that feeling of excitement gets replaced by affection for each other and the feeling that you know each other very well. The couple with children must be close, but perhaps they are distracted by the children.

Now listen to the whole talk again.

Grammar 2: gerunds and infinitives
▶ *CB pages 36–37*

1 Put these verbs into the correct column according to whether they are usually followed by *to* or *–ing*.

enjoy	manage	want	cause
start	prefer	agree	allow
plan	expect	design	decide
attempt	able	use	suggest
avoid	hope	like	

followed by *to*	followed by *-ing*	followed by *to* or *-ing* with little or no change in meaning

2 Complete the sentences by putting the bracketed verb into the infinitive or the gerund.

1 I've always regretted not .... (stay) in touch with him.

2 They got together in 1995 and then both went on .... (become) famous actors.

3 She's got a large house but it needs .... (decorate) to make it more comfortable.

4 If she takes that job it means not .... (see) him for months.

5 I couldn't think who he was, then I remembered .... (meet) him at that party.

6 I'll never forget .... (dance) with her when we were in Italy.

7 I intended to go to the travel agents but I stopped .... (speak) to a friend and forgot!

8 Why don't you try .... (write) her a letter to explain the problem? It may work!

Use of English: key word transformations (Part 5)

1 Complete the second sentence so that it has a similar meaning to the first sentence, using the word given. Do not change the word given. You must use between three and six words, including the word given.

TIP! Make sure you include all the necessary information in the gap.

1 She said she'd come round so I'm sure she's on her way now.
   MUST
   She said she'd come round so .... on her way now.

2 What a pity he couldn't come.
   WISH
   I .... come.

3 I managed to finish the preparations in time.
   SUCCEEDED
   I .... the preparations in time.

4 It isn't necessary to call him as he already knows about it.
   HAVE
   You .... call him as he already knows about it.

5 When he spoke to me he agreed that I wasn't responsible.
   FAULT
   When he spoke to me he agreed that ....

6 She didn't want to join in with the singing.
   TAKE
   She didn't want .... the singing.

7 Anya didn't come to the dinner yesterday evening so perhaps she was ill.
   MUST
   Anya didn't come to the dinner yesterday evening so .... ill.

8 She'll probably end up marrying him!
   CHANCES
   The .... end up marrying him.

Writing: a contribution to a longer piece (Part 2)

About the exam: In Part 2 of the Writing exam you may have the choice of writing a contribution to a longer piece. This may be a contribution to a book, a research project, etc. You will have to write 220–260 words.

Strategy
1 Decide on the purpose of the contribution. Think about who the target reader is and what they need to know.
2 Work out the best, clearest order of presenting the information.

1   Read this task.

You receive this letter from a friend:

> I'm writing a book on the different ways each country relates to the older generation. Could you send me a contribution on your country for my book? I need to know about attitudes to older people in your country and if you think these attitudes will change in the future.

2   Who is the target reader? Read the task again carefully.

1 someone you know
2 a single person you don't know
3 a lot of people you don't know

3   What do you think your contribution should be like?

1 a letter to a friend
2 an article from a magazine
3 a section of a book
4 a report

4   What can you include in your contribution?

• your personal view of the older generation
• what you think is the general or typical opinion
• supporting reasons for a general or typical opinion
• examples from your life
• the name of the country you are referring to
• your opinion supported by general facts
• what you think should be done in the future

5   Read this sample answer and underline the objective language (the language that distances the writer from the text).

In the UK attitudes to older people are not very positive, and this has been the case for a while, but these attitudes may change in the future as the population gets older.

It is clear that not everybody thinks the same, but there are certainly many negative attitudes to older people in the UK. This can be seen in the way that people are cared for when they are older in that they are often put into homes or left on their own rather than living with their families. Many families do not seem to consider that older people have any wisdom or anything to offer them and think that visiting the older members of their family is a duty rather than a pleasure. At the same time, many older people also find it harder to get jobs because companies are less willing to employ them.

However, in the future I think attitudes to older people will begin to change. The population in the UK is getting older, so younger people will be in the minority and will become more dependent on older people. Also many older people in the UK are very active and even do extreme sports or travel to faraway places, so this will make younger people think differently about them.

Overall, I would say there are negative attitudes to older people in the UK, but there are signs that this is changing and that attitudes in the future will be more positive.

Improve!

Always start your paragraphs with a topic sentence so the reader can follow the argument in your writing.

6   Write your own contribution to the task in Exercise 1. Write your answer in 220–260 words.

Reading: gapped text (Part 2)
▶ CB pages 46–47

About the exam: In Paper 1, Part 2, you read a text with missing paragraphs. After the text you find the missing paragraphs in a jumbled order. You decide where they go in the text. There is always one extra paragraph that does not fit anywhere.

Strategy
1 Look carefully for linking words and check what comes after the gap as well as what comes before.
2 Check that your completed text has a logical argument, story or thread running through it.

1 Look at the paragraphs A–G which have been removed from the text below. Match each one to the topics below.

a) the amount of surgery done
b) older people
c) Is surgery bad?
d) changes in society
e) growth in the market
f) two different approaches
g) people needing to look younger in some situations

Use the information above to help you link the paragraphs which have been removed.

Who will be beautiful in the future?

It seems that the older we get as a society, the harder we are all trying to look youthful.

Cosmetic surgery and other anti-ageing **procedures** like Botox are booming. Even at a very conservative estimate, Britons are spending £225 million a year on such procedures, about half of which are concerned with trying to look younger.

1 [   ]

'We get quite a lot of people who are in the media or very competitive jobs in the City, and they just feel as soon as they look a bit tired, that these younger guys and younger women are snapping at their heels, trying to chase them out of their jobs. There still is this feeling that youth and beauty are rewarded in some way in society, and I think they actually are.'

2 [   ]

'The respect for the **wisdom** of ages has gone. What people have got to do is look competitive with other people in the marketplace. People will change their jobs several times in their lifetime, and move to a new local area when they retire. So to be accepted into all these new groups, judgements are made on appearance. All these pressures fit together.'

3 [   ]

Tim Westall of marketing consultancy April Strategy doesn't see this changing, but he thinks it is possible that society will start projecting a 'more mature expression of beauty' as we get older, although it is more likely it will express contradictory attitudes to age.

4 [   ]

Robert Diamond of the Diametric marketing consultancy concurs that we will probably see contradictory images of beauty and maturity in future, as advertisers **wake up to** the potential value of the over-50s' market.

5 [   ]

Continuing innovation in techniques and products available also appears likely to have an impact, with procedures becoming ever more simple, cheap – and therefore appealing. 'Treatments have become less risky, easier, in many cases more affordable and **accessible to** everyone,' says Wendy Lewis. 'People are looking to start early, have smaller things done in bundles, and ease into the ageing process without necessarily looking like they have had work done.'

6 [   ]

'If people are living longer, healthier, happier lives, and their concerns are being spread to things like controlling weight, exercise, smoking, etc. – if it's making people happy at the end of the day, and it's not harming anybody else, then that seems good,' he said. 'In fact, I think some of the things we accepted in the past were probably wrong, such as that people should sit down in their carpet slippers when they reach a certain age.'

From BBC News at bbc.co.uk/news

2   You are going to read an article about plastic surgery. Six paragraphs have been removed from the article. Choose from the paragraphs A–G the one which fits each gap (1–6). There is one extra paragraph which you do not need to use.

A   'Expect the beauty industry to continue to focus on youth,' he says. 'But expect smart marketers to talk about "making the best of who you are" rather than trying to make you become someone different. **Take-up of** cosmetic surgery falls after 45 – older women are more interested in looking good for their age than trying to look a different age,' he says.

B   But is this situation going to change? Surely as the population ages further over coming decades, we are going to start accepting our looks and seeing old as beautiful? Angus McGrouther, Professor of Plastic and Reconstructive Surgery at Manchester University and the UK's first professor of plastic surgery, thinks that fundamental changes in society mean the cosmetic surgery genie will never be put back in the bottle.

C   'There are two **mindsets** that operate, two attitudinal camps,' he says. 'One is about seeking physical perfection – "the L'Oreal woman". There's another which is about beauty from within, about your radiance being the **embodiment of** your life and your spirit and your character – don't over-adorn, and don't mask.'

D   Even if we do still see youth as the main **indicator of** beauty, and continue nipping, tucking, abrading and filling, is that necessarily a bad thing? Professor McGrouther wonders whether it may be a positive sign.

E   According to the British Association of Cosmetic Doctors, 40,000 vials of Botox – enough to treat 150,000 patients – were sold in 2004, with the market growing by 30–40 percent a year.

F   Wendy Lewis, a beauty consultant, explains this by saying, 'Cosmetic surgery is an **epidemic** today. It is exploding [and] the desire for youth, beauty and perfection shows no signs of slowing down.' Simon Withey of the British Association of Aesthetic Plastic Surgeons says all aspects of cosmetic surgery are becoming more popular, for various reasons – among them that people are feeling an intense social pressure to look younger, especially in certain types of work.

G   However, the number of people 'having things done' to look younger remains small. A recent survey by TGI, published by Keynote Research, found that only 7 percent of all women would even consider having a facelift, and 4 percent of men a hair **transplant,** while only 11 percent of women would consider having Botox, and 4 percent of men.

3   Who do you think this article was written for?

a) plastic surgeons

b) the general public

c) cosmetic products companies

4   Check you know the meaning of these highlighted words from the text. Use a good dictionary, such as *The Longman Exams Dictionary*, to help you. Match the adjectives in the box to the words.

fixed	kidney	complex	received
widespread			

1   Plastic surgery can involve undergoing .... **procedures** which can be dangerous.
2   Everybody is worried that there may be a .... **epidemic** of avian flu.
3   I think it is .... **wisdom** that you should not be overweight if you are having an operation.
4   She will have to undergo a .... **transplant** within the next 72 hours.
5   He's got a very .... **mindset** and refuses to consider new ideas.

5   Read through your completed text and underline any references or linking words which helped you complete the task.

Vocabulary 1: science and medicine
▶ *CB page 42*

1 Quiz: Are you sympathetic to science?

Use these words to complete the questions, then do the quiz.

symptoms	breakthrough	scans	advances
diagnosis			

1 Do you think more money should be spent on scientific research?
   a) Only on projects which are working towards a scientific ....
   b) Yes, any and all research is valuable.
2 When you go to the doctor do you expect:
   a) an accurate .... immediately?
   b) a long discussion about your ....?
3 Do you think that .... in science:
   a) have only benefited the world?
   b) have caused more problems than they've solved?
4 If you had to have a series of .... for a medical problem, would you:
   a) be relieved that there is the technology to give doctors more information?
   b) be worried about the long-term effects on your health?

See how you did by checking the Key.

2 Read this article, then use the word given in capitals to form a word that fits the space. Check your spelling very carefully.

YOUR FUTURE IN THE MIRROR!

The wicked queen in 'Snow White' had a magic mirror that told the (**1**) .... (TRUE). French scientists have *gone one better*. They have a mirror that will present you with ugly (**2**) .... (REAL) – five years on. They have fashioned a looking glass that will offer a (**3**) .... (REFLECT) of the future, after years of no exercise and lots of junk food have *taken their toll*, according to *New Scientist* today. Researchers at Accenture Technology, near Nice, have devised a television screen with (**4**) .... (POWER) image-processing technology linked to spy cameras around the house that will monitor the time spent watching television and paying sly visits to the fridge. Software will assemble a picture of the (**5**) .... (LIKE) effects of the day's diet and exercise. At the touch of a button, the computer-(**6**) .... (POWER) mirror will reveal the future you, five years on. One part of the program will calculate the extra (**7**) .... (WEIGH). Another will contemplate the *ravages of time* on the face. The idea is to *deliver a warning* now: this is the digital mirror as personal (**8**) .... (TRAIN) and nutritional coach. 'Technology can be quite persuasive,' laboratory (**9**) .... (DIRECT) Martin Illsey told the magazine.

© Guardian News & Media Ltd 2005

3 Use these verbs in capitals from the text above to make nouns. Be careful – some words may remain the same.

1 The .... (ASSEMBLE) voted in favour of the health service changes.
2 They used a heart .... (MONITOR) to track how fit he was.
3 The news that we should be exercising for 30 minutes a day was a .... (REVEAL) to me!
4 After much .... (CONTEMPLATE), I decided not to give up my diet of junk food.
5 They used a new electronic .... (DEVISE) to calculate how much body fat she had.

4 Use the italicised expressions in the text in Exercise 2 in the correct form to complete these sentences.

1 The surgeon .... about the dangers of smoking.
2 Some scientists are very competitive and always think they can .... than their colleagues.
3 It can be very hard for models to accept the .... on their beauty.
4 If you eat a bad diet it will eventually .... on your health and you will get ill.

5 Check you know the meaning of these words. Use a good dictionary, such as *The Longman Exams Dictionary*, to help you. Which of these are classed as alternative medicine?

homeopathy ☐
psychotherapy ☐
keyhole surgery ☐
chiropractic ☐
acupuncture ☐
biopsy ☐
aromatherapy ☐

Listening: short texts (Part 1)

About the exam: In Paper 4, Part 1, you will listen to three short conversations. You have to answer two multiple-choice questions on each conversation. You will hear each conversation twice.

Strategy
1 When you listen for the first time, try to decide on the communicative purpose of each speaker.
2 Concentrate on general meaning, not specific words.
3 Don't select an option because you hear the same word in the conversation. It may be there to distract you!

1   Listen to the first extract below and answer these questions:
a Is the man: explaining / persuading / agreeing?
b Is the woman: disagreeing / apologising / complaining?

2   You will hear three different extracts. For questions 1–6, choose the answer (A, B or C) which fits best according to what you hear. You will hear each extract twice. Use the second listening to check your answers.

Extract One

You hear two people talking about an old television programme.

1 What is the man's opinion of the TV programme?
   A He was confused by the storylines.
   B He felt the science was unconvincing.
   C He thought the acting was weak.

2 Why does the woman compare the programme to a modern TV programme?
   A to show the level of progress in our understanding of science
   B to emphasise the lack of imagination of the programme makers
   C to illustrate the similarities in what we expect from a programme

Extract Two

You hear part of a radio interview with a woman who is attending a science conference.

3 What does she say is unusual about the conference?
   A the quality of the speakers
   B the range of topics covered
   C the efficiency of the organisation

4 Why is she attending the conference?
   A to understand a new area of business
   B to meet people in her field of work
   C to learn how to give presentations

Extract Three

You hear two people on a science programme talking about genetics.

5 Why has the man changed his view of genetic research?
   A as a result of investigating a particular project
   B because of the way research is now managed
   C due to participating in a research programme

6 What does the woman feel about genetic research?
   A worried about what will happen in the future
   B concerned at the lack of government control
   C anxious about the speed of developments

3   Listen to the extracts again and decide on the correct meaning of each of the following words and phrasal verbs.

Extract One
1 far-fetched   a) unbelievable
                   b) a long way away
2 moved on   a) progressed
                   b) changed place

Extract Two
3 go about   a) walk round
                   b) organise
4 engaging   a) get someone's attention
                   b) employ someone

Extract Three
5 chaotic   a) busy
                   b) disorganised
6 pace   a) length
                   b) speed

Grammar 1: conditionals 1
▶ *CB pages 44–45*

1   Which sentence (i–iv) is about something that:

a) is always true?
b) is possible?
c) is not true in the present and is unlikely or impossible in the future?
d) is imaginary in the past?

i) If he had had a decent night's sleep he would have performed so much better.
ii) If you don't get enough sleep, you become ill.
iii) If we spent a third of our lives sleeping, we could accomplish so much more.
iv) If you've ever stayed up all night studying, you'll know how badly it can affect you.

2   Match the clauses in A to the clauses in B to form sentences.

A

a) **Had she known** she was going to live that long,
b) **Supposing you had** the chance to have yourself cloned,
c) **If** space travel **were to** become less expensive,
d) **Imagine you had** smok**ed** until you were 80,
e) **If you will** just take a seat,
f) **If you happen to** be going to that science conference,
g) **If** her condition **should** change in any way

B

1 please be so kind as to notify me immediately.
2 would you do it?
3 could you possibly get some information for me?
4 the doctor will be with you in a moment.
5 would you consider booking a holiday in orbit?
6 would you bother to give up?
7 she would certainly not have retired so early.

3   Decide which one of the pairs of sentences below is an example of the following uses of conditionals.

Which sentence:

1 is more formal?
   a) Had she realised her research would have been used in this way, she would never have published it.
   b) If she had realised her research would be used in this way, she would never have published it.

2 makes a request more polite?
   a) If you happen to watch that science programme, can you record it for me?
   b) If you watch that science programme, can you record it for me?

3 emphasises that something is a chance possibility?
   a) Supposing you had a chance to travel in space, would you go?
   b) If you had a chance to travel in space, would you go?

4 makes an event sound more hypothetical?
   a) If you lived to be 200, life would probably still hold some surprises!
   b) If you were to live to be 200, life would probably still hold some surprises!

5 is a more polite form?
   a) If you just hold the line for a moment, I'll put you through to the laboratory.
   b) If you'll just hold the line for a moment, I'll put you through to the laboratory.

Use of English: gapped sentences (Part 4)
▶ *CB page 51*

1   Think of one word only which can be used appropriately in all three sentences.

TIP! At least one sentence in each set of three will use a fixed phrase or expression. (This may have a different meaning from the core word.)

1
You can get to the Biology department by taking the .... to the fifth floor.
You drive me mad – you never .... a finger to help when I'm ill.
I've given him a .... to work every day this week, but he never offers me money for petrol.

2
The football team .... themselves very professionally on overseas tours.
It is important that you wear safety equipment when you .... an experiment.
He's hoping to be able to .... the orchestra when they tour next month.

3

In some jobs, it can be really hard to make a decent
....

The drug is tested on .... animals, which I think is appalling.

I'm doing a survey on jobs. Do you mind if I ask you what you do for a ....?

4

You shouldn't .... your nose into other people's business!

Once you have a plan, you should .... to it and stop changing your mind.

She said she would .... by her husband even though he's going to prison.

5

The version he told me was a complete .... of lies.

I find it really hard to .... lightly when I travel – I always take too much.

I think they can .... 50,000 people into the stadium, but it would be really crowded.

Vocabulary 2: collocations and fixed phrases
▶ *CB page 50*

1   Complete the crossword.

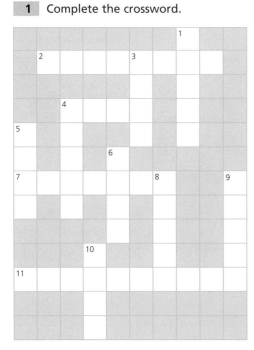

Across

2 to .... a webpage (to help you find it again)

4 a .... of lies

7 to .... experiments

11 to .... your work

Down

1 .... of identity

3 to .... a good living

4 a .... of view

5 to .... into computers (an illegal activity)

6 to .... a muscle

8 to .... your ankle or a .... of fate

9 a .... of curiosity

10 to .... your breath

2   Use the parts of the body below to complete the sentences, then match each sentence to the correct meaning for each highlighted phrase.

| finger(s)   ear(s)   eye   nose |

1 She's not very well so you'll need to **keep an** .... **on** her.

2 I'm **up to my** .... in work at the moment; I haven't got a minute to spare.

3 You shouldn't **stick your** .... **into** other people's business.

4 I'll **keep** my .... **crossed** for you when you have your operation.

5 She's **got a good** .... **for** detail so she'll do well in the sciences.

6 I try to advise him but **it** just **goes in one** .... **and out the other**.

7 You never **lift a** .... to help me – it's not fair!

a) forget information as soon as you hear it

b) look after someone

c) make no effort

d) be very busy

e) hope something will happen in the way you want

f) become involved in something that does not concern you

g) good at noticing a particular type of thing

Grammar 2: conditionals 2
▶ *CB pages 48–49*

1   Choose the correct option in each sentence.

1 *Provided that / Supposing that* the current is applied regularly, the device will function.

2 *Were / Even if* plastic surgery much cheaper, I suspect many more people would consider it.

3 *Only if / As long as* he continues to work hard, he should succeed in medicine.

4 *Provided that / Even if* genetic research were to be controlled carefully, I still think it is wrong.

5 *Supposing that / As long as* you could have any surgery you wanted, what would you change?

6 *Even if / Only if* I was desperate, would I consider plastic surgery.

2   Complete the second sentence so that it has a similar meaning to the first sentence, using the word given. Do not change the word given. Use between three and six words, including the word given.

1 What would you have been if you had never studied to be a doctor?
   IMAGINE
   .... to be a doctor, what would you have been?

2 Might you give up working if you won the lottery?
   SUPPOSING
   .... you give up working?

3 I didn't realise I could catch malaria so I didn't take any tablets.
   HAD
   .... catch malaria, I would have taken some tablets.

4 If I had a facelift, what would you think?
   WERE
   .... a facelift, what would you think?

5 If you need any help, do not hesitate to call.
   SHOULD
   .... do not hesitate to call.

Use of English: key word transformations (Part 5)

1   Complete the second sentence so that it has a similar meaning to the first sentence, using the word given. Do not change the word given. You must use between three and six words, including the word given.

TIP! Think carefully about whether the word you are given involves focusing on a verb change or whether it is part of an expression you are expected to use. If the word you are given is a noun, then it is likely that you have to use an expression, such as in no. 5 below.

1 It's possible that getting stuck in traffic made him late.
   MIGHT
   He .... because he got stuck in traffic.

2 I won't do the analysis unless you clear up the lab.
   LONG
   I'll .... you clear up the lab.

3 The money must be repaid if the project is not completed.
   BACK
   You .... if the project is not completed.

4 'I have had Botox injections,' the actress admitted.
   CONFESSED
   The actress .... Botox injections.

5 He said that he hadn't performed surgery for a while.
   PRACTICE
   He said .... performing surgery.

6 It would be a good idea to speak to a consultant first.
   SUGGEST
   I .... to a consultant first.

7 I only invited you because I thought you wanted to come.
   WOULDN'T
   I .... I thought you didn't want to come.

8 You do realise you may fail your exams!
   DANGER
   Are you aware that you .... your exams?

Speaking: three-way discussion (Part 4)

About the exam: In Part 4 of the Speaking test the examiner will ask you some questions related to the topic you discussed in Part 3. You will have a three-way discussion with your partner and the examiner. It is important to develop or expand what you say, not to just say 'yes' or 'no'.

Look at the task. Listen to the recording of two candidates, Stefan and Rosa, answering a question in Part 3. Decide which candidate is better.

Tick what the better candidate did:
● expanded their answer
● used effective intonation
● used a range of language

Writing: article (Part 1)
▶ *CB page 52*

About the exam: In Part 1 of the Writing exam you may have to write an article. You will have to write 180–220 words.

Strategy
1 Look carefully at the instructions and make sure you deal with each point.
2 Plan your writing so that you write enough on each point.
3 Remember to make your article interesting and persuasive.

1   Read this task.

You are studying at a college in the UK and recently attended a science conference. You have now decided to write an article about the conference for your college magazine.

Read the conference advert below together with some notes you have made. Then, using the information appropriately, write an article explaining what you thought about the conference, giving reasons why and persuading other students to attend next year.

Science for young people

Come and find out how exciting science can be!

Internationally famous speakers.

Opportunity to watch experiments.

Get ideas at our careers desk.

16TH–18TH MARCH
CARDIFF CONFERENCE CENTRE

---

notes:
● lots of new topics & information
● met other students – used English!
● careers desk useful
● experiments amazing (too many people)
● expensive food!
● centre too far from town

Write your article in 180–220 words. You should use your own words as far as possible.

2   Underline the three things you have to do in your article.

3   Read this example article. Does it cover the three points? What is the focus of each paragraph?

Do you think science might be boring? Well, I can assure you you're wrong! I went to a science conference for young people in Cardiff and it really opened my eyes to what's going on in science now and what job opportunities there are in science.
The conference was held for three days in March. The speakers were from everywhere round the world, which was interesting, and in some of the rooms you could watch experiments being performed and see the results! This was exciting and gave you a real feel for the subjects.
Unfortunately, there were too many people in some cases, so it was hard to see. The careers desk was brilliant as they had lots of information. In fact it was so useful that it is worth attending for this alone.
My only criticisms were the food, which was very expensive – but you could easily take your own packed lunch or go outside the centre to eat – and that the centre was a bit far from town, so I hope they have it in a better venue next time. I strongly advise you all to go to this and see exactly what the possibilities are. It's completely changed my views of what I'd like to do and it may change yours too!

4   Choose the best title for the article in Exercise 2.
a) Do you like science?
b) Science IS interesting!
c) Report on the conference.

5   In what two ways is this article different from a report or an essay?

┌─ **Improve!** ◀─

Use persuasive, lively language in articles:
● Use words like *strongly advise*, *urge*, *must*.
● Use adverbs, e.g. *strongly*, *completely*, *absolutely*.

UNIT
5 Thrills and skills

Vocabulary 1: sport
▶ *CB page 61*

1 Underline the correct words in each of the texts below. Use a good dictionary, such as *The Longman Exams Dictionary*, to help you.

THE BAY STADIUM

We offer a range of sports, all taught by *professionals / amateurs* who have worked in the sport for several years and offer expert *instructing / coaching*. We offer trial days where we provide you with the *kit / uniform* and you can practise getting that ball into the back of the *box / net*! Come and give it a go!

DOWNSIDE FOOTBALL CLUB

We're giving our *spectators / audience* the opportunity to *umpire / referee* a football match! All you have to do is control the game and the players with your *whistle / blower*, such as when you spot a *block / foul*, and keep the time. Come along on Saturday and give it a go, if you think you're brave enough!

2 Find six expressions in the wordsearch grid to complete the definitions below.

K	P	B	E	M	O	C	F	A	D	R	E	C	O	R
C	L	O	S	E	M	O	U	L	L	O	S	R	Y	U
M	A	L	A	S	T	M	I	N	U	T	E	A	L	C
O	Y	O	P	E	A	E	W	S	P	E	T	B	C	K
B	E	F	A	T	K	B	A	C	L	A	P	S	E	E
A	L	L	T	O	G	A	S	P	O	M	R	A	N	L
L	S	M	I	N	T	C	M	A	N	P	R	O	S	O
S	E	T	B	A	C	K	I	Y	W	L	A	S	T	M
O	C	G	C	F	A	C	N	E	S	A	L	S	R	A
R	O	R	K	U	T	R	U	C	E	Y	I	W	O	R
A	R	O	A	L	S	E	T	A	R	E	C	O	R	D
N	D	N	P	L	A	Y	E	Y	E	R	K	B	R	E

1 someone who fails to win a competition (7 letters)
2 a problem that delays or prevents progress (7)
3 to become successful or popular again (8)
4 happening or done as late as possible (10)
5 someone who works well with other people (10)
6 to achieve the best result in a sport or competition that has ever been achieved (10)

3 Put the words below into the correct sentences.

tackle	race	caught	volleyed	draw
serve	finishing	score	saved	

1 He tried to .... but the goalie .... the goal so the match was a ....
2 In the tennis final, she had to .... first but she .... the ball straight into the net.
3 In rugby you are expected to .... your opponent and it can get quite rough!
4 It's important to set an even pace when you .... against somebody otherwise you may run out of stamina before you get to the .... line.
5 He was declared out when one of the fielders .... the ball.

4 Match each of these sports to the venues.

1 tennis   a) circuit
2 ice skating   b) course
3 football   c) court
4 Formula 1   d) pitch
5 golf   e) rink
6 rugby   f) stadium

Grammar 1: intensifiers / modifiers
▶ *CB page 55*

1 Which of the modifying adverbs can be used with gradable adjectives and which with ungradable? One adverb can be used with both types of adjectives.

slightly	absolutely	rather	relatively	fairly
really	terribly	unbelievably	completely	
quite	totally	incredibly		

gradable, e.g. cold	non-gradable, e.g. freezing	both

2 These modifying adverbs are typically used with certain adjectives. Match the adverbs on the left to some of their typical collocations on the right. Use a good dictionary, such as *The Longman Exams Dictionary*, to help you.

a) significantly
b) greatly
c) highly
d) entirely
e) fully
f) utterly

i) new / believable / clear
ii) different / higher / longer
iii) competent / recovered / booked / aware
iv) unusual / distinguished / successful / effective
v) miserable / ashamed / ecstatic
vi) appreciated / increased / reduced

3 Use a collocation from Exercise 2 above to complete the following sentences.

1 His excuse for missing training was .... so he wasn't penalised.
2 We trained for three hours in the pouring rain – I was .... by the end of it.
3 Ticket sales were .... by offering four matches for the price of three.
4 After his playing career, he went on to become a .... speaker.
5 The strokes in squash are .... from those in tennis.
6 All the trains to the match were .... – we couldn't get a ticket.

4 Choose the correct adverb for each gap in the following text.

When I went to see Italy play in the World Cup I had an **(1)** .... fantastic time. The weather was great – it had been **(2)** .... wonderful for a few days and on the day of the match it was **(3)** .... boiling. The match was **(4)** .... brilliant – I have never enjoyed myself so much. It got **(5)** .... exciting as it was a draw at full time so they played extra time. Each team scored a goal in the extra time so the match then went to penalties – I was biting my lip because the atmosphere was **(6)** .... tense. Every time they took a shot, I had to close my eyes because it was **(7)** .... scary. Suddenly I heard a roar from the crowd, I looked up and was **(8)** .... surprised to realise that Italy had won. I was **(9)** .... ecstatic! I was **(10)** .... pleased to see that my favourite player, the captain of the team, had scored the winning goal!

1	**A** extremely	**B** almost	**C** absolutely
2	**A** very	**B** quite	**C** a bit
3	**A** perfectly	**B** utterly	**C** absolutely
4	**A** wholly	**B** relatively	**C** totally
5	**A** really	**B** greatly	**C** absolutely
6	**A** completely	**B** unbelievably	**C** entirely
7	**A** very	**B** a bit	**C** perfectly
8	**A** absolutely	**B** extremely	**C** wholly
9	**A** remarkably	**B** greatly	**C** utterly
10	**A** perfectly	**B** doubly	**C** completely

5 When you have checked your answers to Exercise 4, make a list of the adjectives, with their modifiers, from the text above and try to remember them as typical collocations.

Reading: multiple matching (Part 4)
▶ *CB pages 56–57*

About the exam: In Paper 1, Part 4, the questions are not in the same order as the information in the texts.

Strategy
1 Read through all the texts quickly. You don't need to read the texts in detail.
2 Look for words and expressions that <u>mean</u> the same as, but are not identical to, key words in the questions.

1   Read the text on sports coaches quickly and match each section of the text to these headings.

1 Understanding and motivating players
2 Teach life skills along with sports skills
3 Are we having fun yet?
4 Winning isn't everything
5 Be tough but fair

2   The words on the left appear in the questions below. Match the words and expressions from the questions (a–h) to the words or expressions with a similar meaning from the text (i–viii).

a) focus
b) be honest
c) consult
d) enjoyment
e) routine
f) sense of humour
g) spirit
h) be successful

i)   pleasure
ii)   get results
iii) repetitive and ordinary
iv) morale
v)   tell it straight
vi) concentration
vii) ask
viii) see the funny side

What makes a good SPORTS COACH?

What should a coach care about most: winning, teaching, or giving everyone a chance to play? Here's what you told us.

A Winning was a loser in our survey: only 9 percent of you said a coach should care most about winning. 'When you are a good coach, winning or losing is secondary to you. You care more about the morale of your team,' said Daniel, a football player. Most of you respect coaches who put winning in perspective and teach players it's just one part of the game. Naturally, you want to win, but you also want the pleasure of playing well, learning and working as a team. Daniel told us, 'A good coach isn't obsessed with winning but will motivate you and your team to want to win.' 'The best lesson I learned from a coach is that losers give it their best, but winners get the results,' Brett, a tennis player, said. Brett is realistic about the fact that some parents and coaches can push kids too hard, though. 'If I were a coach, I would find out who wants to play and who is playing because of their parents.'

B A coach has to understand a player's weaknesses and strengths. 'They need to know the sport and the athletes well enough to make good choices for the athlete,' said Shannon. Talent for building a player's confidence is also important. Lots of you told us about coaches who have turned your game around. Arielle used to play soccer and she was small and the other kids always picked on her. 'But my coach said that, even though I couldn't kick the ball down the field, I was fast enough to be at the other end to receive it. She said that I should forget about what other people think and stick to what I can do. The rest of that season I was the best midfielder on the team.' So how would you work with your players? Arielle said, 'I would start by asking the players what their goals are. Then talk with them and lay out a plan for the whole year.'

C Coaches who are realistic about what a person can achieve are the kinds of coaches you look up to. Stephanie, a volleyball player, told us a good coach has 'the ability to tell it to you straight or give you the facts without making you feel bad'. Stephanie said that when her coach told her she hadn't made the team, 'he told me why and what I could do to improve, and he said it in a great way. I learned there's a bad way to give an athlete bad news and there's a good way.' 'You want a coach who pushes you to reach your goals in the right way. He should train the team hard, but encourage instead of yelling,' said Spence. How would you handle things as a coach? 'I'd let them know they're doing well but not so much to make them overconfident,' said Spence. Most of you wouldn't be afraid to get tough when it's needed. Spence said, 'I'd let them know that if they're not doing their job, they're going to be given a telling off.'

D 'Besides just coaching, they share wisdom and insight on the world based on personal experience,' said Alex, who told us about his high school wrestling coach. 'It helps having someone besides a parent who's an adult that you can talk to in some situations.' Alex learned the power of positive thinking from her coach, something she can apply away from the sporting field. 'If you mess up, you have to shake it off and concentrate again. Always think about what you will do, not what you won't.' Most of you said the best lesson you'd learned from a coach is 'never give up'. Charley told us, 'We all have bad days and bad competitions and it's OK to be upset, but when you wake up the morning after, you need to set new goals and have a new direction.' So what would you do? 'If I was a coach, I would train my players hard,' said Charley. 'But I would be willing to help any of the players with schoolwork or problems.'

E Almost all of you wanted your coaches to have an ability to see the funny side of things. 'My soccer coach is a role model; you can crack jokes with him and he will crack them back,' said Kelly. You also had ideas on fixing the stuff that wasn't so appealing about your sports. Team drills can be boring, and you'd try to figure out a way to make them more enjoyable. 'I would have at least one drill that was different every week,' said Anna, 'And do a variety of drills.' 'My basketball coach would never punish us with running because he saw no point in making us hate something we should love,' Katelyn said. But you're realistic – sometimes practice needs to be repetitive and ordinary. Katelyn said the best lesson her coach taught her was, 'Fine to enjoy yourself but the boring stuff is what you learn from.' And she offered this advice, 'You practise more than three times the amount that you play in a game, and if you're dreading practice, the sport isn't for you. Find something that you love unconditionally, all the time!'

This information was provided by KidsHealth, one of the largest resources online for medically reviewed health information written for parents, kids, and teens. For more articles like this one, visit www.KidsHealth.org or www.TeensHealth.org.

©1995–2007. The Nemours Foundation

3 For each of the questions, choose from sections A–E. In which section are the following mentioned?

The effect of a coach getting involved with other aspects of players' lives	**1**
A player being helped to recognise their strong point	**2**
The importance of understanding why people are playing a sport	**3**
The need for a coach to show honesty in their dealings with players	**4**
A recognition that routine is essential for sporting success	**5**
The importance of creating the right spirit in a team	**6**
The belief that some exercises can make you feel negatively about the sport	**7**
The change a coach promoted in a player's attitude	**8**
The desire for a coach to drive players forward	**9**
The importance of non-sporting skills to coaching	**10**
The fact that enjoyment does not depend on success	**11**
The desire for coaches to have a sense of humour	**12**
The importance of staying focused, despite setbacks	**13**
The suggestion that a coach should consult players	**14**
A description of different ways of talking to players	**15**

4 Complete these sentences using the expressions below, taken from the texts.

> put it in perspective (A)   turn it round (B)
> look up to (C)   get tough (C)   shake it off (D)
> figure it out (E)

1 I tried to teach myself how to ski but I just couldn't ....
2 If you lose a game, you have to learn to .... and come back fighting!
3 They were losing badly but after half time they managed to ....
4 If you lose, you need to .... and realise it's not life or death!
5 I really .... players who manage to keep their cool on the pitch.
6 If you teach sports you will sometimes need to .... to get the best out of your team.

Listening: multiple choice (Part 3)
▶ *CB page 63*

Strategy
1 Read the first part of the questions only (not the options/alternatives).
2 In each case think carefully about what you are being asked to listen for (e.g. a reason, an agreement, a result, etc.).
3 When you listen, make sure you concentrate on what you are listening for.

1   Look through the six questions on the task below. Decide what you are being asked to listen for. Circle the correct alternative.

For example, in question 1: 'According to Michael, the level of money in football is causing a problem because …', you have to listen for the reason why it is a problem.

1 *problem / (reason) / suggestion*
2 *purpose / suggestion / reason*
3 *reason / problem / purpose*
4 *suggestion / cause / reason*
5 *problem / reason / suggestion*
6 *reason / purpose / cause*

2   You will hear part of a radio interview in which a sports journalist is talking about footballers' pay. For questions 1–6, choose the answer (A, B, C or D) which fits best according to what you hear.

1 According to Michael, the amount of money in football is causing a problem because
   A too many poor quality matches are televised.
   B the game has switched from its working man's roots.
   C it has weakened international competition in the game.
   D the high gate and kit charges have reduced the fan base.

2 Michael claims that the high levels of pay for footballers have come about because of
   A companies wanting players to market their brand.
   B the demand for the televising of matches.
   C clubs fairly rewarding the talent of their players.
   D a desire to prevent top players going to other clubs.

3 Michael says that a valid argument against paying footballers so much is that
   A they are inadequate role models for young people.
   B their salaries are disproportionate to the task.
   C the rich clubs fail to support the poorer clubs.
   D their jobs are less important than those of other workers.

4 Some people feel footballers' salaries are justified because footballers
   A have their whole lives put under pressure.
   B undergo a lot of pressure on the pitch.
   C have a short working life span.
   D lack an alternative career because they missed school.

5 Michael suggests that the solution to the problem of pay is to
   A pay players according to how well they perform.
   B base pay on the percentage of fans the club attracts.
   C create a pay scale with a reasonable top limit.
   D share income from broadcasting across all the clubs.

6 Michael thinks that the profits from football should be used for
   A new sports facilities across the country.
   B involving and teaching children in sports.
   C funding sports scholarships in poorer countries.
   D subsidising an international pay scale for players.

3   Listen again and check your answers.

Vocabulary 2: prefixes

1   Add a prefix to the word in brackets to form a word that fits the space.

Think carefully about how you spell the words.

| un- | dis- | im- | il- | over- | ir- |
| under- | anti- | out- | in- | | |

1 Selling tickets for more than their value is .... (LEGAL)
2 It is .... for a manager to tell a coach what to do with the team. (APPROPRIATE)
3 He has to meet a lot of people but he hates it because he's very .... (SOCIAL)
4 He's so rude – my efforts to help him improve were completely .... (APPRECIATED)
5 They were .... from the match for cheating! (QUALIFIED)
6 The Manchester fans .... the Chelsea fans by 2 to 1! (NUMBERED)
7 She's always boasting about what she's won – she's so .... (MODEST)
8 I think top footballers are grossly .... (PAID)

Use of English: word formation (Part 3)
▶ *CB pages 58–59*

1 Read the text below. Use the word given in capitals to form a word that fits the space. There is an example at the beginning (0). Be careful! Sometimes you have to add a suffix as well as a prefix.

TIP! Check spellings carefully, especially double consonants.

DID COCA-COLA WIN THE WORLD CUP?

In the 2006 World Cup, Coca-Cola came out on top according to data gathered by FIFA's official research **(0)** *organisation* (ORGANISE). A global consumer research study showed the soft drink **(1)** .... (MANUFACTURE) as the most recalled of all FIFA sponsors. This result must have pleased Coca-Cola, although a more qualitative **(2)** .... (ASSESS) shows that Germany, the country itself, was the ultimate World Cup winner.

The Fanfests, a German innovation that allowed the many **(3)** .... (FORTUNE) fans who were unable to obtain tickets to congregate and watch matches in city centres, were a huge success. However, the football fan and the **(4)** .... (OCCASION) TV viewer were both identified as 'losers'. The lack of atmosphere at the final, apparently driven by the **(5)** .... (RESPONSIBLE) selling of too many corporate seats at a cost to the real fans, suggested that, as football becomes more **(6)** .... (PROSPER) as a business, it is losing its passion at both club and global competition level. In addition, broadcasters were criticised for their **(7)** .... (ABLE) to make football more accessible to those not steeped in the game.

Overall, though, the mood was **(8)** .... (OPTIMISM) for the future. The lessons from World Cup 2006 should turn into positive **(9)** .... (ACT) that brings football to a wider audience without further diminishing the atmosphere of one of the greatest **(10)** .... (SPORT) events in the world.

Speaking (Part 3)

About the exam: In Paper 5, Part 3, you will have to discuss some options and make a decision with your partner.

Look at this task. Look at the six pictures showing the benefits of practising sports. Say in what way you think each is a benefit and decide which two offer the greatest benefits.

1 Listen to two students discussing the task. Tick the language they use.

In my opinion ……	So, have we decided?
Would you go along with that?	I'm not sure I agree.
And what else?	Right, are we agreed then?
What I mean is ……	How do you see it?
Is that OK with you?	Shall we say ……

2 Put the expressions above with these functions.

1 giving an opinion

2 asking the other person for their view

3 coming to a conclusion

Grammar 2: comparatives

1   Use the adjectives in A together with words or phrases from B to form suitable comparatives in the sentences below.

A: nearly as	much	the most	than	
far less	as	enough		
B: boring	healthy	well known	near	
fit	young	early		

1 The match was .... I've ever seen – I fell asleep!
2 Beckham is looking .... these days. He must have been training hard.
3 There's no doubt that professionals in sports like karate are not .... the top players in football. In fact, very few people have heard of them!
4 Swimmers have to get up .... the rest of us to train in the morning.
5 Eating sugar is .... than getting energy from carbohydrates.
6 Tennis players .... 16 can start playing professionally.
7 I was at the back so I couldn't get .... to see the goals.

2   The chart shows typical earnings per week for a professional in a variety of sports. Use the comparative expressions and prompts in brackets below to make sentences describing the information in the chart. The first one has been done for you.

sports professional	typical earnings per week
fencer	£50
climber	£65
table tennis player	£125
surfer	£300
rider	£1500

1 significantly more (earn + riding / climbing)
   .Riders earn significantly more than climbers.............
2 not enough (climbers + earn + to live on)
   ....
3 considerably less (earn + fencers / surfers)
   ....
4 by far (riders + earn)
   ....
5 too (fencers + earn + to get by)
   ....
6 the .... sport is riding (earning)
   ....
7 not nearly as (earn + climbers / surfers)
   ....
8 the .... the sport, the .... the salary (prestigious + high)
   ....

Check the answers carefully so you can see the different ways of making comparisons.

Use of English: open cloze (Part 2)
▶ *CB page 62*

1   Read the text below and write in the word that best fits each space. Use only one word in each space. There is an example at the beginning (0).

THE PRIZE!

Wimbledon, the **(0)** .*most*... prestigious tennis championship in the world, was the last major tournament to agree to pay equal prize money to the men's and women's champions. In the lead-up to the decision, current and past players were becoming increasingly outspoken. Several leading names **(1)** .... the women's game claimed that officials at Wimbledon were not doing nearly **(2)** .... to address the problem. In the past, players and critics alike attacked officials for **(3)** .... recognising the unfairness of the women receiving considerably **(4)** .... prize money. What may have prompted the decision was that players had threatened to **(5)** .... further action, possibly even refusing to play. **(6)** .... year Wimbledon has become more and **(7)** .... popular and is now the richest tournament in the sport's history – but officials were immovable. Why did they take so **(8)** .... to see sense? Their justification was that, as women play only three-set matches, they actually made more money per game than the men. These shorter matches also **(9)** .... that the women are less tired and thus more able to play in the doubles and mixed doubles events – increasing **(10)** .... total earning capacity over that **(11)** .... the men's. **(12)** .... considerations were the fact that Wimbledon can charge more for corporate hospitality on men's event days and that more people tune in to watch the men's matches on television. Ironically, women's appearance was probably the factor that forced Wimbledon officials to cave in – the **(13)** .... of Anna Kournikova successfully attract **(14)** .... numbers of people to watch the women's game. As these media stars become better known through advertising campaigns, their appeal has translated **(15)** .... the numbers that win the economic argument!

Writing: report (Part 2)

About the exam: In Paper 2, Part 2, you may have the choice of writing a report. The style of your report will contribute towards your marks.

Strategy

1 Look at what the question asks you to write about and think carefully about what points you need to include. Imagine you are the target reader – what do you need to know?
2 Organise the information into topic paragraphs.
3 Remember to concentrate on register and style.

1 Read the task below. Underline the separate parts of the report. How many sections do you think the report should have?

The sports centre you attend is concerned that it is not attracting enough young people to join in with competitive sports. You have been asked to write a report for the management committee detailing why members are not taking part in competitive sports and providing suggestions for encouraging them to do so.

2 Choose the best title for the report.

a) Competitive sport: popular or not? An overview
b) Reasons why students don't participate in sport
c) The current situation regarding competitive sports and recommendations for the future

3 Read this sample report and fill in the missing headings for each paragraph. Choose from the headings below.
- Sports done in school
- Current situation
- Recommendations
- Conclusion

The aim of this report is to examine the reasons why students are reluctant to take part in competitive sports and to make recommendations for ways of encouraging more students to participate.

a) ....
Most young people enjoy team sports because they are a social event. They like playing with friends and are less interested in open competition. They are keen on fitness and training in the gym, but some are totally uninterested in sport. It also appears that although many enjoy activities

like swimming, they are put off by the current state of the changing rooms, which they feel were dirty and unattractive.

b) ....
Students want to socialise, so sports competitions should be run at times when as many as possible can participate and watch. At present they happen on Saturdays when many students are reluctant to return to college – this should be changed.

The changing rooms around the swimming pool must be improved for those who are currently discouraged from using them because of the state they are in.

The college could run teams for different year groups and offer a prize annually. This would provide motivation as everyone likes to be a winner.

Most importantly, students lack information and should be made more aware of the importance of sport for health and well-being. I recommend that leaflets should be circulated as part of an overall fitness awareness campaign.

c) ....
If these recommendations are implemented, I feel sure that there will be a marked increase in the popularity of competitive sport.

4 Look at paragraph b). Underline the evidence used by the writer to support each recommendation.

5 Which statement connected with reports below is *not* true?

1 The conclusion should link clearly to the rest of the report with an appropriate linking word or phrase.
2 Reports should state their aims in the first paragraph.
3 The writer should not include his or her opinion until the conclusion.
4 A report uses dramatic and informal language.
5 Recommendations should be supported by evidence.

> **Improve!**
>
> Remember to keep your report objective by using, for example, structures like the passive.

6 Write your own answer to the task, using information from a college or centre you know. Remember to follow the advice in the statements you chose in Exercise 5 and to use your grammar checklist to check your work. Write your answer in 220–260 words.

UNIT
6 Family ties

Listening: multiple matching (Part 4)

Strategy

1 Make sure you complete both tasks. Use the second listening to check your answer.
2 Don't pick an answer just because you hear the same word as in the options – listen for a paraphrase.

1 Match each relative below with the paraphrases.

a) mother	i) my aunt or uncle's son or daughter
b) sister-in-law	ii) my husband's or wife's mother
c) cousin	iii) person who gave birth to me
d) niece	iv) my mother's new husband, not my father
e) grandfather	v) my husband or wife's sister
f) mother-in-law	vi) my mother or father's brother
g) uncle	vii) my mother or father's father
h) stepfather	viii) the daughter of my sister or brother

2 You will hear five short extracts in which people are talking about a family connection. You will hear the recording twice.

3 Complete these expressions to do with relationships from the listening above using the words in the box. Then match the completed expressions to the meanings used in the listening.

| hand | there | knit | way | go |
| gathering | down | | | |

a) up and	i) meeting
b) to get your own	ii) inconsistent
c) close-	iii) know and support each other
d) come and	iv) support
e) a family	v) exist then don't exist
f) to give someone a	vi) help
g) to be .... for someone	vii) do what you want

4 Complete the sentences with the following phrasal verbs from the listening in Exercise 2.

| hit it off | tied up with | make it up |
| get together | | |

1 As soon as I met him we really .... – we're so similar!
2 I haven't seen you for ages – we must .... soon.
3 She hasn't called because she's very .... her new boyfriend.
4 You ought to .... with her; she didn't mean to make you cross.

TASK ONE

For questions **1–5**, choose from the list **A–H** the family member the person is speaking about.

TASK TWO

For questions **6–10**, choose from the list **A–H** the attitude each speaker expresses.

While you listen you must complete both tasks.

A aunt			A I wish I lived closer to this person.		
B nephew	Speaker 1	**1**	B I regret arguing with this person.	Speaker 1	**6**
C mother	Speaker 2	**2**	C I hope I can help this person.	Speaker 2	**7**
D father-in-law	Speaker 3	**3**	D I get on well with this person.	Speaker 3	**8**
E stepmother	Speaker 4	**4**	E I wish I had taken this person's advice.	Speaker 4	**9**
F cousin	Speaker 5	**5**	F I'd rather rely on this person than on my friends.	Speaker 5	**10**
G brother-in-law			G I worry about what this person thinks of me.		
H father			H I regret not being kinder to this person.		

Vocabulary 1: word + preposition collocations
▶ *CB page 71*

1   Choose the correct preposition.

ARE TWINS THE CLUE?

People have been constantly fascinated by twins – our sense of self is so strong that we are riveted by the notion that you can have somebody else who appears exactly the same as you. Studies *with / into* twins and their behaviour have focused on the role that genes have *in / on* determining qualities such as optimism, religiosity, etc. According *by / to* many of these studies, the environment has a greater impact *with / on* behaviour than previously thought and much time has been spent on looking at precisely what behaviour is dictated *on / by* our upbringing and what *on / by* our genes. Studying twins, brought up separately and apart, allows researchers to decide *about / on* the balance in the nature vs nurture debate. Personally, I'm more convinced *by / with* the nature argument – but this could lead *to / for* families round the country blaming themselves for the faults in their children!

2   What is the common preposition that follows each group of words?

A	B	C	D
result	pay	coincide	benefit
specialise	apologise	compare	refrain
confide	apply	contrast	suffer

E	F	G
congratulate	refer	boast
influence	confess	worry
insist	react	learn

3   Complete the gaps with a verb + preposition from Exercise 2.

1   My family were great and held a big party to .... me .... passing my exams!
2   My daughter finally .... having broken the vase!
3   When I finish university, my dad wants me to .... a position in a bank.
4   I think I'd like to .... biology as that's what my mum did.
5   My brother's failure had a big .... how hard I worked.
6   My grandad has been in hospital lots because he .... diabetes.
7   I don't think you should .... not having enough money – mum will pay!

4   Complete the gaps with the correct preposition. Be careful – some gaps need a verb, noun or adjective + preposition and some need phrasal verbs.

CELEBRITY RIVALRY

There have been a lot of celebrity sisters in the spotlight in the last few weeks. We thought we were seeing double when Monica Cruz showed **(1)** .... with Penelope at the Oscars. And at Nickelodeon's 20th Annual Kids' Choice Awards, Jamie Lynn Spears was looking very grown **(2)** .... and just like older sister Britney. It must be very odd for the more famous sisters to suddenly be sharing the limelight **(3)** .... flesh and blood. No matter how well you get **(4)** ...., when the 'other woman' on the red carpet is your sister the potential **(5)** .... rivalry is huge. Monica Cruz, for example, is launching a fashion line with Mango, a move which has undoubtedly been helped **(6)** .... her sister's fame. While Penelope seems happy **(7)** .... her sister's success, behind closed doors does it bother her that her sister is seemingly riding her coat-tails? When Jamie Lynn Spears made her red-carpet appearance, one magazine posed the question, 'Does she look like Brit at her best?' And as anyone who saw the picture will know, the answer has to be yes.

It could be a recipe **(8)** .... disaster. But, according **(9)** .... psychologist Ben Williams, it doesn't have to be. 'When problems come in it's usually because of jealousy or parents who favour one more than the other. But if the relationship is a good one they will probably be very supportive and give advice and help because they will have learned **(10)** .... their own mistakes. It's support and collaboration versus rivalry and competition.'

Check your answers, then underline the phrasal verbs. Check the meaning in a good dictionary, such as *The Longman Exams Dictionary*.

Grammar 1: wish
▶ *CB page 70*

1   Match the following sentences to when we use them.

1 I wish I had a car.
   Is this wish about: a) the present   b) the past?
2 I wish he wouldn't call me all the time.
   How do you feel: a) sad   b) irritated?
3 I wish I could stop biting my nails.
   Do you think you will stop: a) yes   b) no?
4 I wish I had helped my mother.
   Is this wish about: a) the present   b) the past?
5 If only I could talk to him.
   Is this wish: a) strong   b) weak?
6 If only I hadn't argued with him.
   Is this wish about: a) the present   b) the past?
7 It's time we left.
   Is this wish about: a) the present   b) the past?
8 I'd rather take my brother to the party!
   Do we want this to happen: a) now   b) in the future?
9 Suppose he asked you out?
   Will this event: a) definitely happen   b) possibly happen?

2   Complete the following sentences using the appropriate form of the verb in brackets.

TIP! Make sure you read the whole sentence before deciding on the verb form.

1 I know Anna wishes she .... (have) another baby, but the doctor says it might not be possible.
2 If only I .... (not + get) so angry with Patrick last time we met.
3 I'd rather we .... (wait) before telling Billy he's going to have a little brother.
4 I wish you .... (visit) your grandmother more often – you must call her.
5 Don't you sometimes wish you and dad .... (not + get married) when you were so young?
6 It's high time you children .... (start) helping round the house.
7 I wish I .... (not + live) so far away from the rest of my family – I hate it!
8 Suppose you .... (have) triplets instead of twins. Do you think you would have been able to manage?

3   Look at the main verb used with regret in these sentences.

1 She **regrets telling** him that she didn't like his mother.
2 I **regret not looking** after my father when he was ill.
3 He **regrets having agreed** to go to the wedding.
4 I **regret to inform** you that your application is unsuccessful.
5 He **regrets his decision** now.
6 She **regretted what** she had done.

a) Which of these functions applies to each of the sentences above?
   – feeling sad about an event or action that has happened.
   – a polite formal way to express refusal.
b) When did the main event in each sentence happen?
   – past.
   – present or future.
c) Which form of *regret* is different from all the others?
d) Is there a difference between:
   She **regrets telling him** that she didn't like his mother.
   She **regrets having told** him that she didn't like his mother.

4   Put the correct form of *regret* with the verb in brackets in the following sentences.

1 She said that she .... (not + be) closer to her mother when she was alive.
2 We .... (say) that we are unable to attend the anniversary celebrations.
3 They .... (tell) her that she could live with them.
4 I .... (take) on the job but it's too late now.

5   Write new sentences for these situations using expressions of hypothetical meaning.

Your brother keeps borrowing your clothes.
1 I wish ....
   You would like to travel round the world.
2 If only ....
   You would like to have a bigger family.
3 I wish ....
   You would prefer you and your fiancée to have a big wedding.
4 I'd rather ....
   You think your sister should get a job.
5 It's time ....
   You regret not calling your dad to apologise.
6 I wish ....
   You regret working when your kids were young.
7 If only ....
   You want to suggest that you and your sister buy a present for your dad together.
8 Suppose ....?

Vocabulary 2: easily confused words
▶ *CB page 77*

1 Fill the gaps in the clues below with commonly confused words. Use a good dictionary, such as *The Longman Exams Dictionary*, to help you. Then complete the crossword.

Across
1 .... your hand if you know the answer.
3 If you don't pass exams, it can make you .... confidence in your ability.
6 You need to .... the material flat on the table.
7 The .... on the children's behaviour was astonishing.
8 From the evidence, we can .... that the victim knew the burglar.
9 Police had to be called in to .... the crowds.
12 We couldn't sell anything because the house was full of .... junk.
13 I've got a very short .... – I forget everything!
14 You shouldn't leave a child .... in the house.

Down
1 There has been a .... in consumer prices this month.
2 She did not mean to .... that he was lying.
3 My tooth feels .... and wobbly – I'd better go to the dentist!
4 This decision will .... our lives for ever.
5 The jewels are .... so they are kept in a secure gallery.
6 I always .... awake worrying on the night before an exam.
9 You should .... that all the doors are locked securely.
10 Don't you get .... being on your own all day?
11 I bought a model of the Eiffel Tower as a .... of Paris.

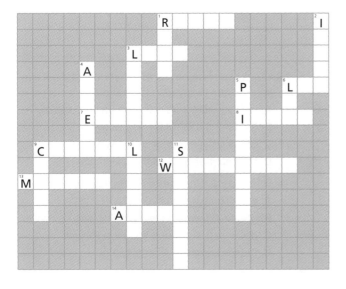

2 Underline the correct word in each sentence.

1 He made an *allusion / illusion* to the fact that I had caused the argument.
2 I don't know why she was so upset – I told her it was nothing *personnel / personal*.
3 How do you intend to *precede / proceed* with this plan to save money then?
4 The police *ceased / seized* the goods as soon as they came in the country.
5 I'm close to my uncle and he's always been my *confidant / confident*.
6 From the look on his face, she *expected / suspected* that he was lying to her.
7 I didn't want to *except / accept* the award for the worst performance!
8 Are we packed and *already / all ready* to leave?

Use of English: key word transformations (Part 5)
▶ *CB pages 76–77*

1 Complete the second sentence so that it has a similar meaning to the first sentence, using the word given. Do not change the word given. You must use between three and six words, including the word given.

1 She waved until the train could not be seen any more.
   SIGHT
   She waved until the train ....
2 I regret speaking to him like that.
   WISH
   I .... to him like that.
3 I'm phoning because my son is too ill to talk to you.
   BEHALF
   I'm phoning .... my son, who is ill.
4 She isn't in so I assume she went to the party.
   MUST
   She .... to the party.
5 She should get him to do more housework.
   HIGH TIME
   .... him to do more housework.
6 I thought you wanted me to invite him.
   IMPRESSION
   I was .... you wanted me to invite him.
7 We need to know how genes determine behaviour.
   ROLE
   We need to know what .... behaviour.
8 Javier and I are completely different.
   COMMON
   I .... Javier.

Reading: short texts (Part 1)

Strategy
1 Make sure you understand what the question or 'stem' is asking you.
2 Read the text quickly and find the words which lead to the answer.

1 Underline the words in each of the questions 1–6 which tell you what to focus on. The first one has been done for you.

2 Read these three texts which are all about family and connections. For questions 1–6, choose the answer (A, B, C or D) which best fits according to the text.

SMALLER CIRCLES

An American study of behavioural trends has identified **a marked decline** in relationships outside the family that are strong enough to allow a person to divulge their deepest worries. It also found that the number of people who say they have no one with whom they can discuss important matters has more than doubled.

Researchers said that the trend towards greater social isolation is a result of people working longer hours, living in less neighbourly communities, joining fewer clubs and seeking advice from sources such as the Internet, sociologists believe. The survey found that both family and non-family confidants had dropped, with the loss greatest in non-family connections.

Lynn Smith-Lovin, Professor of Sociology at Duke, said that the evidence clearly showed a damaging shift. 'This change indicates something that is not good,' she said. 'Ties with a close network of people create **a safety net** for our society. These ties lead to civic engagement and local political action.' The study **paints a picture** of Americans' social contacts as a 'densely connected, close, homogeneous set of ties slowly **closing in on itself,** becoming smaller, more tightly interconnected, more focused on the very strong bonds of the nuclear family'.

FIND YOUR FAMILY!

Many people are interested to know where they came from and thanks to the Internet, researching your family history is now so much easier. To trace your ancestry and find out when, where and how your relatives lived, follow the advice below and enjoy this fast-growing and increasingly popular hobby.

How successful you are in researching your family history is determined by a number of factors, many of which are outside your control – the survival of records, how common your surname was, your *line 10* family's mobility, their social status and level of literacy, and the possibility of transcription errors. However, success can also depend on your tenacity, keeping an open mind and not taking anything for granted, being methodical, approaching a problem from more than one angle and corroborating any evidence you may find.

Before you begin your family history research, it is a good idea to focus on what you want to achieve. Do you wish to pursue the paternal (male) line with its continuity of surname, or the maternal (female) line, or perhaps even verify a family legend? You may find that the decision is made for you, if the research proves difficult. The golden rule in family history research is to try to work backwards from what you already know. As such, family history truly does begin at home and you may be surprised at how much information you can gather from within your extended family. Then contact us and, for a small fee, we can help you access the records you need.

www.ScotlandsPeople.gov.uk

1 Research has found that relationships outside the family have declined in the USA <u>because of</u>
   A features of modern lifestyles.
   B an unwillingness to trust outsiders.
   C the rise in the number of nuclear families.
   D smaller neighbourhoods.

2 Lynn Smith-Lovin implies that the reduction in outside contact is a disadvantage for
   A families who want to be more neighbourly.
   B individuals who may feel isolated.
   C communities and the way they are run.
   D local clubs which are trying to expand.

3 The writer mentions factors that might be outside your control in lines 10–13 to illustrate
   A why you might have to give up your search.
   B the time it might take you to get answers.
   C obstacles you may need to overcome.
   D the importance of careful planning.

4 Before contacting the company, you should have
   A done some research already.
   B got an agreement from your family.
   C developed a schedule for your research.
   D found out where records can be accessed.

The Positives and Negatives of Birth Order

First-borns are natural leaders and often high achievers. The majority of politicians, spokespersons and managing directors are first-borns. They often come in two flavours: compliant nurturers and caregivers or aggressive movers and shakers. Both are in control; they just use different methods. As a rule, first-borns are picky, precise people who tend to be punctual, organised and competent. The negatives are that they are often moody and occasionally lack sensitivity. They can be intimidating, particularly by pushing people too hard or refusing to take no for an answer. Sometimes they can be a bit 'know-it-all', and often they are poor at delegating, largely because they don't trust other people as much as they trust themselves. They also tend to be bossy, perfectionists and overly conscientious.

line 18   Last-borns are the world's cheerleaders. They have strong people skills and love to entertain and talk to others. They make friends easily and immediately make others feel at home. They're extroverts, energised by the presence of other people and probably not afraid to take risks. However, last-borns tend to get bored quickly. They have a strong fear of rejection and a short attention span. When the fun stops, they've had enough and want to check out. To some extent they're self-centred. They may harbour unrealistic expectations of finding a relationship that is always fun – and, of course, such relationships simply do not last.

5 The writer mentions jobs that first-borns do to show that
  A if you are as determined as a first-born then you can make it to the top.
  B the qualities first-borns have make them more successful than others in those jobs.
  C first-borns are naturally bossier than other people.
  D the position you are born in may dictate which job you do.

6 What does the writer mean by 'cheerleaders' in line 18?
  A people who tend to rush round and do lots of activities
  B people who are extroverts and like showing off
  C people who are optimistic and enjoy the social side of life
  D people who can be fun but who can also have a tendency to be superficial

3 Identify what type of text each of the texts is and where you would find them.
a) an analysis in a popular pyschology magazine
b) advertising information available on a website
c) an article in the 'society' pages of a newspaper

i) Smaller Circles
ii) The Positives and Negatives of Birth Order
iii) Find Your Family!

4 Look at these fixed phrases in 'Smaller Circles' and tick the best meaning in the context.
1 a marked decline   a) a noticeable decrease
                      b) noticeably worse
2 a safety net   a) a system that exists to help you in difficulty
                      b) threads or wires to catch something
3 to paint a picture a) to use paints to show a design
                      b) to describe something
4 to close in on itself a) to move closer to something in order to attack it
                         b) to think about oneself only

Which meaning is literal (physical or real) and which is metaphorical (expressing an idea) in each case? Put L or M next to each of the meanings above.

5 Find these words in 'Find Your Family!' and 'The Positives and Negatives of Birth Order'. Look carefully at how they are used in the texts. Put them into the correct columns.

| picky | moody | trace | bossy | mobility |
| check out | corroborating | | verify | cheerleaders |

colloquial language	academic language

Use of English: open cloze (Part 2)

1 Read the text below and write in the word which best fits each space. Use only one word in each space. There is an example at the beginning (0).

WILL THE CRADLE ROCK?

It is (0) .....*a*..... fact of modern life that in Europe and the USA people are having fewer children than (1) .... parents and grandparents did. In the States the current birth rate is 2.1 children per woman. In Europe the average is 1.5 children per woman. So (2) .... is this happening? In a recent poll, many people said that they wanted to have more children but they believe that they could (3) .... afford to. (4) .... they were asked how many children they intended to have, some people said one child, though (5) .... majority said two. Of course, some people (6) .... want to have children are unable to do (7) .... One woman told researchers she was worried (8) .... not having enough money to pay for their education. Another family said that they had had a lot of children because they were considered a benefit to the farm they lived on. In the city, (9) ...., children are not (10) .... an obvious benefit as this. The additional cost means that many young men are not keen to have lots of children (11) .... the fact that their wives may well (12) .... A further reason is that some young people, in these countries especially, are worried that their families may split up and do not want to inflict this (13) .... their children. It is also the (14) .... that, increasingly in Europe and the USA, both halves of the couple have to work in (15) .... to maintain the lifestyle that they want for their children.

2 Underline all the examples of substitution and mark where there are ellipses in the text in Exercise 1. Where there are ellipses, decide what words are missing.

Grammar 2: substitution/ellipsis
▶ *CB pages 74–75*

1 Choose the correct response for each of the statements.

Neither do I.   So have I.   So do I.   So am I.
If you can't, I will   I'd love to

1	**A:** I'm going to Italy in June.	**B:** ....
2	**A:** I've got two older sisters.	**B:** ....
3	**A:** Would you like to come to dinner?	**B:** ....
4	**A:** I'm not sure I can help her.	**B:** ....
5	**A:** I think your dad's really great.	**B:** ....
6	**A:** I don't like her new boyfriend.	**B:** ....

2a Match each of the sentences on the left with a sentence on the right.

a) Can we have steak for dinner tonight?	i) I don't think <u>so</u>.
b) He locked his car keys in his car.	ii) That's why I go there so often.
c) Has she seen him recently?	iii) If you want to.
d) Are you going to fail your exam?	iv) I don't know how.
e) We always have great food at	v) Such behaviour is my gran's. unacceptable.
f) She's always fighting.	vi) I hope not.

2b Underline words which substitute a clause or mark where there are ellipses – i has been done as an example. Be careful – one sentence has two substitutions.

Writing: competition entry (Part 2)

About the exam: In Paper 2, Part 2, you may have the choice of writing a competition entry.

Strategy
1 Plan your reasons or arguments carefully to fit the judges' requirements.
2 Remember to have a strong concluding paragraph to make the judges pick you or your nominee!

1 Read the details of this competition.

Competition for an ambassador for children

We are looking for an ambassador for children. This person will have to get on well with young people and be able to represent them and their interests. Do you know someone who could do this? It could be somebody famous or even a member of your own family. If so, write to us telling us about this person, saying why you think they could do this job and giving reasons why your nominee should be selected.

2 Which of the following do you think the judges need to know?

- the name of a person
- how you know this person
- a physical description of the person
- a description of the person's character
- information about the person's work history
- information about any connection this person has with children
- why the person wants to be selected
- why this person would be better than other nominees

3 Read this sample answer.

I would like to nominate Angelina Jolie as an ambassador for children.

Angelina Jolie is a famous Hollywood film star and she would make an excellent ambassador for children for several reasons. First of all, she is very famous so wherever she went to talk about children or represent them, people would pay attention because they know her. Secondly, she is very beautiful so she would make people notice her and any children she met would like her a lot. Thirdly, she is famous for travelling the world and adopting children from all over the world. Not only does she love children and have their interests at heart, but also she is very conscious of the problem for children in different parts of the world. In addition, she is very rich so she could undertake a lot of tasks herself without much need to be funded.

Angelina Jolie should be selected because she would be better than the alternatives. A sports person may not be popular with girls and someone who was not famous would not be very good at meeting important people and representing children's interests. Also some people who might be quite good are too old, like Madonna - Angelina has a very youthful appearance and could be more in touch with young people. Other people are too tied up in their careers to be able to devote enough time to the job.

4 Choose the best concluding paragraph.

a) I think you should pick Angelina Jolie because I like her a lot.
b) All in all, I definitely think Angelina Jolie would be the best person and I urge you to appoint her in this role.
c) You must choose Angelina Jolie as the alternatives are hopeless.

5 Underline the language of persuasion in the sample answer.

6 How many reasons for selecting her nominee does the writer give in the sample answer?

Improve!

Use a variety of descriptive adjectives to show a range of vocabulary.

7 Write your own competition entry for the task in Exercise 1. Write your answer in 220–260 words.

Reading: multiple choice (Part 3)
▶ *CB pages 82–84*

Strategy
1 Make sure that you read the first part of the question very carefully.
2 Check that the option you select is correct when matched with the first part.
3 Your complete answer must match what is written in the text.

1 Read this extract from a text and the question underneath. Which option is correct and why are the other options incorrect? Underline the words in the first part of the question which are important.

I think graffiti is a very important and admired art form. Whether or not it will become more so depends on a number of factors, such as whether it can come up with new ideas and progress artistically or whether the gangs who indulge in it broaden so they're not just teenagers, who seem to eventually grow out of it. But it's been around a long time now and the endless cycle of it being done then wiped away will eventually wear the artists down.

1 According to the writer, graffiti is unlikely to become more popular because
   A the artists are moving on to other art forms.
   B too much of it is regularly removed.
   C it fails to change with the times.
   D it only appeals to a certain age group.

2 You are going to read an article about graffiti. For questions 1–7, choose the answer (A, B, C or D) which you think fits best according to the text.

1 What does Artist Tango24 think about the current status of graffiti?
   A He thinks its success will be short-lived.
   B He is optimistic that it will return to its roots.
   C He approves of its increasing success as an art form.
   D He is proud that it can now be seen in galleries.

2 According to the writer, the Romans
   A used graffiti to record their history.
   B wrote graffiti that was often unintelligent.
   C were unaware of the consequences of their graffiti.
   D thought graffiti was an essential decoration to public buildings.

3 Banksy says that the problem with graffiti is that
   A it involves taking a lot of risks.
   B it is appreciated for the wrong reasons.
   C it will never be recognised for its artistic value.
   D it is hard to get work accepted by British galleries.

4 What does the writer say about cleaning costs in paragraph 4?
   A The costs have escalated year on year.
   B Council money could be better spent on other things.
   C Taxpayers are unaware that they are paying for the cleaning.
   D There are hidden costs involved in cleaning the graffiti.

5 Alan Best is concerned about the effects of graffiti because
   A removing it involves destructive processes.
   B it can never be fully removed from a building.
   C it is having a significant impact on the environment.
   D the paint in the graffiti can be harmful to the people who remove it.

6 What is Best's attitude to 'paint-eaters'?
   A They are unsuitable for historical buildings.
   B They can only be removed from a building with chemicals.
   C They are too damaging to the buildings they are used on.
   D They are an unsatisfactory solution in the long term.

7 Why will the new coating mentioned in the last paragraph disappoint taggers?
   A It will prevent them from spraying graffiti on the walls.
   B Their graffiti will not remain on buildings for very long.
   C They will no longer be able to target certain buildings.
   D They will be more likely to be caught spraying buildings.

3 Find words or phrases in the text that have the same meaning as the following.

1 secret and illegal (para 1)
2 felt sexually attracted to (para 2)
3 without knowing or realising (para 2)
4 very large and impressive (para 4)
5 push a hard object into something (para 5)
6 getting less and less (para 6)
7 invented (para 7)

URBAN ART OR MINDLESS VANDALISM?

Graffiti can be both – enlivening our cities on one hand,
costing a fortune to clean up on the other.

Graffiti is gaining ground as an acceptable art form. In London, train company Thameslink recently invited graffiti artists to improve Tooting station with a full-scale, graffiti mural. Some pieces have made it into art galleries and many councils create designated spaces where artists have permission to express themselves. Artist Tango24 says, 'Graffiti is mainstream nowadays, you see it in music videos, promotions, advertising, pretty much anywhere. Hopefully, in another five to ten years, it'll be underground again.'

Graffiti isn't new. Ruins from ancient civilisations show that the Romans, Greeks, Mayans and Vikings were at it thousands of years ago. The Romans carved graffiti into their walls and monuments, and examples were preserved at Pompeii when Vesuvius erupted, burying the town. Romans etched everything from people they fancied to insults, quotes, magic and politics into their walls, unwittingly leaving clues for today's archaeologists about Roman street life.

Nowadays, taggers, as graffiti artists are sometimes known, take greater risks for their art. 'For the dedicated graffiti vandal, danger is often part of the thrill,' reckons the British Transport Police, which says that attempts to spray difficult surfaces such as bridges or trains in sidings put both the sprayer and others in danger. Graffiti artists like Banksy, whose works have been displayed in US art galleries, might agree. 'People look at an oil painting and admire the use of brushstrokes to convey meaning,' he says. 'People look at a graffiti painting and admire the use of a drainpipe to gain access.'

But spare a thought for the people who have to clean it up. Graffiti is on the increase and the costs of removing it are epic. Britain's rail system spent over £5 million erasing graffiti in 2005, while taking trains out of service for clean-up caused disruption and delays. London Underground workers devote 70,000 hours a year to cleaning graffiti, at a cost of at least £10 million. A further £38 million would pay for replacements for graffiti-etched windows on every Tube train. Town councils each spend tens of thousands of pounds of taxpayers' money removing illegal art.

Whether you find graffiti expressive or excessive, it damages building surfaces and impacts on the environment. Colourful paints and permanent markers, including acrylic, water-based and nitro combinations, soak into buildings' porous surfaces and attack the minerals. 'Graffiti removers also dig in with lots of elbow grease, wire brushes and even more chemicals,' says Alan Best, who runs eco-company Green Concept. 'A high-pressure hot-water jet system is then used to finish the job.' Cleaners blast scalding water or steam through a lance, rinsing a cocktail of minerals, mortar and paint and chemical residues into the environment. Shadow traces of the graffiti are often left behind on walls. The stone or brick has now deeply absorbed both the removal chemicals and the water. This water expands as it freezes in winter, and works with the paint chemicals to further weaken the building's surfaces.

Councils and other organisations can slap anti-graffiti coatings on buildings and monuments to make the removal job easier. Graffiti artists call these coatings 'paint-eaters'. Polyurethane-based protection products are permanent and repel graffiti. The drawback is that they are expensive and you can see them clearly, making them unsuitable for some stone buildings. 'Environmentally speaking, these are petrochemical-based products that use up dwindling oil resources, and are cleaned with solvents, which then have to be properly disposed of,' says Best. Silicone-based products and waxes, together with polysaccharides and fluoropolymer-based products, are known as 'sacrificial' protection. This layer absorbs graffiti and is easier to shift. But organisations like British Heritage are reluctant to use sacrificial coatings to protect monuments after finding that they aren't completely effective and they changed the mineral's appearance.

Best worked with scientists to create a new anti-graffiti coating that is clean, water-based, safe and inexpensive. They cooked up a safe, water-based coating containing nano-particles – particles a few billionths of a metre wide. These particles coat the building surface in an incredibly thin layer, a few atoms thick. They stop paints, oil or water getting in, but still allow the bricks or stone to breathe. A micro wax coating goes on next. If taggers strike, then hot water will wash off the spray paint along with the wax, while the nano-coating underneath stops water penetrating the surface. The new eco-friendly graffiti protection is already a hit with health authorities, churches, schools and the police, although it could come as a disappointment to the taggers.

Grammar 1: the future
▶ *CB pages 85–87*

1   Match the highlighted language used to express the future in A to the meanings in B.

A

1 His work **is due to** be exhibited at the gallery next year.

2 Anyone wishing to take photographs today **is to** get permission from reception beforehand.

3 He's **on the point of** withdrawing his work if they don't increase his fee.

4 You'd better call her. I'm sure she **won't have been notified** yet that she's been entered for an award.

5 By the end of this month the gallery **will have welcomed** over 80,000 visitors.

6 **Will you be teaching** the children art tomorrow afternoon?

7 By the end of this year the government **will be investing** more in the arts than it has ever done before.

B

a) expresses certainty that something has (or has not) happened

b) makes a polite enquiry

c) says something will be complete by a particular time in the future

d) says something will be in progress in the future

e) refers to the next moment

f) indicates a previously scheduled time

g) indicates a formal arrangement

2   Choose the best alternative to complete each sentence.

1 '*Will Reinhart be exhibiting / Will Reinhart be on the point of exhibiting* at the Royal Academy this summer?' she asked.

2 By the end of the decade, fewer children *will have studied / will be studying* art in school than today.

3 Be quick! The prize-giving is *about to start / due to start* in five minutes.

4 Photographs *are not to be taken / will not have been taken* inside the gallery.

5 Don't tell me the result! I know he *will win / will have won* again!

6 Sssh! The auctioneer *is on the point of starting / will be starting* the sale.

7 By the end of this year, I *will have sold / will be selling* more paintings than I did last year.

3   Complete the second sentence so that it has a similar meaning to the first sentence, using the word given. Do not change the word given. Use between three and six words, including the word given.

1 If they don't agree to give him more publicity, he's going to cancel tomorrow.
POINT
He's ...., if they don't agree to give him more publicity.

2 The plan is for the programme to go live at 6 o'clock tonight.
DUE
.... live at 6 o'clock tonight.

3 People who arrive late must wait until the interval before entering the theatre.
ARE
People arriving late .... until the interval before entering the theatre.

4 She will be upset that she wasn't asked.
BEEN
She will be upset not .... asked.

5 When he planned the project, I know he took account of the problem.
WILL
I know he .... the problem when he planned the project.

Vocabulary 1: phrasal verbs
▶ *CB page 81*

1 Search for the verbs that go in the gaps to complete the phrasal verbs. (One verb appears twice!)

O	T	P	G	O	E	T	K
S	T	H	I	N	K	G	P
E	O	U	T	B	B	S	W
T	E	M	K	R	R	O	O
M	C	O	M	E	I	U	S
W	O	I	N	K	N	G	N
S	G	K	G	N	G	H	O
E	O	G	H	T	O	T	U
G	S	W	O	R	N	I	N

1 We need to .... **up** a new idea to get more visitors.
2 I'm trying to .... him **round** to my way of thinking on art.
3 When the conservatives .... **to** power, they intend to invest more in art.
4 At the opening party, we .... **out** the artist so we could chat to him.
5 It's easy to .... **off** an artist if he changes his style.
6 He .... **about** painting as many landscapes as he could.
7 The surface of the painting had been .... **away** by the dust.
8 He had to .... **away** to study as his college didn't do the course he wanted.

2 Put the correct form of these phrasal verbs into the most appropriate gaps below, then do the quiz.

TIP! Look at the answers to help you decide.

deal with   fall out of   go about   get out of
turn someone on   put something into   think of
come across

Are you sensitive to art?

1 Does modern art ....?
   a) not at all   b) definitely

2 Do you think graffiti will .... fashion?
   a) no   b) yes

3 How do you think artists should be ....?
   a) as a waste of time   b) as creative geniuses

4 How do you think we should .... art in school?
   a) drop it from the curriculum
   b) have lessons every day

5 What do you .... seeing a modern painting?
   a) absolutely nothing   b) a thrill

6 When you .... a piece of sculpture in the street, what do you do?
   a) ignore it   b) take a closer look

7 Do you think cities should .... more money .... sponsoring modern art?
   a) no   b) yes

8 How do you think we should .... modernising cities?
   a) renovate the old buildings
   b) invest in new, innovative buildings

Find out how sensitive you are to art by checking the answers in the Key.

Check you know the meaning of all the verbs by using a good dictionary such as *The Longman Phrasal Verbs Dictionary*.

Listening: sentence completion (Part 2)
▶ CB page 80

1   Look at this text and underline the words that have a parallel meaning to the highlighted words in the gapped sentences below. Then complete the gaps using words from the text.

There are several museums which are interesting to see for the buildings alone. The significant ones are normally vast and located in capital cities. However, the latest designs can more than match these historical buildings. It seems their success depends on the money that is poured into them. But this is recouped through foreign visitors who potentially come and stay in the town.

1 It is worth going to **some** .... just to see the buildings.
2 The **important** buildings are **usually** .... and in capital cities.
3 The **newest** .... are as good as older buildings.
4 The success of new buildings **relies on** .... invested in them.
5 Investment can be recovered from the .... **tourists** who may visit the town.

2   You'll hear a travel report on the radio about the Guggenheim Museum in Bilbao, in northern Spain. Listen and complete the sentences. You do not need to write more than two words.

THE GUGGENHEIM, BILBAO

The plans for building the museum faced some
(1) .... when first proposed.
The museum has turned Bilbao into an important
(2) ....
The town has undergone significant **(3)** .... since the museum was built.
The museum reminds many people of a **(4)** ....
The appearance of the museum changes depending on the **(5)** ....
Some people visit the museum only to look at the
(6) ....
There are wonderful **(7)** .... from the museum.

3   Listen again and check your answers.

4   Put these words from the listening text into the correct gaps in the sentences below.

mascot	rundown	backwater	head for
heights	regenerating	knock-on effects	

1 The building is so .... that it will have to be demolished.
2 We are .... the town centre by investing heavily in new buildings.
3 Boxton is such a .... that it hasn't even got a post office!
4 Building the museum in the town centre had some very positive ....
5 He didn't go up the Empire State building as he has no ....
6 Lots of towns have a .... that they bring to football matches and festivals.

Vocabulary 2: words with similar meaning
▶ CB page 87

1   Choose the most suitable word to complete each sentence. Use a good dictionary, such as *The Longman Exams Dictionary*, to help you.

1 Art investors are people who have .... a great deal of wealth.
   A collected   **B** hoarded   **C** accumulated   **D** gathered

2 The painting was sold by the government even though it was a .... of national pride.
   A symbol   **B** sign   **C** logo   **D** trademark

3 The main .... of young designers is how to make money while creating something original.
   A obsession   **B** preoccupation   **C** fascination
   D absorption

4 The shop had a wonderful window ....
   A show   **B** exhibition   **C** presentation   **D** display

5 I don't understand his .... for acting like that at all.
   A motivation   **B** ambition   **C** purpose   **D** drive

6 She .... his face to see if he was telling the truth.
   A examined   **B** scrutinised   **C** inspected
   D checked

Use of English: word formation (Part 3)
▶ *CB page 88*

> **TIP!** Remember to look for negative meanings. Check whether the word needs to be plural or singular.

1 Read the text below. Use the word given in capitals to form a word that fits the space. There is an example at the beginning (0).

A career in graphic design

Graphic design comes in where words and visual images are used to convey ideas and **(0)** ..*information*.. (INFORM). So graphic design features in lots of different areas, including advertising, **(1)** .... (PUBLISH), signage, packaging, corporate identity (a company's image and logo) and multimedia. At its heart, graphic design is about drawing and **(2)** .... (PRESENT) skills and also the ability to handle colours, lettering and patterns. But it uses a lot of new technology so, **(3)** .... (ALONG) these skills, it requires a high degree of computer **(4)** .... (LITERATE) and even mathematical skills.

Graphic communications designers work on a wide range of projects or can become **(5)** .... (SPECIAL) in, for example, typography (print), illustration, packaging, corporate identity or magazine design. There is also an **(6)** .... (END) demand for designers specialising in television and video graphics and in digital/new media as this is a growth area.

Although more and more organisations are recognising the importance of good design, Britain has the largest number of graphic design higher education courses in Europe and this means that entry to the profession is **(7)** .... (COMPETE). However, in graphic design there are more **(8)** .... (OPEN) than in any other area of design – in advertising agencies, design studios, in-house company departments and **(9)** .... (CONSULT) as well as in the freelance sector. In addition to basic design skills, courses usually cover advertising, typographic design, print technology, illustration, new media and computer-**(10)** .... (AID) design.

Design Council www.designcouncil.org.uk

Speaking: three-way discussion (Part 4)

About the exam: In Part 4, the three-way discussion, it is important that you use a range of language and don't repeat yourself.

Look at this typical question that you could be asked:

Do you think children should be taught more about art in school?

Look at these words and phrases you may need to answer this question. Write at least one synonym for each word or phrase. Your synonyms can be words or phrases. Use a dictionary to help you.

beneficial	....
rewards	....
creative	....
a waste of time	....
it should be	....
because	....

Now listen to two students answering the question. How many synonyms can you hear? Check the audioscript on page 158.

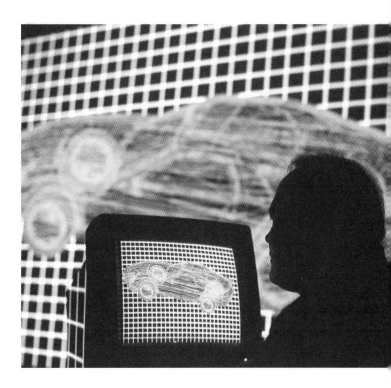

Grammar 2: verb patterns
▶ *CB pages 88–89*

1 In six of the sentences below a verb has been followed by the wrong pattern. Find these sentences and correct them.

1 He encouraged me entering the art competition.
2 Although the design seemed familiar, I couldn't remember to see it before.
3 Something made me stop in front of the strange building.
4 Even though funding for design is very poor in the UK, art students continue to create good designs.
5 I wouldn't risk to ask him to the opening if I were you.
6 Many people have attempted explain his complex sculptures.
7 The teacher helped her overcoming her difficulties with life drawing.
8 I was about to pay for the art books when I realised I'd forgotten bring my wallet.

2 Complete these sentences in your own words, using an appropriate verb pattern.

1 I sometimes regret ....
2 My parents would let .... when I was twelve.
3 My teacher encouraged ....
4 I don't think I would ever dare ....
5 I sometimes miss .... as I did it a lot when I was younger.
6 I expect .... until I retire.
7 Something I know I should try .... is ....
8 What I hope to avoid .... is ....

3 Complete the second sentence so that it has a similar meaning to the first sentence, using the word given. Do not change the word given. Use between three and six words, including the word given.

1 Breathing slowly results in you feeling calmer.
   MAKES
   Breathing slowly .... calmer.
2 'You really shouldn't argue about your results,' he said.
   ADVISED
   He .... about my results.
3 Designers have to try not to replicate other people's work.
   AVOID
   Designers have to .... other people's work.

4 She said she wouldn't fund my art course if I didn't work harder.
   THREATENED
   She .... my art course if I didn't work harder.
5 You didn't tell me that the exhibition was finishing today!
   NEGLECTED
   You .... the exhibition was finishing today!

Use of English: key word transformations (Part 5)

1 Complete the second sentence so that it has a similar meaning to the first sentence, using the word given. Do not change the word given. You must use between three and six words, including the word given.

TIP! Remember you MUST NOT change the form of the word you are given. Think carefully about whether the word is part of a fixed phrase.

1 We started our journey at 6 o'clock in the morning.
   SET
   We .... at 6 o'clock in the morning.
2 I'm sure her career will be successful.
   SUCCESS
   I'm sure .... her career.
3 I've never climbed Mount Snowdon, but I'm going to have a go.
   ATTEMPT
   I'm going .... Mount Snowdon.
4 He's going to blow the whistle in the next minute.
   ABOUT
   He .... the whistle.
5 I can never remember people's names.
   MEMORY
   I .... people's names.
6 I was very sorry that I hadn't taken the job.
   REGRETTED
   I .... the job.
7 Nothing interesting ever happens in my town.
   ORDINARY
   Nothing .... ever happens in my town.
8 He was sacked because he was incompetent.
   GROUNDS
   He was sacked .... incompetence.

Writing: review (Part 2)
▶ *CB page 90*

About the exam: In Paper 2, Part 2, you may be asked to write a review of something you have seen or heard, saying whether or not you would recommend it to others.

Strategy
1 Don't include too much description – this should be brief!
2 Make sure you include a recommendation, even if it is that you don't recommend people to buy or see it.
3 Give strong reasons for your recommendation.

1 Read this task.

An English language magazine is asking readers to submit reviews of buildings people can visit. Write a review of a building you know, explaining why it is important to the region or town where it is located and saying whether or not you would recommend visitors to your area to go and see it.

2 Tick the points you think you should include in this review:

a) brief details about your chosen building
b) a detailed description of the building's location
c) reasons for its importance to the town or region
d) how it compares to other similar buildings
e) why others should or shouldn't go and see it

3 Read this sample answer and underline the language the writer uses to recommend. Remember, there may also be some negative recommendation.

CARDIFF'S SPECTACULAR VENUE

Would you bother going to visit a football stadium? No, I thought not. Well, the Millennium Stadium in Cardiff may change your mind!

The Millennium Stadium is a spectacular architectural and engineering triumph. Funded by government money, it was built for the year 2000 to allow the capital of Wales to have a suitable venue for its great passion – rugby. It is built in the heart of the city and has wonderful white arches that reach towards the river and a roof that opens or shuts depending on the weather. Although intended for sport, it is also now a major concert venue and inside has a feeling of intimacy despite its size.

It has proved to be critical to the regeneration of Cardiff as up around it have grown the pubs and clubs that support visitors to the matches. On match days the stadium is the living heart of the city, with spectators being only a stone's throw from all the amenities the city has to offer. It has not only brought extra work to the city but also been an inspiration to the people of the city.

I suggest you go and visit the stadium – walk round the outside and admire its curves. However, I wouldn't recommend visiting it when it is empty, so get yourself a ticket for a match and see what 70,000 people enjoy!

Can you think of any other language you could use to recommend or not recommend something?

4 Reviews are normally written in the chatty style of an article. Underline all the informal expressions or expressions which are like spoken language in the sample review.

5 Write your own review for the task in Exercise 1. Use the strategy advice to help you. Write your answer in 220–260 words.

► Improve! ◄

Use more variety of structures for recommending.

Ways to recommend:
I recommend
I strongly suggest
You would be mad to miss this ....
I cannot praise .... highly enough
This .... is a must-see

Ways to not recommend:
It's not worth ....
I wouldn't bother ....

UNIT

8 What keeps us going

Listening: short texts (Part 1)

Strategy
1 Underline the words in the question that tell you what you are listening for, e.g. *What does the man think …, What do the speakers agree …*
2 Don't be distracted by individual words that you hear. Concentrate on general meaning.
3 Use the second listening to check your answers.

1 Underline one or two words in each question that tell you what to focus on. Check the answers in the key before you continue.

2 You will hear three different extracts. For questions 1–6, choose the answer (A, B or C) which fits best according to what you hear. You will hear each extract twice. Use the second listening to check your answers.

Extract One

You hear two people discussing a book on how to do well in an interview.

1 According to the man, what is the most useful aspect of the book?
   A the examples it uses
   B the advice it gives
   C the clear organisation of points

2 What is the woman most concerned about?
   A The book is useless for people who already have a job.
   B Readers will copy the techniques given in the book.
   C The author is unknown in the business community.

Extract Two

You hear part of an interview with a businessman called Nigel Frame.

3 What is Nigel's opinion of people who are ambitious?
   A He appreciates what they can bring to a company.
   B He wonders whether they annoy their colleagues.
   C He thinks they are often careless in their work.

4 How does he feel about the people who work for him?
   A proud of their performance
   B satisfied about their relationship with him
   C grateful for their commitment

Extract Three

You hear two people talking about their work situations.

5 Why did the woman decide to leave her company?
   A her colleagues were unpleasant
   B her salary was unsatisfactory
   C her opportunities for promotion were limited

6 What do the two speakers agree about?
   A You should tell your boss if you are unhappy.
   B Once a job has become boring, it's time to leave.
   C It's best to change jobs frequently.

3 Complete these sentences with the correct form of the phrasal verbs from the listening texts in Exercise 2.

to end up	to pick up	to be fed up
to be put together	to be on	get on with

1 The project .... in a rather disorganised fashion so we couldn't find what we needed.
2 I didn't .... the mistakes in that document so thanks for bringing them to my attention.
3 What .... you .... at the moment because I'm sure we can match that if you work for us?
4 He was so hopeless that I .... doing the job myself just to get it done in time.
5 I .... really .... in my job so I'm looking for a new one.
6 He's very quiet – he just sits and .... his work and doesn't disturb anyone.

Vocabulary 1: compounds: verb + preposition

1 Use these words with the prepositions below to make compound nouns. Remember the preposition may go in front of or after the word. Write the nouns in the correct column. There is an example to help you. See how many words you can make. Use a good dictionary, such as *The Longman Exams Dictionary*, to help you.

TIP! There are over 30!

let	draw	lay	set	break	print	come
fall	take	cut	turn	look	put	

out	in	back	over	down	through	up
outlet						

2 Match these compound nouns with their meaning.

A follow-up   i) something you say suddenly that expresses a strong emotion, especially anger

B outburst   ii) the ability to understand and realise what people and situations are really like

C upkeep   iii) something that is done to make sure that earlier actions have been successful

D rundown   iv) the process of keeping something in good condition

E insight   v) a review or summary

3 Use one of these words with one of the prepositions to make a compound adjective.
Then match each adjective to the nouns they usually refer to.

out	in	under	over

A ...depth   i) chairman / president / MD

B ...going   ii) workers / women / profession

C ...loaded   iii) study / report / analysis

D ...paid   iv) factory / office / project

E ...staffed   v) with work / with information / with problems

4 Most compound nouns need to split into verb + preposition to become a verb (e.g. *to take over, to lay out, to cut back* in Exercise 1). Some verbs from compound nouns remain as a single word. Which single preposition fits in all the gaps below to make single-word verbs and nouns?

1a) We need to ......grade the software on the computer every two years.

  b) I've booked economy but I wondered if I could have an ......grade to business class?

2a) I wondered if you could give me an ......date on what's happening on the project?

  b) I'm sorry, we don't have your current address – we need to ......date our records.

3a) She caused a huge ......set when she refused to continue with the project.

  b) I was very ......set at the way he spoke to me!

4) Make a list of other things that can be ......graded or ......dated. Use your dictionary to help you.

5 Complete each gap with one of these words from Exercises 1–4.

drawback	input	outcome	insight
underpaid	outgoing	indepth	

MOTIVATING MILLIONAIRES

How can a contemporary football coach expect to **make any real impression on** the very wealthy young men in **elite** football teams like Manchester United? The problem is how to motivate people who have enormous salaries; it's the opposite of many managers, who are trying to motivate their **(1)** .... workers. One football coach did an **(2)** .... study in the USA, where million-dollar contracts to sportsmen have been **commonplace** for years, to see how their coaches solved the problem. He found that looking at this gave him a real **(3)** .... into dealing with millionaire athletes. He said, 'It's a matter of trying to instil selflessness. For the best **(4)** ...., you have to make them feel it's "we" rather than "me" that matters. When I took over my current job I found that the **(5)** .... coach had mainly just analysed the opposition and how best to operate against them. But I felt I needed to reassure people and **resolve their doubts** about themselves and their place in the club. And once the training session is over, what really makes a difference is my personal **(6)** .... whereby I take a real interest in the players. One **(7)** .... is that a lot of players now don't want to **start at the bottom.** They want an assistant manager's job at least. But you only get experience through working your way up through the ranks.'

6 Match the highlighted expressions in the text above with these meanings.

1 Learn a job by working in the most low-level position first.

2 Make somebody feel more confident or sure of themselves.

3 Normal, usual, typical.

4 Have an effect on somebody.

5 Best, most skilled or most experienced.

Grammar 1: indirect speech

1 How do you change the following into reported speech? Match 1–11 with reported speech changes a–g.

1 past or present tenses

2 modals

3 references, e.g. here

4 things that are still true

5 reporting in the present, e.g. says

6 wh- questions

7 do etc. questions

8 requests

9 offers

10 orders

11 future tenses

a) no change

b) shift back a tense

c) make more distant, e.g. *there, that, those*

d) use *would*

e) use *if* or *whether*

f) switch order of object and verb

g) use *told* + 'to' infinitive

2 Put these sentences into reported speech.

1 'Will you be able to come to the conference next week?' Tom asked Alice.

2 'Do you need a lift to the airport tomorrow?' she asked me.

3 'Who did you speak to when you phoned last week?' the woman asked her.

4 'I may have to leave early this afternoon,' Sandra explained.

5 'You should take a few days off,' said the doctor.

6 My boss is always asking me, 'Where is my diary?'

7 'Have you seen my report?' Tim asked Lynn.

8 'I find it very difficult to do presentations,' Simon said.

3 Complete the second sentence so that it has a similar meaning to the first sentence, using the word given. Do not change the word given. Use between three and six words, including the word given.

1 'Have you sent your application in yet?' I asked him.

   IF

   I asked him .... application yet.

2 He said to me, 'Maria phoned yesterday.'

   HAD

   He told me .... day.

3 'I'll help you with the project,' he said.

   TOLD

   He .... me with the project.

4 'Can you come next week?' she said.

   FOLLOWING

   She asked me .... week.

5 'Call him this afternoon,' he said.

   TOLD

   He .... afternoon.

6 She asked me, 'What do you want me to do later?'

   WANTED

   She asked me .... later.

Vocabulary 2: work qualities

1 Put these qualities into the most appropriate column.

> sociable   able to work independently
> pushy   has good judgement   reliable
> willing to follow set procedures   imaginative
> cautious   conformist   flexible   aggressive
> trustworthy   assertive   has common sense
> courteous   thoughtful   frivolous   indecisive
> conscientious   laid-back   realistic

positive	neutral	negative

2 Match each of these qualities to their meaning.

1 communicative

2 competitive

3 cooperative

4 creative

5 decisive

6 practical

a) determined to be more successful than other people

b) good at making decisions quickly and with confidence

c) good at dealing with problems and making decisions based on what will really work

d) willing to work with someone else to achieve something you both want

e) able to talk easily to other people

f) using imagination to produce new ideas or things

3 Use these affixes to create opposites of the words in Exercise 2.

> im-   in-   un-

4 Which qualities from Exercise 2 above are necessary for each of these jobs?

1 computer games designer
2 flight attendant
3 nurse
4 professional footballer

Speaking

Look at the three photos. They show people in different work situations. Write down how you think the people in each photo are feeling. Think about why the people in the photos might enjoy or not enjoy their work. Make a list of aspects of work you could talk about. Check what you write against the suggestions in the Key.

Use of English: multiple choice cloze (Part 1)
▶ *CB page 96*

1 Read the text below and decide which answer (A, B, C or D) best fits each space. There is an example at the beginning (0).

HORSES FOR COURSES

American psychologists have been looking into how a child's position in the family can **(0)** ..*B*.... his or her selected career.

It would appear that first-born and only children are more likely to be high achievers, **(1)** .... professions such as law, finance, engineering or medicine. According to Professor Frederick Leong, co-author of the psychologists' report, the **(2)** .... is for them to head towards 'cognitive and analytical' work. Professor Leong puts this **(3)** .... to the fact that parents are likely to be more over-**(4)** .... towards first-born or only children. Examples of famous names demonstrating this include many politicians.

Younger siblings, on the other hand, are more likely to be **(5)** .... to take up more creatively based or outdoor-based occupations, such as landscape gardening, fashion, music and art, as **(6)** .... by Oscar Wilde, Yehudi Menuhin and Madonna.

Professor Leong's overall explanation is that 'parents typically **(7)** .... different demands on and have different **(8)** .... of children, depending on their birth order. Parents of only children may discourage physical or outdoor activities because they are more fearful of physical **(9)** .... to their child. That, and the fact that they get more time and attention from their parents than children with siblings, may be why only children are more likely to be academic.'

He points out how the **(10)** .... often happens in larger families. 'As they have more children, parents become more open and relaxed, and that may allow younger children to take more **(11)** .... If the first-born or only child wants to be a poet, that may concern parents. But by the fourth child, parents may not **(12)** .... as much.'

www.childalert.co.uk

0	**A** involve	**B** <u>affect</u>	**C** effect	**D** concern
1	**A** pursuing	**B** chasing	**C** driving	**D** tracking
2	**A** trend	**B** direction	**C** bias	**D** tendency
3	**A** on	**B** up	**C** down	**D** over
4	**A** guarding	**B** protective	**C** covering	**D** watchful
5	**A** destined	**B** intended	**C** designed	**D** fated
6	**A** exhibited	**B** displayed	**C** depicted	**D** exemplified
7	**A** rest	**B** plant	**C** fix	**D** place
8	**A** prospects	**B** expectations	**C** outlook	**D** possibilities
9	**A** hurt	**B** loss	**C** harm	**D** suffering
10	**A** alternative	**B** counter	**C** converse	**D** contrast
11	**A** risks	**B** gambles	**C** hazards	**D** ventures
12	**A** oppose	**B** mind	**C** dispute	**D** contend

Reading: gapped text (Part 2)
▶ *CB pages 94–95*

Strategy
1 Read through the whole text first to get an idea of how it develops.
2 Try to guess what information is missing in each paragraph.
3 Check that the paragraph fits with information before *and* after the gap.

1   The following topics are mentioned in the article. Read the article through quickly and decide the order in which these topics are discussed.

a) identifying strengths and weaknesses
b) finding your passions
c) dealing with weaknesses

2   Read the article again. Six paragraphs have been removed from the article. Choose from the paragraphs A–G the one which fits each gap (1–6). There is one extra paragraph which you do not need to use.

Discover your Passions

*Lynne Franks talks about **marrying** your passions and natural gifts with your business ideas.*

Thinking about a career change but wondering what to do? My advice is to use your passions to guide you in your choice. Sometimes your passions can be the most obvious things. What makes you <u>light up</u> inside when you think about doing it? And is there a way to combine this pleasure with your existing professional experience and skills?

1

And for those of you who aren't currently working, do you want to go back to your last job or training or do you want to <u>move into</u> a totally new career? Is there a way of taking elements of your experience and combining them with more of your personal values and gifts and somehow **forging** that into a single career?

2

Just to make sure we're not overlooking any passions that you've <u>let go of</u>, let's also look at your preferred activities and hobbies as a child and a teenager. For example, when I was a child, I was always the organiser of the other neighbourhood children's games, and I loved dancing and reading. When I was a teenager, I was still organising everyone's social activities, dancing, reading and writing.

3

And I'm not the only one who has managed to forge a career from her natural inclinations. A friend of mine spent much of her childhood and teenage years on the telephone to all her friends advising them on their parent or relationship problems. Needless to say, she grew up to become a psychologist. Another, now a successful interior designer, told me she used to love making furniture for her toys when she was small, using her mother's sewing machine to make little curtains and constantly redesigning her bedroom as a teenager.

4

Sometimes it's difficult to be very objective about yourself, so after making your list of your strengths and weaknesses <u>check</u> them <u>out</u> with your **nearest and dearest** as well as your work colleagues. Choose people who you know will tell you the truth so you can get an honest assessment of what you're good at.

5

Similarly, having a sense of humour in just about any situation is obviously a plus, but not to take situations seriously when they obviously need to be is surely a minus. What we have to learn to do is either to turn our weaknesses into positives, or just <u>weed</u> them <u>out</u>.

6

It's all common sense, but it's amazing how we sometimes ignore our essential personality traits and inner qualities when we take on a particular job or plan our working life.

A

Of course, one person's strength is another person's weakness. It's just a matter of balance and context. You may prefer writing to speaking to people and see that as a strength, as one of my friends does. However, even though that does make her a good writer in a job, it also means she is unable to deal with people face-to-face, which is clearly a weakness.

B

Let's look first at how you enjoy spending your time, what excites your soul. To find out, make a list of 20 activities that you enjoy doing the most. These can be professional or personal. They could include going for a walk, dancing, going to art galleries, meeting people or surfing the Internet.

C

Once you've defined what you really enjoy doing with your time, you can then look at your strengths and weaknesses. Once you have honestly assessed your passions, skills and problem areas, a picture will **emerge** of how you can use what you've got and what kinds of things you would love to create a **thriving** business from.

D

This story illustrates how you may just have to accept these failings and **take** this **into account** when you are planning your future. If you don't enjoy crowds, create a business where you don't have to deal with any.

E

So, as you begin to plan your new business, consider where your weaknesses could become positive attributes. For example, if you are always restless, think of a business that requires a lot of travelling. If you don't like being with adults very much but love children, why not create a business based on childcare or children's education.

F

Of course, for many of you, just transferring your professional career from employee **status** to freelance seems the easiest way to start your own business. But does your current or former job make you happy enough to want to continue doing the same work, especially when you are working for yourself?

G

Now I am an adult and I am still doing the same things. I've <u>come to</u> appreciate that amongst my gifts are people skills, organising events, absorbing information and writing – all ideal skills for a person with a career in public relations, journalism and public speaking, who loves to dance whenever possible.

3 Match the highlighted words in the article and title with these meanings. Use a good dictionary, such as *The Longman Exams Dictionary*, to help you.

1 appear
2 close relatives
3 building a strong relationship between
4 consider
5 official legal position
6 combining two different ideas
7 very successful

4 Complete these sentences with the correct form of the underlined phrasal verbs in the article above.

1 If an idea isn't working out you need to .... it and think of something else.
2 After a lot of effort, I've .... realise that I wasn't meant to be a doctor.
3 When you develop a plan you should .... it .... with colleagues to see if it works.
4 Although I graduated in IT, I decided to .... a completely different type of work.
5 At work, managers need to .... the people who aren't making an effort and get rid of them if necessary!
6 I .... when I think about my new job – I'm so excited.

Grammar 2: reporting words
▶ *CB pages 99–100*

1   Rewrite these sentences in reported speech using one of the reporting verbs in the box.

> **TIP!** Remember that you won't need to repeat all the words in the original sentence.

> apologise   accuse   suggest   warn
> promised   complained   remind   refuse

1 'It was you who took the report off my desk, wasn't it?' she said.

    ....

2 'I hate having to work overtime,' he said.

    ....

3 'I will definitely finish the report by Friday,' she said.

    ....

4 'I'm not going to work with him,' she said.

    ....

5 'Be careful you don't take on too much work,' she said.

    ....

6 'Don't forget to ask questions in the interview,' he said.

    ....

7 'I'm sorry I didn't come to the meeting,' he said.

    ....

8 'Why don't you make a list to help you organise your time?' she said.

    ....

2   Put the correct form of the verb in brackets into the gaps together with a preposition, if necessary.

1 He advised me .... (wear) a suit.
2 I decided .... (go) on a training course.
3 She thanked me .... (help) her with the work.
4 We agreed .... (meet) on Friday.
5 I congratulated her .... (get) the new job.
6 He told me .... (speak) to the new manager.
7 They invited me .... (attend) the conference.
8 He denied .... (forget) about the work.

3   Think of one word only which can be used appropriately in all three sentences.

1

I ran into him by ....
I had the .... to apply for a promotion.
Sometimes you need to take a .... if you want to succeed.

2

I lost my presentation notes and had to do it from ....!
I've got a very poor short-term ....
If my .... serves me right, he said he would call us.

3

We have had overwhelming .... for the new MP3 player we launched last month.
The trade union's sudden .... for a pay increase needs to be dealt with immediately.
The goods were produced on .... so we did not have to pay for warehouse space.

4

The .... of the factory can be converted into a car park.
I objected on the .... that it would cost too much.
We need to look carefully at the .... for the suggested change.

5

I need more .... at using the computer software.
I worried about my interview as I'm a bit out of ....
The .... of dumping waste directly into the sea needs to be stopped.

Writing: letter of application (Part 2)

About the exam: In Paper 2, Part 2, you may have the choice of writing a letter of application. You will have to write 220–260 words to a specified reader. You will be expected to use a greeting and an expression for signing off appropriately.

Strategy

1 Make sure you understand what the requirements of the job are and plan your answer to address these.
2 Remember that in the opening paragraph of your letter you must state clearly why you are writing.
3 Think about your target reader and try to persuade him or her that you are the best person for the job.
4 Don't include irrelevant information.

1   Read this announcement from a sports magazine.

> ## Be a Sports Coach to Children
>
> We run holiday sports camps for children and we are looking for students to work during the holidays to help organise activities for the children. You must be able to teach sports and be good at English. Write to us telling us about your experience, what you think the qualities of a good sports teacher are and why you would like to do this job.

2   Tick the points you think you should include in this letter of application.

a) why you need a job

b) why you are writing

c) why you would be good at the job

d) where you saw the job advertised

e) a description of your personality

f) an outline of your experience

g) why you want the job

h) the qualities of a good sports teacher

3   Read this sample letter.

Dear Sir

I am writing to apply for the job you advertised in the sports magazine on Saturday for a sports coach for children in the summer.

I am an 18-year-old girl and I have just finished school. I am looking for a job in the summer and I think this job would be ideal for me.

I enjoy working with children and have three younger brothers and sisters, so I am used to entertaining children. In addition, I speak good English and have just taken my Cambridge advanced exam. At school I did lots of sports such as basketball, tennis and running and I used to do some training for younger students in the school.

I think a good sports teacher is able to show the technical side but also is patient and calm with the children. I think I have all the skills you need and I would very much enjoy doing this job.

I am able to work the whole summer. I can be contacted at home on 01786 450 876 and am available for interview all next week.

I look forward to hearing from you.

Yours faithfully

NB: This letter is 189 words.

4   Did the sample letter include the relevant points from Exercise 2? Put the relevant points in Exercise 2 into the best order. Use the example letter to help you.

5   Which two things should go in the final paragraph of a letter of application?

a) details of how to get in touch with you

b) details of your availability for interview

c) an explanation of why you will be waiting for a response

6   Match the tenses with what they are often used to express in a letter of application.

a) past

b) present perfect

c) present

d) future/would

i) your skills and current activities

ii) your hopes and desires

iii) previous work or experience that is relevant

iv) the process of you acquiring your current skills

Underline examples of each in the example letter above.

— Improve! ◄—

How could the sample letter be improved? Think about the number of words used and the amount of information given.

7   Write your own response to the task in Exercise 1. Make a plan, using Exercises 2, 5 and 6 to help you. Write your answer in 220–260 words.

Vocabulary 1: travel

1 Do this travel quiz, then check your answers at the bottom of the page.

Do you travel well?

1 You are going on holiday and your plane is **held up**. Do you
   a) shout at the airline employees?
   b) **chill out** with a cup of coffee?
   c) complain to the people you are travelling with?

2 You visit a country where you don't speak the language. Do you
   a) **switch off** and refuse to communicate with anyone?
   b) buy a phrase book and try to use it?
   c) speak very slowly and use mime?

3 You get to your hotel and the room is dirty. Do you
   a) call the reception and ask for a maid immediately?
   b) wipe a few surfaces and then go and **soak up** the sun?
   c) **check out** and go somewhere else?

4 You **set off** on an excursion but forget your bag. Do you
   a) insist everybody **turns back** so you can get your bag?
   b) decide to just enjoy it but not eat or buy anything?
   c) borrow money, etc. from the trip organiser?

2 Use the verbs in bold in the quiz in the correct form to complete these sentences.

1 I always .... when people start showing me their holidays snaps!
2 When I'm on holiday I .... by lying in the sun and reading.
3 When we .... they tried to charge us extra for room service.

All As – you are too tense to enjoy holidays. Learn to relax!
All Bs – your holiday could be a disaster, but you will enjoy it!
All Cs – you have the right balance to get what you want and enjoy the holiday.
Mixed answers – you can't decide if you enjoy travelling or not!

4 We .... from the house so late that we missed the plane.
5 On holiday I like to just wander round a city and .... the atmosphere.
6 We were .... for hours during an air traffic controllers' strike.
7 On the climb, the weather was so bad that we decided to .... and try again the next day.

3 Match one of the advantages on the right to each type of holiday.

A package holiday   i) You can pay for your holiday while you are on it.

B fly-drive holiday   ii) You can do something exciting or learn something new.

C tailor-made holiday   iii) You can travel light and without a plan.

D self-catering holiday   iv) You can travel cheaply and experience outdoor life.

E house exchange   v) You can live in a typical family home.

F backpacking   vi) You can relax as everything is organised for you.

G camping   vii) It should be the most romantic holiday of your life!

H working holiday   viii) You have the convenience of a car when you arrive.

I activity holiday   ix) You can eat what you want, when you want.

J honeymoon   x) You don't have to follow the crowd.

4   Choose the most appropriate adjective in each sentence. Use a good dictionary, such as *The Longman Exams Dictionary*, to help you.

1   The view from the Empire State Building is absolutely *picturesque / spectacular*.
2   New York has some *breathtaking / dramatic* views from the top of the Empire State Building.
3   The south-west corner of India has very few visitors and is one of the most *unspoilt / bustling* parts of the country.
4   It was a very *picturesque / exotic* village, with old-fashioned shops and a green.
5   Angel Falls in Brazil is one of the most *historic / dramatic* waterfalls in the world.
6   The Spice Islands are an *exotic / historic* mixture of sights and scents.
7   This is a *historic / romantic* spot where Europeans first set foot on American soil.
8   Marrakech has a *bustling / breathtaking* central square where crowds gather in the evening.
9   Prague is supposed to be for lovers and is famed as one of the most *spectacular / romantic* cities in the world.

5   Decide which alternatives are *not* possible in the text below.

As travel agents, we recommend *advance / provisional* bookings as you get better prices on holidays, so if you can plan ahead you may even get a good price on a holiday in *high / low / peak* season when resorts are at their busiest. Normally in *off / peak* season hotels get very booked up, so even if you're not sure what you want to do it's worth making a *confirmed / provisional / last-minute* booking to hold your place as you can always cancel it. Another option is to make a *last-minute / provisional* booking a few days before you travel as you can get some very good deals. Just click on our links below ......

Listening: sentence completion (Part 2)
▶ *CB page 109*

Strategy
1   When you listen for the **second** time, check:
   a) that the word you have written fits the sentence grammatically
   b) that you have spelt the word correctly
   c) that you write only what you hear; do not change the word(s).

1   You will hear a journalist talking about an ancient town called Machu Picchu in Peru. As you listen you must complete the sentences. Look at question 1 in Exercise 2 below.
- Decide what type of information is missing, e.g. a noun, a number, etc.
- Listen to the first part of the listening (up until the pause) and write your answer.
- Look at your answer – is it the correct form? Have you spelt it correctly?

Now decide what type of information is missing in questions 2–8.

2   Listen to the rest of the report and complete sentences 2–8.

MACHU PICCHU

A new bridge to Machu Picchu has created access to the site by **(1)** ....

There are concerns that the site will be ruined by the **(2)** .... of tourists.

The bridge will end a period of **(3)** .... for residents.

Previously, farmers had to endure a long drive over **(4)** ....

A bridge used to exist before it was destroyed in a **(5)** ....

The central government has made **(6)** .... , which have been rejected.

The mayor has dismissed concerns conservationists have raised about **(7)** ....

The mayor claims that the rail company is using the conservationist cause to preserve its **(8)** ....

© Guardian News & Media Ltd 2007

3   Listen again and check your answers.

4   Write down the reasons for and the reasons against the bridge mentioned in the report. Listen again if necessary.

Reasons against the bridge	Reasons for the bridge
1	1 ....
2	2 ....
3	3 ....
4	4 ....

Reading: multiple matching (Part 4)
▶ *CB pages 106–108*

Strategy
1 Read through the texts quickly first to get the gist of what each is about.
2 Remember the questions are a summary of what is in the text, so look for information that matches the summary.

1 You are going to read five short reviews of cities. To practise strategy 2 above, read through the texts (A–E) and look for information that answers questions 1 and 2. Which texts say that you can experience shops that are different from anywhere else?

2 For questions 3–15, choose from the texts (A–E). The texts may be chosen more than once.

In which review are the following mentioned?

A unique shopping experience	1
	2
The particular atmosphere created by the city's population	3
The contrast between rich and poor	4
The transformation the city has undergone	5
	6
	7
The unexpected vibrancy of the city's economy	8
The uniqueness of the city	9
The city's ability to change	10
The overwhelming beauty of its location	11
	12
The limitless choices it offers	13
The variety of centres within the city	14
The spectacular views it offers from a high point	15

Cities of charm

Different cities offer different pleasures

A Miami

Far and away the most exciting city in Florida, Miami is a stunning and often **intoxicating** and beautiful place. Awash with sunlight-intensified natural colours, there are moments – when the neon-flashed South Beach strip glows in the warm night and the palm trees sway in the breeze – when a better-looking city is hard to imagine. Away from the beaches and the tourists, the **gleaming** skyscrapers of downtown herald Miami's proud status as the site of many international banks' Latin American headquarters. Even so, it's the people, not the climate, the landscape, or the cash, that make Miami so **noteworthy**. Two-thirds of the 2 million-strong population is Hispanic, the vast majority of which are Cuban. Spanish is the predominant language almost everywhere – in many places it's the only language you'll hear. Just a hundred years ago Miami was a swampy outpost of mosquito-tormented settlers. Since then, much has changed, for two very different reasons. First, the gentrification of South Beach helped make tourism the lifeblood of the local economy again in the early Nineties. Second, the city's determined wooing of Latin America brought rapid investment, both domestic and international.

Adapted from www.roughguides.com

B Buenos Aires

Argentina's vibrant, wonderfully **idiosyncratic** capital, Buenos Aires, is the third largest city in Latin America. Famous for its tango, football and European-style architecture, it also holds hidden gems, including picturesque cobbled neighbourhoods, sophisticated shopping and some of the best and most varied cuisine in the whole continent. Lending itself perfectly to aimless wandering, Buenos Aires is primarily a city of barrios (neighbourhoods), each with its own heart. For many people, these barrios are Buenos Aires' best sights, more intriguing than most museums, churches or monuments, and requiring nothing more than a bit of time to be enjoyed. More important than the divisions between barrios is the one that exists between the north, where you'll find Buenos Aires' moneyed classes, and the south, which is largely working class. Yet for the tourist, these parts of the city have much to offer. The main draw in the north are the city's best museums and the landscaped parks. The microcentro, or downtown, is a transitional zone, beset by a sometimes **hectic** atmosphere but mellowed by countless welcoming cafés, bookstores and cultural centres. The south is the location for the city's popular

Sunday antique market, as well as the colourful southern port district.

C New York

The most **beguiling** city in the world, New York City is an adrenaline-charged, history-laden place that holds immense romantic appeal for visitors. Whether gazing at the flickering lights of the Midtown skyscrapers as you speed across the Queensboro bridge, experiencing the 4am half-life in the Village, or just wasting the day away in Central Park, you really would have to be made of stone not to be moved by it all. There's no place quite like it – it stands alone. Though you could spend weeks here and still barely scratch the surface, there are some key attractions and pleasures that you won't want to miss. These include the different ethnic neighbourhoods, like Chinatown, and the **celebrated** architecture of Midtown and the Financial District, as well as many fabulous museums – not just the Metropolitan and MoMA, but countless other smaller collections that afford weeks of happy wandering. In between sights, you can eat just about anything, at any time, cooked in any style; you can drink in any kind of company; and enjoy any number of obscure movies. For the avid consumer, the choice of shops is vast, almost numbingly **exhaustive**, in this heartland of the great capitalist dream.

D Tokyo

Tokyo is not one of the world's great sightseeing cities. Yet despite this, Tokyo still has the power to make you go 'Wow!' The sense that nothing here is permanent has produced a city that renews itself at an unimaginable speed, from the **futuristic** new cityscapes of Odaiba or Roppongi Hills to the bustling shopping and entertainment centres of Shibuya and Shinjuku. Since it first flung open its doors to the world back in 1868, Tokyo has been a laboratory for the meeting and synthesis of local and western architectural styles. But if Tokyo has one area that is famous the world over, Ginza is it. The area's reputation for exclusivity stretches right back to the 19th-century Meiji period, when Ginza became the first part of Tokyo to be rebuilt in red brick rather than wood. Sadly, none of the bricks survives, since the area was razed by the great Kanto earthquake. Now there are elegant department stores, traditional shops and Japanese tea rooms. Ginza is also home to the Sony Building. All the latest Sony models are on display and can be tried out. It offers eight floors of entertainment, and the sixth floor is dedicated to PlayStation.

E Sydney

Sydney may not be the capital, but it is the **glitzy**, party-loving heart of modern Australia and the country's biggest metropolis with a population of just over 4 million. Its unique setting, with miles of coastline, a breathtaking harbour and mountainous parklands, is complemented by a warm, tropical climate. The city was inhabited for tens of thousands of years by Aboriginal bands, but the arrival of English explorer Captain James Cook in 1770 changed all that. In 1788 Governor Arthur Phillip settled on Sydney Cove as a colony for British convicts and a trading port on the East India route. Now the crenellated harbour is the spine of the city, and a good way to get an idea of its layout and a ringside view of some of the city's most extravagant residences is on a harbour cruise. Also here are Sydney's two most famous icons, the Sydney Harbour Bridge connecting the CBD with the north shore, and the great sails of the Sydney Opera House. If vertigo isn't a problem, try climbing the bridge: the panorama is amazing.

3 Why do articles which describe places, such as the ones here, use so many adjectives?

a to show you the variety of feelings and responses you will experience in the places described

b to follow a tradition of how places and destinations are usually described

c to help you understand how the writer feels and responds to what he is describing

4 Match highlighted adjectives in the texts to meanings. Use a good dictionary, such as *The Longman Exams Dictionary*, to help you.

1 very busy or full of activity
2 unusual and modern
3 important or interesting enough to deserve attention
4 exciting and attractive because of being connected with wealth and fashion
5 making you feel happy, excited and unable to think clearly
6 attractive and interesting
7 famous
8 with unusual or unexpected features
9 extremely thorough and complete
10 shining softly and cleanly

Grammar 1: review of narrative tenses
▶ *CB page 105*

1   Choose the correct tense from A, B or C below.

1973 **(1)** .... the year I **(2)** .... London for the first time and I **(3)** .... by the city. My friend, Gillian, and I found a small hotel just off Holland Park Road. By an amazing coincidence, it was the same hotel in which Gillian's father **(4)** .... five years before – and they **(5)** .... him! Near the hotel there were several buses, none of which ran particularly regularly in those days. Every morning we **(6)** .... one of these buses to Oxford Street and **(7)** .... hours looking in shop windows at wonderful things. Gillian also liked to go to Knightsbridge, where there were even more expensive shops, such as the famous Harrods. The only things we could afford to buy there were beautiful linen handkerchiefs, which we **(8)** .... to our friends when we **(9)** .... to Canada. Gillian's older brother, who **(10)** .... London earlier that year, **(11)** .... us a list of places to visit. We happily retraced his steps, sometimes stopping for a cup of tea in one of the cafes which he **(12)** ....

1 A is	**B** was	**C** had been
2 A was visiting	**B** had visited	**C** visited
3 A have been bewitched	**B** was bewitched	**C** was being bewitched
4 A stayed	**B** was staying	**C** had stayed
5 A had remembered	**B** have remembered	**C** remembered
6 A would catch	**B** were catching	**C** have caught
7 A spent	**B** have spent	**C** spend
8 A were giving	**B** gave	**C** are giving
9 A got back	**B** were back	**C** were getting back
10 A has visited	**B** was visiting	**C** had visited
11 A give	**B** had given	**C** has given
12 A had been recommending	**B** was recommending	**C** had recommended

Vocabulary 2: dependent prepositions
▶ *CB page 108*

Complete the crossword with the prepositions that go with the nouns and adjectives below.

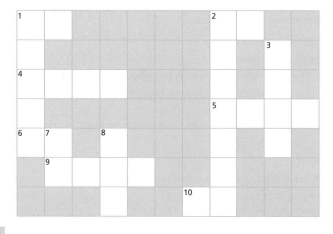

Across
1 excellent ...... something
2 captivated ...... somebody/something
4 power ...... somebody/something
5 fascination ...... something
6 related ...... something
9 different ...... each other
10 dependent ...... somebody/something

Down
1 nervous ...... something
2 similarities ...... two things something/somebody
3 do research .... something
7 typical ...... somebody/something
8 concerned ...... somebody

Use of English: word formation (Part 3)

1 Read the text below. Use the word given in capitals to form a word that fits the space. There is an example at the beginning (0). Check your spelling very carefully.

HOLIDAY HYSTERIA

We've been fascinated by reports yesterday that nannies are **(0)** .*increasingly*. being hired by airlines during the Christmas season to look after children flying alone or who have become separated from their busy parents, who are busy flagging down cabs and buying Christmas gifts.   **INCREASE**

It was reported yesterday that a one-month-old baby was **(1)** .... put through an X-ray machine at Los Angeles airport and left in the **(2)** .... items tray that usually holds watches, mobile phones and keys. The woman who left her son apparently had a lot on her mind. Airport staff claimed this behaviour was completely **(3)** .... but typical of parents during this busy season. Obviously, some parents were very **(4)** .... in coming up with excuses, but not so good at looking after their children.   **APPARENT**   **PERSON**   **ACCEPT**   **IMAGINE**

Another woman was reported to have left her two-year-old son in the car while she went shopping. She left **(5)** .... with the man in charge of the car park that she would be back shortly and not to wake the child. The car park **(6)** .... became worried about what was going to happen after she had been gone for two hours. She was arrested following a **(7)** .... with police, who said that leaving your child in the car park was **(8)** .... to abandoning your child. She claimed she had not wanted to be restricted by having her child with her when shopping. She also insisted on the police officer going back to the shops to pick up her presents.   **INSTRUCT**   **ATTEND**   **AGREE**   **EQUAL**

Researchers say that people **(9)** .... the stress of holidays. It should be a time to enjoy yourselves instead of running **(10)** .... around trying to get everything done. Look at the president. You don't see him breaking with his traditional 9 to 5 schedule. Neither should you.   **ESTIMATE**   **FRANTIC**

2 Underline the adjectives and verbs with dependent prepositions in your completed text above. There are nine.

Speaking: individual questions (Part 4)

About the exam: These are the types of questions you may be asked in Part 4 of the exam:

1 You can learn more if you travel alone. How far do you agree with this?

2 Do you think journeys are more enjoyable than arriving?

3 Some people say there is nowhere left to explore these days. What's your view?

> **TIP!** In Part 4 it is important that you give reasons for your views or give an example to support your view.

1 These are some reasons you might give in answer to question 1 above. Decide if the reasons below agree or disagree with the statement. Write A or D (Agree or Disagree) next to each reason.

i   You may switch off because you are on your own.   ......

ii You are more likely to meet local people.   ......

iii You could be more in touch with your experiences.   ......

iv On your own you'd be less adventurous.   ......

v   You may be too shy to join in with local activities.   ......

vi You'd have plenty of time to read about your destination.   ......

2 Listen to the recording of the sentences above and notice any difference in intonation between the Agree and Disagree statements.

3 For questions 2 and 3 above, write your own lists of reasons to support your views. Remember you can use positive or negative reasons.

Grammar 2: cleft sentences
▶ *CB page 110*

1   We use *wh-* cleft sentences, mainly in conversation, when we want to emphasise the information after the cleft clause. Match the beginnings (a–e) to the endings 1–5 to form complete sentences.

a) I can't be bothered to go to the beach; what I'd really like ....

b) We got back at midnight after a ten-hour flight. What had happened ....

c) Naples is a chaotic city, but what I like about it ....

d) She had forgotten her swimsuit, so what she did ....

e) Flying makes me very tired, so what I do ....

1 was that there was a traffic jam on the motorway.
2 is rest for the day after.
3 is to lie by the pool.
4 was buy an expensive one in the hotel shop!
5 is the sense of freedom it has.

2   Write sentences using emphasis (the cleft construction) with the words in brackets.

Example:

I don't want to go to Paris. (like / go / Rome)
  What I'd like to do is go to Rome.

1 Resorts shouldn't take too many people.
   (should / impose / restrictions)
   ....

2 I don't speak the language very well. (ought to / do / try)
   ....

3 We can't speak to the manager. (could / leave / note)
   ....

4 I haven't got enough cash. (must / go / bank)
   ....

5 I'm sorry but the plane is going to be delayed.
   (can / offer / meal vouchers)
   ....

6 I wish you could come with me to see the waterfall.
   (will / take / photographs)
   ....

Use of English: key word transformations (Part 5)

1   Complete the second sentence so that it has a similar meaning to the first sentence, using the word given. Do not change the word given. You must use between three and six words, including the word given. NB: In this exercise most of the sentences require using the *wh-* cleft. In the actual exam, the task will have more variety of structures.

1 Travel agents don't always get the best price for their clients in my view.
   CONVINCED
   I'm not .... get the best price for their clients.

2 I need a weekend away, so I booked something on the Internet.
   DID
   I needed a weekend away .... something on the Internet.

3 I object to hanging around in airports.
   WHAT
   .... hanging around in airports.

4 I only got my money back after weeks of calling.
   MANAGE
   Only after weeks of calling .... to get my money back.

5 A drivers' strike delayed our train.
   DUE
   Our train .... a drivers' strike.

6 I find travelling exciting.
   WHAT
   .... travelling.

7 I resolved the problem by taking an extra suitcase.
   WHAT
   .... an extra suitcase.

8 It worries me that I don't speak another language well.
   WHAT
   .... I don't speak another language well.

Writing: proposal (Part 1)

About the exam: In Paper 2, Part 1, you may be asked to write a proposal. You will be assessed on the accuracy and range of your language, organisation, style and tone and your ability to persuade the reader of your recommendations.

Strategy
1 List the points you need to cover in your answer.
2 Think about how you can make your proposal persuasive.
3 Make sure you include reasons why your idea or proposal should be accepted.

1   Read this task.

You are studying at a college in Scotland where extensive tourism is affecting the area. You see a notice offering money to help an area affected by tourism and decide to write a proposal about how the area could be improved. Read the notice below and some notes you have made. Then, using the information appropriately, write a proposal to the organisation, describing how tourists use the area, explaining what damage they cause and suggesting how money could be spent on improving the area.

HELP US TO HELP THE PLANET

We want to invest some money in helping an area that is being damaged by tourism. Is there something in your area that could be improved by spending some money to prevent further damage? We will invest in your area if you can convince us that the money will be well spent.

damage to beach
rubbish
too many boats!

2   What should be included in a proposal for the above?

1 A description of the area you are concerned about.
2 A description of activities you can do in the area.
3 A financial plan of how you will spend the money.
4 An explanation of the problems caused by tourism.
5 How your nominated area is similar to other areas.
6 An outline of what action would help to prevent further damage.

3   Read this sample answer.

I would like to nominate the area which I am studying in to receive some money to prevent it being damaged by tourism. This is an area of beautiful coastline on the north-west coast of Scotland.

Recently more and more tourists have come to the area, mainly families with children. The number of people and especially the children are damaging the sand dunes. These are getting worn away. Also the tourists leave a lot of rubbish on the beach. There is also a small harbour and more and more rich people are bringing their boats down and polluting the water and making a lot of noise.

If we had some money, we could put signs up to protect the dunes and pay for guards to walk along and check them. Also we could pay for rubbish collection on the beach. In addition, we could use money to set up a permit system for boats so we could limit the number in the harbour.

These final paragraphs all 'persuade' the reader in different ways. Which is the best final paragraph? Why?

1 Areas on the coast are being eroded by so many tourists walking there. It's disgraceful. Your money would help us repair the path and control the tourism. This is why you should give some money to us.

2 The area depends on tourism for its income, but the tourists come for the natural beauty so they will disappear if the area becomes more damaged. The solutions I have suggested are simple and economical but would be very effective, so I urge you to support our area by investing in these solutions.

3 So we have a lot of problems. I'm very grateful that you are willing to invest money in this problem. Please give the money to our area to stop the problems I have outlined. If you do, we will make a sign to say this is what your organisation has done.

4   What headings would you give each paragraph in the sample answer above? Use the ideas for the report headings in Unit 5 to help you. You could also look at the Writing sections in Unit 8 of the coursebook.

┌─ **Improve!** ◄─
│ Part 1 tasks always include an element of
│ persuasion. In a proposal, make sure you give
│ reasons and use formal persuasive language.
└

5   Write your own answer to the task in Exercise 1. Remember to use both content and language to persuade the reader. Write your answer in 180–220 words.

Reading: gapped text (Part 2)
▶ *CB pages 118–119*

Strategy
1 Sometimes you need to work out the order of events in a text to help you decide which missing paragraph to choose. For example, events may not always be described in chronological order.
2 Look carefully at substitution to help you work out where the missing paragraphs fit.

1 Look through the text and the missing paragraphs. Go carefully through each paragraph and underline any words or phrases which refer backwards or forwards in the text. Look especially for time phrases, abstract nouns, definite articles and pronouns.

2 Read the article again. Six paragraphs have been removed from the article. Choose from the paragraphs A–G on page 81 the one which fits each gap (1–6). There is one extra paragraph which you do not need to use.

3 Use these adjectives (in bold in the text) to complete the sentences. Use a good dictionary, such as *The Longman Exams Dictionary*, to help you.

indolent	stunning	fruitless	epic	prize
agape	elusive	vicarious	towering	barren

1 Deserts are very beautiful, but some people find them .... and unappealing.
2 The scenery in the Hindu Kush is absolutely ....
3 He had an eventful and .... journey – he was very brave to undertake it.
4 The koalas are the .... exhibit in the zoo. Everybody wants to see them.
5 The men in the tribe had a .... journey to find water, returning empty-handed.
6 The mountains formed .... peaks, so high that we couldn't see the summits.
7 I got a .... satisfaction from watching my children learning to surf.
8 The tourists, exposed in the small car, had their mouths .... in horror as the lion emerged from the bushes.
9 In the afternoon the bears are very ...., lying around on rocks, soaking up the sun.
10 Our tour guide proved very .... so we had to go round the city by ourselves.

CHASING THE SNOW LEOPARD

A tour guide describes his attempts to find the snow leopard.

As an adventure tour guide, I have run some fairly ambitious trips in my time: riding horses blind across the mountains of Kyrgyzstan; travelling into the centre of the Sahara; leading a group safely through Afghanistan. But offering to take a party of ten on a two-week holiday into the snowy reaches of the Hindu Kush, in mid-December, to find a snow leopard made me wonder if I had finally met my proverbial. They say a good guide is a lucky guide; for this trip to be even partially successful, I knew I would need that commodity in spades.

1

This was worrying news. Surrounded by **towering** mountains, Chitral province is only accessible by dirt roads over high mountain passes or by an extremely unreliable, weather-dependent air service. With the passes now closed, our only option was to fly.

2

I have been to Chitral many times, I even have a house high up in the valley where the festival was taking place, but I have never been in winter. Like other summer destinations, this is a time when tourism is non-existent and life returns to its natural

indolent rhythms. As I stepped off the plane, I breathed in deeply and smiled. Whatever happened with snow leopards, I knew now I could relax … just being in this **stunning** place was privilege enough.

| 3 |

Mark had spent three **fruitless** years in Nepal trying to capture one of these increasingly rare animals on film for David Attenborough's series *Planet Earth*, and was now getting desperate. I told him that I knew exactly where it had been seen and that the spot was extremely accessible. Mark travelled to Chitral that winter and shot the exceptional film we were all so lucky to see on our TV screens last year. And if he could get to see it, why couldn't we?

| 4 |

We found Mark and the rest of the BBC crew in the same place they shot their **epic** footage – this time making a film for Natural World – with a row of impressive lenses pointing west across the river. But although there were plenty of markhor (wild goats) to watch, there was no sign of the **prize** animal.

| 5 |

When we arrived at the same time the following afternoon, Mark gave me the thumbs up. I jumped out of the Jeep and clambered up the slope. 'She came out half an hour ago and has been sitting there ever since,' he said, pointing to the dappled rocks a hundred yards beyond the river. I stared, mesmerised, mouth **agape**. As I looked around at my group, all of whom were beside themselves with excitement, I felt an enormous sense of relief.

| 6 |

We continued to watch her and take photographs all afternoon as she prowled this way and that across the mountainside. Then, as dusk fell, she stalked her prey – a young markhor – and made her kill. None of us could have asked for more.

A

The idea of running a trip to Chitral in winter had been brewing for quite some time. In the autumn of 2004, I was called by Mark Smith, the award-winning wildlife photographer, and asked if I knew anything about a snow leopard that had apparently taken up residence just outside Chitral town.

B

Mark told us encouragingly that with the early snow pushing her lower into the valley, there was a good chance she'd appear. But with only four days set aside to catch this **elusive** animal, we would have to be very lucky indeed. As night fell, we returned to our hotel with cold feet and hands and plenty of film left in our cameras.

C

We arrived in Peshawar, Pakistan's border town, on December 10, only to learn that bad weather had hit the mountains earlier than expected and that for the past week all flights to Chitral in the north had been cancelled.

D

It also made me proud of myself. I had been told I couldn't run a snow leopard tour as the chances of seeing one were just too small. Yet here we were on the second day of trying with the snow leopard in our sights. The **vicarious** pleasure I gained from my clients was absolute, I could have hugged them all.

E

This kind of information leaves the tour guide in an awkward position. You have to stay positive, show your group around with enthusiasm and focus, but inside your thoughts are in turmoil. Where will I take them? What will we do?

F

Luck was with us as only a day later we touched down into a winter wonderland, surrounded on all sides by snowy mountains. At one end of the tranquil valley stood the **towering** form of Tirich Mir, the highest mountain in the Hindu Kush, while at the other swept a row of icy peaks. The sky was deepest blue and the air was clean and sharp.

G

Set in a tapered gorge, Tushi is a hamlet of six or seven dwellings half an hour out of Chitral town. On one side is Chitral Gol national park, bordered by the narrow road that leads to Afghanistan and a shallow but thunderous river. Opposite are craggy, **barren** mountains rising up towards snowy peaks.

Listening: multiple choice (Part 3)
▶ *CB page 120*

Strategy
In Part 3, you are often asked about a feeling, opinion or attitude expressed by the speaker. Make sure you read the questions carefully and understand exactly what each question is asking you to listen for.

1 Read through the questions in Exercise 2 and decide what each one is asking you about – an opinion or attitude, a feeling or a fact. You need to look at both the question and the choices.

2 You will hear an interview with Mark Latell, a scientist who works on volcanoes, talking about his job. For questions 1–6, choose the answer (A, B, C or D) which fits best according to what you hear.

1 According to Mark, predictions about volcanic eruptions can be inaccurate because
  A the measuring instruments need to be more sophisticated.
  B reliability is affected by significant variations between volcanoes.
  C scientists need to know more about the history of individual volcanoes.
  D the observation and monitoring of volcanoes needs to be constant.

2 When Mark's team successfully predicted an eruption, he felt
  A grateful to the staff in his team.
  B relieved that they had arrived in time.
  C embarrassed by the thanks he received.
  D surprised the local people responded well.

3 Why might Mark's team visit other eruptions?
  A if they are invited by a government
  B in order to study different volcanoes
  C if there is a national emergency
  D in order to liaise with other scientists

4 Mark denies that he and his team are 'cowboys' because
  A they consider the job to be relatively safe.
  B their families prevent them from taking risks.
  C they plan any expeditions to a volcano very thoroughly.
  D their training has prepared them for the job they do.

5 What does Mark say about his experience on Mount St Helens?
  A He was glad that he was with a colleague.
  B He was excited to have had the experience.
  C He was lucky to escape from such a big eruption.
  D He was pleased at the knowledge his team gained.

6 According to Mark, the next big eruption
  A may occur in an unexpected location.
  B could significantly alter the earth's climate.
  C is bound to be preceded by some warning signs.
  D may be unlike anything we have experienced before.

3 Listen again and check your answers.

 4 These phrasal verbs all appeared in the interview. Listen to the interview again and match each one to the meaning used in the interview.

a) build up	i)	to travel somewhere by plane, implying luxury or excitement
b) come up	ii)	to decide not to do something you have agreed to do
c) jet off to	iii)	to gradually increase in amount, size or strength
d) pitch up	iv)	to continue, especially for a long time
e) back out	v)	to appear on a computer screen
f) go on	vi)	to arrive where someone is expecting you

5 Complete these sentences using the phrasal verbs in Exercise 4 in the correct form.

1 I searched for his website on volcanoes, but nothing ....

2 I'm hoping this summer that I'm going to be able to .... the Caribbean!

3 The explosion was quick, but the noise from the volcano .... for ages.

4 We .... early at the hotel and our room wasn't ready.

5 My friends and I planned to go camping but I didn't have enough money so I had to ....

6 The arguments against flying are slowly .... because we know more now about the damage it causes to the environment.

Grammar 1: countable/ uncountable nouns
▶ *CB page 117*

1 Complete the second sentence so that it has a similar meaning to the first using the word given.

1 I don't understand why we're going to see animals locked in a zoo.
   POINT
   I don't see .... to see animals locked in a zoo.

2 I didn't have a clue how to photograph wild animals.
   IDEA
   I had .... how to photograph wild animals.

3 A local myth claims that the mountain can prolong life.
   POWERS
   A local myth claims the mountain has .... prolong life.

4 We were prevented from climbing the mountain by the officer in charge of the reserve.
   AUTHORITIES
   We were prevented from climbing the mountain ....

Vocabulary 1: linking words/text referring words

1 Put the following linking words and text referring words into the correct gaps in the text. Capitalise if necessary.

in fact	while	this searching behaviour
this task	however	this time delay
the controversy	alternatively	

DANCING FOR THEIR DINNER

In the 1960s, zoologist Karl von Frisch proposed that honeybees use dance, the 'waggle dance', as a coded message to guide other bees to new food sources.

He claimed that when a honeybee worker discovers a good feeding site, she informs her nest mates through a dance that describes the distance and direction of the feeding site. **(1)** ...., von Frisch's experiments also showed that bees that had attended the dance (recruits) took far longer to get to food than would be expected. **(2)** .... caused other scientists to argue that the recruits found the food source simply by tracking down the smell that they had picked up from the dancing bee. **(3)** .... it was suggested that recruits simply followed the dancer when she flew back to the food. **(4)** .... has persisted because no one could show exactly where the recruits flew when they left their hives.

Scientists have now repeated the experiment using a radar. First, they watched the waggle dance in a glass observation hive and identified recruits. They then captured these recruits as they left the hive, attached a radar transponder to them, and then tracked their flight paths using the radar. **(5)** .... most recruited bees undertook a flight path that took them straight to the vicinity of the feeding site, where they then proceeded to search for its exact location, using odour and other cues. **(6)** .... accounts for the time lag that caused the original controversy. **(7)** .... the bees' success at **(8)** .... has now been proven, it is still a matter of debate as to whether or not this 'bee communication' constitutes a language!

Bees for Development www.beesfordevelopment.org

Vocabulary 2: the natural world

1 Every year some animals are pushed further towards extinction while others recover their numbers. They are either wildlife winners or losers. Decide which of the following animals are winners and which are losers, then check your answers over the page.

1 the polar bear	4 the harlequin frog
2 the African grey parrot	5 the giant panda
3 the Bengal tiger	6 the red squirrel

Winners or Losers?

A THE POLAR BEAR: LOSER

The polar bear's **grip** on the Arctic ice is slipping and the world population of about 25,000 bears is expected to fall by 30 percent over the next 50 years. The main cause is that the polar pack ice is melting fast; in summer it is now separated from land by a wide belt of sea. This means that the 'fat time', when the bears can catch seals easily, is decreasing. It also forces the bears to swim, using up their fat reserves. The result: drowned and starving bears, and fewer baby bears to replace them.

B THE AFRICAN GREY PARROT: WINNER

The future looks brighter thanks, ironically, to bird flu. In Britain the trade in wild birds was put on hold in 2005 after bird flu was diagnosed among quarantined animals. With its 'perfect mix of brains and beauty', this most popular of talking parrots is in huge demand, but the import ban is protecting it. One of the world's most intelligent birds, it is said to have the intellectual capacity of a five-year-old, but the emotional development of 'a particularly terrible two-year-old'.

C THE BENGAL TIGER: LOSER

Half a century ago there were tens of thousands of tigers in the wild jungles and swamps of the Indian subcontinent. The most recent estimate is around 1500, but even that may be over-optimistic. The reason for the downfall is poaching. Every part of a tiger is potentially valuable, from its whiskers to its tail. Most valuable are the skins, worth £7600 each on the black market. A crackdown by police and customs has reduced poaching, but the outlook for the mighty Bengal tiger looks **bleak**.

D THE HARLEQUIN FROG: LOSER

Sixty-five of the many species of these brightly coloured tropical frogs have disappeared since 1980. They inhabit high, humid forests in Central and South America and the deadly agent seems to be a fungal disease which smothers the skin of the frog and kills it. This may occur because weather in frog country is changing – days are getting cooler, nights warmer, and periods of drought are becoming more frequent. According to experts, disease is killing the frogs, but climate change is **pulling the trigger**.

E THE GIANT PANDA: WINNER

The Chinese have finally **cracked** how to breed the giant panda, the symbol of endangered species the world over. Captive animals normally lack sex drive and stubbornly refuse to mate. But Wolong research centre in south-west China has got around the problem by showing them videos of mating pandas. This year a record 27 baby pandas were born in captivity and China plans to create 'bamboo corridors' from one panda sanctuary to another to enable the animals to roam more widely.

F THE RED SQUIRREL: LOSER

Experts now believe that the vast sums of money spent in the UK on trying to control the non-native grey squirrel and preserve the native reds are **a waste of time**. The grey is not only bolder, stronger and greedier, it also spreads a virus that kills the reds but spares fellow greys. The best hope for the red squirrel is on islands around Britain where there are no greys. Likely sanctuaries are the Isle of Wight, the Isle of Arran and Brownsea Island in Poole Harbour. That is, if the grey squirrel doesn't find its way to them on board the ferry!

Peter Marren, ©The Independent, 28 December 2006

2 Find words in the texts which mean:

1 areas where an animal is protected and cannot be hunted (texts E and F)
2 to walk or travel for a long time with no clear purpose or direction (text E)
3 illegally catching or shooting animals (text C)
4 kept apart from others in case the animals are carrying a disease (text B)
5 a supply of food and warmth that animals store in their body to be used in the winter (text A)
6 a long period of dry weather when there is not enough water for animals to live (text D)

3 Metaphors are a way of describing one thing as something different and suggesting that it has similar qualities to that thing. The words in a metaphor have a literal meaning and a metaphoric meaning. Look at these highlighted metaphors in the texts and decide which meaning is intended. Which one intends both meanings?

1 grip … is slipping	a) losing tight hold
	b) losing power or control over something
2 … looks brighter	a) appears light and shining
	b) appears successful or promising
3 bleak	a) without anything to make you feel hopeful
	b) cold and unpleasant
4 to crack	a) to break so something has lines on the surface
	b) to find the answer to a problem
5 to pull the trigger	a) to be the thing that causes a serious problem
	b) to fire a gun
6 waste	a) when something is not used in an effective way
	b) unwanted materials or substances

4 Look back at the Reading texts in Unit 9. How many words or expressions can you find that are used metaphorically? Check your answers in the Key.

Use of English: gapped sentences (Part 4)

1 Think of one word only which can be used appropriately in all three sentences.

TIP! Usually one of the sentences uses the word in a fixed phrase or expression, so remember to look carefully at the words on either side of the gap.

1
I can't get the top off this bottle – my .... isn't strong enough.
The new manager asked a lot of questions in order to get a .... on what was happening.
We haven't got a very good .... on the environmental problems we are creating.

2
First you have to .... the eggs into the bowl.
We must do something about filling that .... in the wall before it lets in rain.
She's amazing – she managed to .... the problem as soon as I gave it to her!

3
.... products must be put in the appropriate bin for recycling.
We must eat the chicken today or it will go to ....
Trying to save energy in our homes is a .... of time unless everybody does it.

4
Could you do me a .... and give me a lift?
I'm not in .... of reducing the time we quarantine animals from abroad.
Cuts in taxes always .... rich people!

5
He had an .... in his car but he's ok.
I bumped into her by .... when I was shopping.
It is no .... that he got the job – his brother is the manager!

Use of English: open cloze (Part 2)
▶ *CB page 121*

1 Read the text below and write in the word which best fits each space. Use only one word in each space. There is an example at the beginning (0).

THE UNGRATEFUL FOX

Scientists who argue for the benefits of having animals around tend to focus more on the advantages they bring **(0)** ....*in*.... terms of stress-release and proto-parenting. I have **(1)** .... doubt there is merit in all their assertions. But, **(2)** .... struck me recently that the curious incidents that filled my childhood may offer one or two unheralded arguments in favour **(3)** .... spending our lives close to animals.

When I was eleven, for instance, my father and I found a fox cub injured in the woods nearby and brought it home. We nursed it **(4)** .... bottled milk for a few weeks. We converted an old sideboard **(5)** .... his home, even gave him a name, Carlo. No one was **(6)** .... enthusiastic about our new charge than my father, **(7)** .... was fired by memories of his own childhood when he too had reared a stray cub. I remember sensing that our shared responsibility for this poor creature had brought **(8)** .... closer.

(9) .... morning I woke up to discover the fox had battered **(10)** .... way out of the sideboard and fled. He was gone but he hadn't forgotten. A week later an already more mature-looking Carlo reappeared in a roadside hedge near our lane. Rather idiotically, I assumed he'd come back to say thanks. So, unbelievably, **(11)** .... my father. As he kneeled down to stroke the fox, Carlo bit him **(12)** .... hard he almost severed a finger. I'd **(13)** .... seen so much blood. **(14)** .... is a memory that has been locked away ever since, a piece of family lore. Naturally, neither my father **(15)** .... I have ever trusted a fox since.

© Guardian News & Media Ltd 2007

Grammar 2: preparatory *it* (subject and object)
▶ *CB pages 122–123*

1 Rewrite these sentences using *it* as a preparatory subject.

e.g. *That birds migrate so far is amazing.*
 It's amazing that birds migrate so far.

1 To think how little we are doing to protect our planet is uncomfortable.
2 That the panda has managed to survive is extraordinary.
3 To experience watching animals in the wild is incredible.
4 When we finally try to control the damage we are doing, it will be too late.
5 To realise how much we pollute the oceans is difficult.
6 To put your hands through that cage at the zoo was dangerous.

2 Match the two halves of these sentences and insert *it* (object) in the right place.

e.g. *(0) I found exciting (00) to take part in the safari.*
 I found it exciting to take part in the safari.

a) I can't stand when	i) to understand the problem of endangered animals.
b) The politician made clear	ii) that is not their responsibility to save energy.
c) The charity made easy	iii) people won't even try to recycle things.
d) Most people think	iv) leave up to me to walk the dog!
e) I wish you wouldn't	v) that global warming was a serious issue.

Speaking: (Part 3)

About the exam: In Part 3 of the exam, after you have discussed the choices you will have to reach an agreement with your partner.

Which of the following phrases are the best ones to use to conclude your discussion with your partner?

So, are we agreed then? *What I'm trying to say is …*
What do you mean by that? *Right then, let's decide …*
Do you know what I mean? *Is that how you see it?*
Right, is that ok with you? *So, shall we say ……*
Ok, which one(s) shall we *Could I just add …*
 choose to …

What do all the concluding phrases have in common? Listen to examples of how to use the phrases on the CD.

Writing: report (Part 1)
▶ *CB pages 125–126*

About the exam: In Paper 2, Part 1, you may be asked to write a report. You will be marked on organisation and style as well as language.

Strategy
1 Make sure you use the information you are given in your report.
2 Think carefully about what your target reader needs to know.

1   Read this task.

You are studying at a college in the UK. Recently the college paid for you to attend a conference on the environment as part of your course.

Read the email from your teacher, the conference programme and some notes you made below. Then write a report for your teacher describing your experience of the conference, suggesting how it could be improved and saying whether or not you would recommend other students to attend.

From: Mrs Giles
Subject: Environment conference

I hope the conference was useful for your course! Can you write a report giving your impressions of it and saying whether or not you think the college should continue to pay for students to attend.
Anna Giles

Are We Doing Enough?

Choice of seminars *seminars overbooked*

Lecture: Are the solutions working?
no interpreters

Meet representatives from environmental organisations
too little time to speak to representatives

Free information
Useful handouts

2   The words in bold in the question are the instructions for what should be included in your report. How many points do you need to cover? How many headings do you need in your report?

3   Make notes on a sample plan. Use the information in the question.

Section title/paragraph heading:	Include:

4   Choose the best topic sentences to introduce each section.

1a) This reports tells you whether or not you should send students to the conference next year.
1b) The aim of this report is to assess the usefulness of the environmental conference to future students.
2a) Some aspects of the conference were good.
2b) There was quite a lot of the conference that I found interesting.
3a) There are various improvements that could be made which would make the conference more effective.
3b) Some things needed improving such as the seminars, not having interpreters and making more time to speak.
4a) In conclusion, I would say that you should send students to the conference.
4b) Overall, it is probably worthwhile sending students in the future, especially if improvements can be implemented.

Check your answers with the key, then decide why the suggested answers are the best.

> ─ **Improve!** ◀
>
> Remember to use linking words (see page 83) to make your sentences more complex.

5   Write a report as outlined in Exercise 1. Use your notes in Exercise 3 to help you. Write your answer in 180–220 words.

UNIT

11 Always on my mind

Vocabulary 1: expressions with *take*, *mind* and *brain*
▶ *CB page 131*

1 Complete the crossword with the words that fill the gaps in the clues.

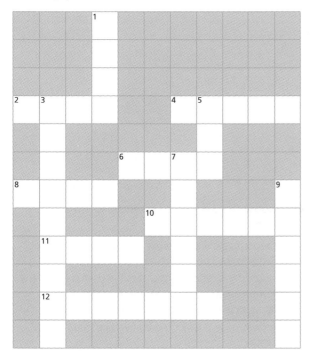

Across

2 r.......... your brains

4 s.......... your mind

6 put your mind at r..........

8 m.......... up your mind

10 take someone's b.......... away

11 t.......... your mind off something

12 take somebody for g..........

Down

1 p.......... someone's brains

3 take a.......... of somebody

5 p.......... someone's mind at rest

7 take everything in your s..........

9 c.......... your mind

2 Complete the sentences with these expressions.

| brain child   brainwave   brain drain |
| brain teaser |

1 Britain is suffering from a .... with many graduates going to live in other countries.

2 The mystery was a real .... but we eventually solved it!

3 The festival was very original and was the .... of an old rock star.

4 I've just had a brilliant ....

3 Replace the underlined words in each sentence with one of the expressions in the box. Use a good dictionary, such as *The Longman Exams Dictionary*, to help you.

| bear in mind   walking on air   cheer up |
| a piece of one's mind   in the depths of despair |
| down in the dumps   on top of the world |
| at the back of one's mind |

1 I thought she behaved so badly that I told her what I thought of her.
   I thought she behaved so badly that I gave her
   ....

2 The news about my new job made me feel really happy.
   The news about my new job made me feel as if I was
   ....

3 He looked so glum that everyone told him to be happier.
   He looked so glum that everyone told him to
   ....

4 When my boyfriend and I split up, I was very, very unhappy.
   When my boyfriend and I split up I was
   ....

5 What I couldn't stop thinking about was that he might be with someone else.
   .... was the thought that he might be with someone else.

6 You should consider the fact that he may not want to come to the wedding.
   You should .... that he may not want to come to the wedding.

7 She came with us to the party, but she looked rather miserable the whole time.
   She came with us to the party, but she looked rather
   .... the whole time.

8 I've just got a new girlfriend so I'm feeling extremely happy.
   I've just got a new girlfriend so I'm feeling
   ....

Listening: short extracts (Part 1)

Strategy
You will have only a limited time to read through the questions before you listen, so make sure you read the first part of each question and know what you should be listening for.

1 Read the first part of each question 1–6 below. Underline the key words in each of these and circle the most important word that tells you what kind of information (e.g. reason, purpose, etc.) to listen for. Question 1 has been done as an example.

2 You will hear three different extracts. For questions 1–6, choose the answer (A, B or C) which fits best according to what you hear.

Extract One

You hear part of an interview with a woman who is a psychologist.

1 The woman thinks people want to be liked because
   A it is part of the human survival instinct.
   B we have wider social circles than we used to.
   C approval is important for our mental health.

2 What is the woman's attitude to people who fear rejection?
   A She disapproves of the fact they are self-centred.
   B She thinks they are lazy about helping themselves.
   C She criticises them for blaming their parents.

Extract Two

You hear two people talking about how to deal with feeling unhappy.

3 What made the woman get involved with helping other people?
   A the appeal of the organisation she chose to work for
   B the enjoyment of the people she worked with
   C the rewards she got after she had helped people

4 What do the two speakers agree about?
   A It's possible to help yourself if you are feeling down.
   B You need outside help to make you feel better.
   C Everybody experiences ups and downs.

Extract Three

You hear two people discussing how they remember things.

5 The woman decided to do a course to improve her memory in order to
   A achieve one of her ambitions.
   B improve her everyday life.
   C change to a different career.

6 How does the man feel about his bad memory?
   A worried that he can't improve his memory
   B relieved that his memory is not getting any worse
   C concerned that he can't remember recent events

3 Match these phrases from the listening extracts to their meanings. Listen again to make sure you understand the context.

Extract One:
put into perspective
   a) to give something its correct importance
   b) to be influenced by your experiences

focus in on oneself
   a) to become very inward-looking
   b) to concentrate successfully on improving oneself

Extract Two:
sort themselves out
   a) succeed in making arrangements
   b) deal with all their problems

it's not the end of the world
   a) it's not as bad as you think
   b) it's not the point at which you have to stop

Extract Three:
get to grips with
   a) to start improving your behaviour
   b) to understand or deal with something difficult

a lost cause
   a) desperate
   b) hopeless

Grammar 1: modal verbs 2
▶ *CB page 130*

1 Match the modals in these sentences to the functions a–f below.

1 When I was younger I had to live with my grandparents.
2 I couldn't forget the way he looked at me when I told him I was leaving.
3 He may have got through the interview, but he didn't look happy when he came out.
4 You must have been worried about your future when you lost your job.
5 You should have gone to the doctor earlier if you were feeling ill.
6 I told her she could have come over if she was upset.

a) possibility
b) logical deduction
c) obligation/necessity
d) advice (weak obligation)
e) permission
f) ability

2 Underline the correct modal + infinitive in each sentence.

1 She was very grumpy – she *might have / should have* had a row with someone.
2 His body language was quite negative, so I *wouldn't have / mustn't have* thought he wanted to stay.
3 He hasn't called. I suppose he *could have / can't have* lost his phone.
4 He left early – he *must have / should have* been very keen to get home!
5 If she wanted to be liked, she *should have / must have* been kinder to people.
6 She *can't have / mustn't have* passed the test – she looked really worried when I saw her.
7 He wanted to speak to a psychologist – he *may have / should have* done already but I don't think so.
8 My daughter worked very hard for her exams, so I *needn't have / can't have* worried about her passing.

3 Correct the mistakes in the modals in the following sentences.

1 She thought she was doing the right thing but she can be told beforehand that she wasn't.
2 If she'd prepared her work better, she wouldn't give such a bad presentation.

3 I'm not surprised she's cross with you. In my opinion, you can't have criticised her.
4 He didn't get up in time for his exam and it may be his alarm not going off!
5 She said she had studied really hard, but she couldn't do as she got really bad marks.
6 He mustn't have prepared for his interview well enough.
7 You must had some therapy as you seem so much better now!

Speaking: Part 2

About the exam: In Part 2 of the Speaking exam you will be asked to speak about some pictures for one minute.

Strategy
1 You must talk about what the examiner asks you to talk about. Ask the examiner to repeat the instructions if you are not sure.
2 You have a few seconds to think about the pictures. Think quickly about what you want to say.
3 When you talk, remember not to repeat yourself.

1 Look at this task. These pictures show different feelings. I'd like you to compare two of the pictures and say how you think the people are feeling and why they might be feeling like this.

2 Tick what you could talk about.
What the people look like.
What the people are doing.
What feelings their actions express.
What the people would like to be feeling.
What may have just happened.
What the people are going to do next.

3 Talk about the photos for one minute. Time yourself.

TIP! Even though you have only one minute, don't rush as this can affect your pronunciation, stress and intonation. Speak calmly.

Use of English: multiple-choice cloze (Part 1)

1   Read the text below and decide which answer (A, B, C or D) best fits each space. There is an example at the beginning (0).

WHY ARE THEY SO WEIRD?

When they finally **(0)** ....*B*.... at lunchtime on a Saturday and need a crane to get them up on schoolday mornings, teenagers are not just being lazy. Their biological clocks **(1)** .... on a different time to those of adults, because the hormone melatonin, which **(2)** .... sleepiness, starts to be secreted in the brain much later at night and **(3)** .... later in the morning.

Researchers have found that students do worse in exams when they **(4)** .... them in the morning compared with in the afternoon. 'Teenagers' body clocks can be delayed by between two and four hours, and they don't start to **(5)** .... until at least 10a.m.,' says Professor Russell Foster, a neuroscientist at Oxford University. 'The timetable is not very well thought **(6)** .... It is cruel to impose a cultural **(7)** .... on teenagers that makes them underachieve,' he adds. 'Most schools' regimes force teenagers to work at a time of day that is suboptimal, and many university students are **(8)** .... to considerable dangers from sleep deprivation,' Prof. Foster says.

Teenagers who hide in their rooms may be **(9)** .... and just need to **(10)** .... Strauch, another neuroscientist, says, 'That doesn't mean we are not supposed to have them take out the rubbish and be part of the family. But it does teach us that there are enormous changes going on inside their brains.

'I think the most **(11)** .... thing it teaches us is that they aren't finished yet. That helps us to be a little bit more patient. Teenagers may look grown up but they are not grown-ups. There is still a lot of development **(12)** .... in their brains.'

Julia Stuart, © The Independent, 16 January 2007

0	**A** stand up	**B** <u>surface</u>	**C** raise	**D** come up
1	**A** run	**B** go	**C** tick	**D** perform
2	**A** advances	**B** furthers	**C** develops	**D** promotes
3	**A** waits	**B** lingers	**C** persists	**D** endures
4	**A** sit	**B** fix	**C** place	**D** set
5	**A** act	**B** behave	**C** produce	**D** function
6	**A** about	**B** of	**C** out	**D** over
7	**A** plan	**B** pattern	**C** method	**D** manner
8	**A** exposed	**B** revealed	**C** shown	**D** presented
9	**A** over-excited	**B** over-stimulated	**C** over-aroused	**D** over-animated
10	**A** break off	**B** run out	**C** make off	**D** get away
11	**A** relieving	**B** reassuring	**C** supporting	**D** calming
12	**A** emerging	**B** coming to light	**C** transpiring	**D** taking place

Reading: multiple choice (Part 3)
▶ *CB pages 132–133*

Strategy
1 Read through the text quickly before you look at the questions. Then read the questions and make sure you understand what each question is asking you to consider.

1 Multiple-choice questions usually ask you to consider an opinion or attitude, how somebody feels, what was the reason for or purpose of something or a summary. Read through questions 1–7 on page 93 and decide what each one is asking you to consider.

• the writer's opinion or attitude
• a reason or purpose for something
• a summary of the mentioned text

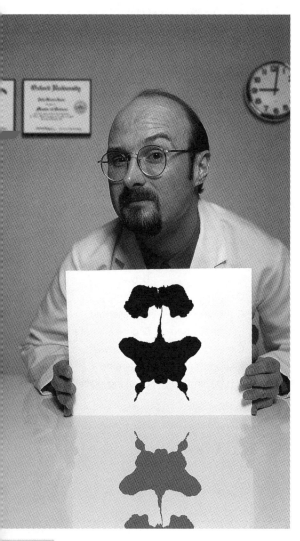

INTERNAL AFFAIRS

Don't underestimate the power of the inner world

People who appear to be attractive, clever and successful can sometimes surprise us when we discover that they are **racked** with insecurities and feel themselves to be ugly, stupid or a failure. And no matter how much you try to **bolster** the self-confidence of people like this, the effects don't last. What could possibly cause this strange difference between what people appear to be to the outside world and what they believe and feel on the inside?

We do not live in one world but in two. The outer world consists of other people, objects and nature, while the inner world is made up of feelings, beliefs and dreams. Sometimes we call the first world reality, but we couldn't be more wrong. Both worlds are equally real. Moreover, when it comes to **determining** how we feel about ourselves, it is the second world that provides the tone and mood music by which we live our lives, not the first.

This is illustrated by one of the most famous psychological tests – the Rorschach, or ink blot, test. I had to practise giving the test to my fellow students when I was training. Examinees are shown a series of patterns, formed by random ink blots. What we see in front of us has to come from our own minds – what psychologists call projection. Our responses thus reveal how we colour the world.

I gave the test first to one woman who looked at the weirdly shaped stains and began to smile. She said she thought it was two funny-shaped clowns, dancing around and waving flowers in the air, and that all around them she saw beautiful butterflies dancing in the sun. The next day I showed the same card to a different woman. Her brow darkened and at first she wouldn't speak. Eventually she whispered that she could see two terrible witches that were shooting machine guns at each other. What for the first had been something enchanting became blood splattering the air around them.

From spending time with these women at the Institute I could see this dramatic difference played out. Both were highly intelligent, attractive and interesting company, but the first had a sunny disposition, always seeing the good in situations. The other spent her time being grumpy, feeling threatened and acting destructively. One came from a secure, loving family and was in constant contact with her parents. The other's father had left when she was twelve and her mother would compete with her to be prettier and more popular with men. This explained their responses to the test. That is the reason why the mood music from our internal worlds proves so insistent. It is a track that is laid down in our childhoods, when we are most sensitive to what others think of us.

It is from our parents and sometimes other close relatives that we hear the chorus that accompanies our developing lives: 'She's a moody one'; 'He'll never amount to anything'; 'She twists everyone round her little finger'. Often these labels do not come from what the child is actually doing but are **projections** from the internal world of the parent. Then, tragically, the label can become a self-fulfilling prophecy.

Good therapy is about uncovering these, often unconscious and ingrained, assumptions and replacing them with a more realistic **appraisal**. But it can be a long and painful process. However, despite these difficulties we do have to deal with that childhood **legacy**; for only if we heal our damaged internal worlds will we be able to enjoy our achievements in the external one. Otherwise our success will be only skin deep.

2 Read the text and decide which answer (A, B, C or D) you think fits best according to the text.

1 In the first paragraph, what does the writer say about people with insecurities?

   A They can never lose their insecurities.

   B They cannot understand what causes their insecurities.

   C They often appear to be very different.

   D The cause of their problem is insoluble.

2 In the second paragraph, the writer claims that our inner world is

   A more real than the outside world.

   B more influential in certain situations.

   C more likely to cause us difficulties than the outside world.

   D more difficult to understand than the outside world.

3 The writer mentions the Rorschach test in the third paragraph to show

   A how the inner world can be studied scientifically.

   B how different we all are in the way we see things.

   C how unrelated the inner world is to the real world.

   D how our inner world affects our perceptions.

4 The writer concludes that the two different women were affected by

   A their past relationship with men.

   B their current interactions with their mothers.

   C their relationship with their parents.

   D the moods of each of their families.

5 According to the writer, what is true when people comment on our personality?

   A The comments may bear no relation to our behaviour.

   B If you say something is true then it will become true.

   C What is said may affect what we are doing at the time.

   D Other people may pass on their prejudices from previous relationships.

6 In the last paragraph the writer is

   A advocating therapy for everybody to make them feel better.

   B explaining how therapy works for most people.

   C suggesting that solutions can be found through therapy.

   D proposing a new therapy for dealing with internal problems.

7 What would be the best subtitle for this article?

   A *Don't underestimate the power of the inner world*

   B *Two women – two views of life*

   C *Why we all need to see a therapist*

   D *The inner workings of the human mind*

3 What job do you think the writer does?

a) a journalist

b) a psychotherapist

c) a university teacher

4 Look at these highlighted words in the article. Both meanings, a and b, given below are possible. Tick [✓] the best meaning in the context.

1	racked	a) to acquire (a number of something)
		b) to suffer (physical or mental pain)
2	bolster	a) to help someone feel better and more positive
		b) to improve on something
3	determining	a) to influence something
		b) to find out facts about something
4	projections	a) a calculation about what something will be in the future
		b) something you imagine to have particular qualities because of your wishes or feelings
5	appraisal	a) a meeting to discuss one's work performance
		b) an opinion judging the worth or value of something
6	legacy	a) something that happens or exists as a result of things that happened at an earlier time
		b) money or property that you receive from someone

5 Match each word in Exercise 4 to the words it collocates with below. Use the meanings above and the article to help you. One set of collocations goes before the word above.

a) educational / political

b) the result / the factors / the way that … / the conditions

c) of someone's fears / of someone's insecurities

d) with pain / with guilt

e) pride / confidence / self-esteem

f) of a situation / standards / life

Grammar 2: emphasis with inversion
▶ *CB page 135*

1 Complete the sentences with the correct form of the verb in brackets. Add any other words that you might need.

1 Rarely .... (read) such a marvellous book about psychology.
2 Only when I saw his face .... (realise) how upset he was.
3 Never .... (witness) such a terrible row.
4 Under no circumstances .... (phone) me at the office.
5 Hardly .... (take) my coat off, when the door bell went.
6 At no time .... (explain) how unhappy he was.
7 No sooner .... (apologise) than she started shouting at me!
8 Not only .... (buy) her flowers but he took her to dinner as well!

2 Use each of the following adverbials and make all other necessary changes to give greater emphasis to these sentences.

Never ...	Not only ...	Rarely ...
At no time ...	Hardly ...	Only after ...
No sooner ...	Under no circumstances ...	

1 She had just started working when a loud bang broke her concentration.
2 I have not often been in greater need of a confidence boost than I am today.
3 He had only met such a fascinating and intelligent person as Madeleine on rare occasions.
4 He forgets people's names and he also finds it difficult to remember the words for common objects.
5 You should not let anyone disturb you under any circumstances unless it is an emergency.
6 Barely a second after she started work, the phones started ringing.
7 She posted the letter and then realised she had forgotten to post the cheque.
8 She did not doubt at any time that he would make her happy.

Use of English: key word transformations (Part 5)

1 Complete the second sentence so that it has a similar meaning to the first sentence, using the word given. Do not change the word given. You must use between three and six words, including the word given.

Note: These sentences all focus on using inversion for emphasis. In the exam, the same structure will not appear in more than one sentence.

1 I've not seen such a fantastic performance before.
NEVER
.... such a fantastic performance before.
2 I had only just arrived when he insisted we went out again.
SOONER
.... he insisted on going out again.
3 She's never been in greater need of a friend than now.
HARDLY
.... in greater need of a friend.
4 They split up and then realised that they did love each other.
ONLY
.... did they realise that they loved each other.
5 You must never disturb someone when they are sleepwalking.
CIRCUMSTANCES
.... disturb someone when they are sleepwalking.
6 I had only just got on the train when it left!
BARELY
.... on the train, when it left.
7 She never doubted that she would be able to meet the challenge.
TIME
.... that she would be able to meet the challenge.
8 I have hardly ever come across such a strange man.
SELDOM
.... such a strange man.

Writing: article (Part 2)
▶ *CB pages 138–139*

Strategy
1 Make your article interesting for the reader by using a wide variety of vocabulary and using devices such as examples, anecdotes and rhetorical questions.
2 Remember to use a chatty style – speak to your reader!

1 You see this announcement in a health magazine.

Lifting Your Spirits?

Many of us think it's possible to make yourself happier when you're feeling sad or down. We want you, our readers, to send in articles on this topic. In your article describe what you do to make yourself feel better when you're sad, explain why this helps you and say why you think it is important to take responsibility for your own happiness.

We will publish the best articles.

2 Read this sample answer.

PICK YOURSELF UP!

Do you ever feel blue or down? Does the stress of life sometimes get to you? Or maybe something happens that puts you in a very bad mood. What can you do to lift yourself out of this?

I don't often feel sad, but when I do sometimes I just want to go to my room and sit and listen to music. This makes me feel better because music affects your senses and your mood and can really cheer you up. Also you can feel part of a larger community if you listen to the radio, for example. But the thing that really makes me feel much better is going to the gym and doing some exercise. This really pushes your body and gets rid of all the stress and also makes you focus on something that is happening now so you can forget about your problems. By the time I leave the gym I feel quite bright and ready to tackle anything.

Everybody feels sad sometimes and you cannot expect other people to listen to you moping and moaning as that will make them sad as well and they will get fed up with you. It's much better to think about what you can do to change your mood – either doing some sport or helping other people. Anything that stops you concentrating on yourself. It's very important that you do this for yourself and then you will always have a strategy for making yourself feel better as you can't always rely on other people to help you.

3 What is a rhetorical question?

a) a question that tricks someone into giving the answer you want
b) a question you ask as a way of making a statement without expecting an answer
c) a question to which there is a certain or definite answer

4 What is the effect of a rhetorical question? Why do we use them in articles?

a) to make readers aware of what the article is about
b) to convince readers that the writer has an answer to a particular problem
c) to persuade readers to continue reading the article

▸ Improve! ◂

The sample answer is repetitive in places. Highlight where you think it is repetitive. Look at the answer key to check how this could have been avoided. Remember in your article to try to make several different points to support your argument.

5 Write your own response to the task in Exercise 1. Remember to make a plan. Write your answer in 220–260 words.

Title:

Paragraph 1

Paragraph 2

Paragraph 3

Vocabulary 1: expressions with *time* and *future*

1 Do the quiz on expressions with *time*.

How important is time to you?

❶ What do you do when you want to kill time?
   a)   read
   b)   watch TV
   c)   phone your friends

❷ What do you consider to be a waste of time?
   a)   going to the cinema
   b)   learning how to cook
   c)   studying history

❸ What do you do when you are pressed for time?
   a)   decide which job to do first
   b)   get very stressed and panic
   c)   ask other people to help you

❹ What do you do if you are not on time for an appointment?
   a)   phone to say you will be late
   b)   do nothing – that's life
   c)   apologise when you arrive

Now check your answers at the bottom of the page. Underline the expressions with *time* in the quiz.

2 Match the expressions using *future* with the situation in which they are most likely to be used.

1 Only we can offer a dynamic **vision of the future**.
2 Nobody can know **what the future holds** now.
3 There is **a serious question mark over his future** here.
4 You need to **consider your future** carefully.

a) a comment after a tragedy
b) a conversation about a child's education
c) a speech to potential investors
d) a discussion at work

3 Put these words for future outlooks into the correct column.

bright	bleak	great	foreseeable
immediate	rosy	near	uncertain	secure
not-too-distant	gloomy	promising	grim

happening soon: the ... *future*	a positive outlook – a ... *future*	a negative outlook – a ... *future*

NB in English we do not say *the next future*

4 Complete these sentences with words and expressions to do with the future from Exercises 2 and 3.

1 The university set out an ambitious ...., with plans to achieve a 10 percent increase in student numbers over three years.
2 I do plan to work in another country – but not in the .... I'm still studying at the moment.
3 He had a job for life at the bank so could look forward to a steady but .... as he knew he wouldn't have to worry about losing his job.
4 I'm afraid that, as you have failed to achieve your sales targets, there is a .... in our company and you may want to start looking for another job.
5 Prices are likely to remain low for the .... I don't know when they'll pick up.
6 His failure to lead the team to victory in the cup means he now faces an .... and cannot rely on staying on as manager.

5   Put the verbs below into the correct gaps to complete the collocations for what you can do to the future. Underline the collocations when you have checked your answers to help you remember them.

> face   determine   shape   forecast   invest in

1   It's young people today who have the creativity and ideas that will .... the future in an entirely new way.
2   Despite the setbacks, he bravely decided to .... the future head on.
3   The way we behave now will .... the future and how successful we are.
4   Studying is a way to .... your future as you will reap the rewards later on.
5   None of us is able to .... the future with any accuracy.

Listening: multiple matching (Part 4)
▶ *CB page 148*

Strategy
1   Listen for the attitudes, opinions or feelings each speaker expresses.
2   Don't panic if you don't understand every word.
3   Use the speaker's intonation as well as what they say to help you.

1   In the listening extracts, you may not hear the same words as the ones on the page. Write down three words or expressions you would associate with the nouns in Task One below.

Example: museum – *precious things, old, valuable*
When you have completed the listening task and checked your answers, play the recording again and check how many words you heard from your list.

2   You will hear five short extracts in which different people talk about visiting somewhere which showed life in the past.

3   Listen again and check your answers.

4   Complete the sentences using the correct form of these phrasal verbs from the listening extracts.

> take round   wander off   head for
> pass through   to be holed up   wipe out

1   We drove via Rome but as we were just .... I didn't get a chance to see much.
2   Some ancient civilisations were .... by simple diseases such as measles.
3   I wish you wouldn't .... like that – I didn't know where you were.
4   We were .... the exhibition by the guide, who told us some really fascinating details.
5   During the First World War, soldiers .... in the trenches for months on end.
6   I'm going to .... the exhibition, so I'll see you later in the café.

TASK ONE	TASK TWO
For questions **1–5**, match the extracts with the place the speaker visited, listed **A–H**.	For questions **6–10**, match the extracts with the aspect of the visit that the speaker was interested in, listed **A–H**.

While you listen you must complete both tasks.

A a museum		**A** the difficulty of the way of life		
B an old house	Speaker 1 [**1**]	**B** the type of diseases that used to be fatal	Speaker 1 [**6**]
C an archaeological site	Speaker 2 [**2**]	**C** the daily life of workers	Speaker 2 [**7**]
D a special celebration	Speaker 3 [**3**]	**D** inventions that revolutionised life	Speaker 3 [**8**]
E a tour of a city	Speaker 4 [**4**]	**E** the way aristocrats treated servants	Speaker 4 [**9**]
F a ship	Speaker 5 [**5**]	**F** the wealth of the community	Speaker 5 [**10**]
G a battlefield		**G** people's attitudes to animals		
H a tomb		**H** physical differences in humans between then and now		

Reading: short texts (Part 1)

Strategy

1 In order to understand the purpose or argument in a text, try to summarise what each paragraph is about. This will help you to find the answers to questions about the writer's attitude or opinion.

1   Read the texts below and choose the summary which best describes the focus of each paragraph.

Text A paragraph 1

a) why claims dismissing astrology are unfair
b) why astrology cannot predict sporting events

Text A paragraph 2

a) how to prove the claims made in astrology
b) why scientists should consider astrology

Text B paragraph 1

a) reasons why the movie will be popular
b) reasons to go and see the movie

Text B paragraph 2

a) how the movie could have been better
b) how the movie differs from the book

Text C paragraph 1

a) the reasons why aliens are interested in us
b) the background to a belief in alien kidnappers

Text C paragraph 2

a) the evidence for and against the existence of aliens
b) problems with the theory of alien kidnappers

2   You are going to read three extracts which are all concerned in some way with looking into the future. For questions 1–6, choose the answer (A, B, C or D) which you think fits best according to the text.

A

Are scientists prejudiced against astrology?

Earlier this month our Science Editor, Dr David Whitehouse, took a **sideswipe** at astrology following reports that footballers were preparing for the World Cup by studying the stars – their signs, in this case, rather than the opposition's strikers. The article infuriated another scientist, Dr Paul Kail of Prague, who says that the claims which astrology makes are just as testable as the claims made by chemists or physicists. For example, astrology claims that people born with Mars in Aries are likely to be more aggressive than average. This is testable. Unfortunately, because of the prejudice of the scientific community, funds for studying astrology are limited. Consequently, much astrological theory is unproven. One could hardly expect otherwise from a tradition which is thousands of years old, but which has only in the last century been subject to scientific analysis.

Astrology will succeed or fail on the basis that the claims that it makes are tested and found to be valid. It cannot be judged on the basis that we don't yet have a **plausible** mechanism for it. Yet scientists **scoff** at astrology because they cannot understand how it could work. This is an irrational approach, not a scientific one. Moreover, it is **putting the cart before the horse**. If at least 20 percent of what astrology claims is proven, then we have something to investigate. Kail says that if astrology cannot be explained by existing laws, then maybe it can tell us something new about the universe. Indeed, any scientist worthy of the name should be open to new ways of looking at the universe, rather than defending existing dogmas.

From BBC News at bbc.co.uk/news

1   According to Dr Kail, how could the theories of astrology be proven?

   A if more time was given to testing the theories
   B if astrology attracted more research funding
   C if scientists included astrology in their own tests
   D if we looked more carefully into the history of the subject

2   Dr Kail criticises scientists for being

   A illogical.
   B derogatory.
   C narrow-minded.
   D stubborn.

B

The Hitchhiker's Guide to the Galaxy

Hey, movie fans – *The Hitchhiker's Guide to the Galaxy* has finally been turned into a movie! Following the radio play, TV series, commemorative towel and books, this is the latest instalment in the sci-fi-comedy franchise. The creatures and sets are inspired and the answer to the sci-fi fan's primal need to see lots and lots of **cool stuff**. For those unfamiliar with the story, everyman Arthur Dent wakes up one morning to discover that his house is set to be demolished to make room for a bypass. Little does he know the entire planet Earth is also set to be destroyed for an interplanetary bypass by the Vogons, a hideous and bureaucratic race of aliens.

Whisked off the planet by his best friend, alien-in-disguise Ford Prefect, Dent embarks on a goofy **jaunt** across the galaxy accompanied by his trusty *Hitchhiker's Guide*, which looks like a really fancy PDA (Personal Digital Assistant). Where the story **stumbles** is in the telling. As books, *The Hitchhiker's Guide* was foremost about brilliant ideas that raised questions about our place in the universe while getting a laugh. The movie has enough trouble figuring out how to get the characters from one fantastical location to the next that Adams's funniest concepts often feel **left in the dust**. One wonders what we could have expected had the creator of this science fiction universe lived to see it with his own eyes.

3 According to the writer, the film's appeal is in its
   A gadgetry.
   B plot.
   C acting.
   D special effects.

4 The writer thinks that the weakest aspect of the film is that
   A it fails to reproduce the locations accurately.
   B it asks too many profound questions.
   C it lacks the originality of the book.
   D it fails to retain the book's humour.

C

Kidnappers from outer space

Aliens are taking millions of people inside their spacecraft, where they are **prodded, probed, scanned** and **implanted** with monitoring devices. The ultimate aim is to create a race of hybrid humans/aliens. Why is so little known about this? Apparently, way back in the 1950s, US President Eisenhower secretly approved a treaty with the aliens. In return for allowing the aliens to build underground bases on US territory and abduct US citizens, the government would get details of advanced alien technology. That's the conspiracy theory. What about the facts?

The idea that millions of people have been abducted is mainly based on the findings of opinion polls. The most optimistic indicates that over 6 million US citizens could be abductees. A problem with the abductions is that they are often recalled through dreams, nightmares and hypnosis. Critics think this shows that people who say they've been nabbed by little green men from outer space are those who easily confuse fantasy with reality. Some people argue that the worldwide consistency of abduction stories, the evidence of implants and the testimony of independent observers proves that it does happen. In fact, the theory raises more questions than it asks. Why would aliens need to abduct millions of people? Why have implants inside abductees eluded X-ray examination? And when video cameras have been trained on people who say they are regularly abducted when asleep at night, the equipment has failed or no abductions occur. Strange …

5 Despite lack of evidence, people believe in alien abductions because
   A the abductions have a historical precedent.
   B they believe officials have agreed to hide the abductions.
   C they think the aliens have a physical presence on earth.
   D so many experiments are conducted on humans by aliens.

6 What is the writer's attitude to the theory of alien abductions?
   A sceptical
   B interested
   C bemused
   D critical

3 What type of text?

a) Match each of these language features to each text (A, B or C) above.

	Text
passive structures	....
rhetorical questions	....
idioms and colloquial expressions	....

b) Match each of these types of writing to each text above.

	Text
a review	....
an academic argument	....
a sensational story	....

c) Decide where each text would be most likely to appear and why. Use your answers to a) and b) to help you.

	Text
a 'True Stories' magazine	....
a national newspaper	....
a website	....

4 Match these meanings to the highlighted words in each text. Use a good dictionary, such as *The Longman Exams Dictionary*, to help you.

Text A

a) likely to be true or successful

b) to do two things in the wrong order

c) a criticism of someone, given when you are talking about something else

d) to laugh at a person or idea

Text B

a) abandoned

b) falls or is unsteady

c) things that people admire

d) a short trip for pleasure

Text C

a) examined something using a long, thin object

b) put something into someone's body by performing a medical operation

c) pushed someone or something with your finger or a pointed object

d) passed an electrical beam over something to form a picture of what is inside

Grammar 1: passives 1
▶ *CB pages 144–145*

1 Match the reasons the passive is used to the sentences below.

a) The agent is unknown or obvious.

b) The focus of the sentence is on the event and not the agent.

c) The agent is people or things in general.

1 Steps will be taken to record the history of the town.

2 The museum was visited by over 1000 tourists last year.

3 The museum was to have been opened by the mayor on Friday.

4 Younger people have been encouraged to visit the museum.

5 The law is to be changed, allowing galleries to open on Sundays.

6 People are taken round the museum by a trained guide.

2 Rewrite these sentences using the passive. Decide if the agent needs to be mentioned or not.

1 He wanted the museum to employ him.

2 I'd like someone to show me round the exhibits.

3 I'm not keen on tourists asking me questions!

4 I'm pleased the director asked me to help with the project.

5 We displayed the exhibits in new glass cases.

6 He'll put the pictures up later today.

7 They have reduced the entrance prices.

Use of English: open cloze (Part 2)
▶ *CB page 150*

1 Read the text below and write in the word which best fits each space. Use only one word in each space. There is an example at the beginning (0).

THE MEMORIES OF OUR SENSES

I went for a wander into town as, after a period of illness, I was going **(0)** ..*back*.. to work the next day and I thought it **(1)** .... good idea to get out and see **(2)** .... I felt. I was going to get stamps to send some things off that have to go **(3)** .... snail mail. Walking along in a world of my **(4)** .... , I was almost there **(5)** .... I was stopped in **(6)** .... tracks by the beautiful tones of 'Il Silenzio'. I thought I had gone back in time, **(7)** .... powerful were the memories **(8)** .... invoked. I looked around for the source of this wonderful sound and there, to my right, was a street musician, scruffily dressed, **(9)** .... belied the equipment he had at his feet and the trumpet that he was playing so beautifully. I listened to him play a **(10)** .... more pieces and then moved on. But I was amazed **(11)** .... the strong images that the piece of music had evoked. And it got **(12)** .... thinking how memories can be provoked by the simplest of things, a piece of music, a smell, pictures. We seem to associate music **(13)** .... memories especially, maybe because it was playing at a specific time **(14)** .... because we had it dedicated to us. **(15)** .... triggers these memories interests me. Which piece of music, smell or whatever makes you remember, and why?

Vocabulary 2: idiomatic language
▶ *CB page 144*

1   Put the words in the box into the most appropriate gaps in the article.

the benefit of hindsight   highly dubious
catch a glimpse   free will   gives weight to
in due course

Historians always claim that we can rewrite history with **(1)** .... so that it accords with our current views of the world. This means that some policies and actions taken by countries in the past that were once praised are now regarded as **(2)** .... Current claims that, in the past, we may have been **acting** solely **in our own best interests** rather than for others **(3)** .... the arguments presented in the newer version of these histories. I wonder what we would think if we could **(4)** .... of our own future? What we would **make of** our actions today? Something which we think of as good and beneficial may, **(5)** ...., be seen as harsh and unfair. One thing is sure – if we are acting from our own **(6)** .... we must be prepared **to take responsibility for** our actions and apologise if what we do has **a negative impact on** others.

2   Use the phrases in bold above to complete these sentences.

1   I never agreed with free university education. I think it's right that students should .... their own costs.

2   I think it's sad that we no longer have free dental care. This could have a very .... the next generation.

3   I wonder what today's kids would .... the idea that we used to give free milk for children in primary school?

4   People always say that compulsory conscription into the armed forces was stopped because it was unfair, but I think we were .... as we needed a professional army!

Speaking: (Part 3)
▶ *CB pages 148–149*

Strategy
1 Remember to talk about each of the pictures.
2 You must reach a conclusion, even if it is that you don't agree.

Look at this task.
Look at these pictures and say how you think each one may have affected the future, then decide which two had the most significant effect on the future.

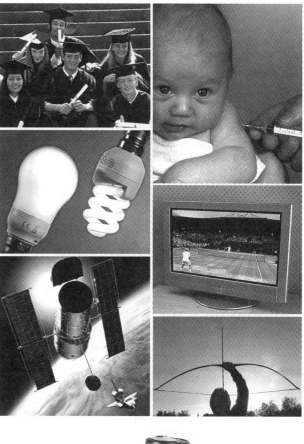

1   Write down one way in which each thing may have affected the future. Then make notes on which two you think were the most significant and why.

2   Now listen to the recording of two students doing the task. Did they agree with you?

Grammar 2: the future in the past
▶ *CB page 147*

1   We can use 'future in the past' structures to talk about intentions in the past. What is the difference between these sentences? Think carefully about what time the speaker is referring to.

Example: *She was going to change her job but she didn't apply in time.*

(Both clauses are in the past; *was going to* refers to an intention up until the application had to be in.)

a) Oh, hi. Sorry, I was going to call you, but I haven't had time.

b) I was going to go to university, but I didn't get the grades.

c) I was going to go and see my gran, but I'm not feeling very well.

Now mark where each sentence should go on the timeline below.

example sentence

past —x— past —— present —— future

2   Match these clauses to make sentences. Use the different linking words to help you. Think carefully about the situation.

1   He was just about to leave
2   I was going to invite her
3   The job would have been done by now
4   She would later become a good singer
5   We were to arrive on

a) and go to the foothills the following day.
b) if there hadn't been unforeseen delays.
c) but there weren't enough places.
d) when the telephone rang.
e) but we were unaware of her talents at the time.

3   Read the text and choose the best alternative. Read the whole text through before you make choices. Be careful – they are not all the future in the past!

WHAT I WISHED FOR …

I never imagined that achieving my dream *would be / was about to be* so difficult. I had it all mapped out and my horoscope predicted my success. I thought I *were to / was going to* be a pop star by the time I was twenty-five. I actually envisaged how I *would get / would have got* there – I imagined writing songs in my room, finding a band and finally recording a disk to send to a music entrepreneur who *was to make / would make* my dreams come true. According to my master plan, I *was to have / will have* a top ten hit at the age of twenty-one and then make it big in the USA. My dream, however, was cut short when I was only sixteen. As I listened to my idols and started trying to imitate them, I *was to be pleased / was pleased* with my progress and offered to play at a school gig. I was excited. But I *had forgotten / would have forgotten* one crucial thing about performing – I had never sung in front of an audience before. Just as I *was about to / would* open my mouth, I went into a kind of shock and nothing came out – I had no voice. I *would have given / was to give* anything at that moment for the floor to swallow me up. Now my friends *joke / will joke* about my thwarted dream.

4   These are comments that were made about the future. They were made by the people in the list below. Match the comments to the people.

Getting it wrong!

A 'I think there is a world market for maybe five computers.' (1943)

B 'This "telephone" has too many shortcomings to be seriously considered as a means of communication. The device is inherently of no value to us.' (1876)

C 'Who the hell wants to hear actors talk?' (1927)

D 'We don't like their (The Beatles') sound, and guitar music is on the way out.' (1962)

E 'Heavier-than-air flying machines are impossible.' (1895)

F 'Drill for oil? You mean drill into the ground to try and find oil? You're crazy.' (1859)

G 'Everything that can be invented has been invented.' (1899)

H 'Louis Pasteur's theory of germs is ridiculous fiction.' (1872)

Decca Recording Company (Music)

Charles Duell at the US Office of Patents (which registers inventions)

The President of the Royal Society (an organisation of scientists)

Thomas Watson, chairman of IBM

HM Warner, Warner Brothers

Workers who were being enlisted to work for an oil company.

Pierre Pachet, Professor of Physiology at Toulouse

Western Union internal memo (USA communications company)

Writing: essay (Part 2)
▶ *CB pages 151–152*

About the exam: In Part 2 of the Writing paper you may have the choice of writing an essay. You will be expected to organise your writing and give your opinion on the topic.

Strategy
1 Think about whether you need to present one or both sides of the argument.
2 Make sure you plan your essay carefully. Organise your ideas into paragraphs.
3 Remember to give reasons or examples to support your views.
4 Spend 10 minutes planning, 30 minutes writing and 5 minutes checking.

1 Read this exam task.

In class you have been discussing how things may change in the future. Your teacher has asked you to write an essay on the following topic:

In the future everyone will be able to shop from home and this will break down communities and make us more and more isolated.

Write your essay in 220–260 words.

2 Write a plan.

Think about your plan in stages:

A How many paragraphs do you need for the essay above and what is the focus of each paragraph above?
B How many words do you need in each paragraph approximately? You have to write the essay in 220–260 words.
C How many reasons can you give in each of your central paragraphs? Remember to think about how many words you have and that you have to include a reason or example to support your view.

3 Make notes for your plan. Write your point, then make notes on your reason. An example has been done for you.

reasons for	reasons against
1 No face-to-face contact – e.g. no conversation as all online; staying at home	

Now check your plan with the example plan in the Key.

4 Use linking expressions to help guide the reader through your essay. Underline the most suitable linking expressions in the extract from a sample answer below.

(1) *On the one hand / At first*, online shopping will save time and money as we won't have to travel to and from the shops. **(2)** *According to me / It seems to me* that this will be better both for the planet and for our stress levels.

(3) *Furthermore / On the other hand*, traditional shops may go out of business and communities may die. The streets may be deserted and become dangerous.

(4) *For this reason / And so*, we should approach the growth of computer shopping cautiously. **(5)** *Personally / It seems to me* that, although people like going on the Internet, they also still enjoy contact with the rest of their community.

(6) *For this reason / It is the case that*, I think traditional shops will survive. **(7)** *Also / But* many people like to see and touch what they are buying, especially with food.

— **Improve!** ◄

Think about the variety of linking words used in the extract above. In which places could you use the following links words in order to show more complex language or a greater range?

From my point of view …   *I believe that …*
In addition …   *This means that …*

13 A way with words

Listening: sentence completion (Part 2)

Strategy
1 Make sure you listen carefully for the endings of words.
2 Don't change the word you hear when you write your answer.
3 The answer will be only one or two words. Don't write more.

1 Do these tasks to help you write the correct answer in the test.

A Listen to the words and spell them correctly. Think carefully about words with double consonants or vowels.

B Listen to the words and write them down, making sure you write the correct form.

C Write one or two words in the gaps. Make sure what you write fits the sentence.
He was very ....
He's got the latest .... of the phone.
We wanted to talk ....
Check your answers in the key.

2 You will hear a woman talking about young people and mobile phone communication. For questions 1–8, complete the sentences.

For young people, the number of calls you make on your mobile reflects your **(1)** ....

The advantage of sending texts is that it allows you to communicate **(2)** ....

The mobile phone can make young people feel **(3)** ....

Having a mobile with you can prevent you from **(4)** .... on the present moment.

People who had their phones taken away did **(5)** .... more than previously.

Conversation can be much more difficult if there is no **(6)** ....

Technology is creating new ways of **(7)** .... among young people.

Over half of young people still **(8)** .... face-to-face.

3 Now listen again and check your answers.

4 Choose the correct meaning for the following words and expressions for the listening text. Use a good dictionary, such as *The Longman Exams Dictionary*, to help you.

1 etiquette
　　a) a way of behaving
　　b) the formal rules for polite behaviour

2 come to light
　　a) appear suddenly
　　b) a fact that becomes known

3 confer
　　a) to give someone a particular honour or right
　　b) to discuss with other people

4 tricky
　　a) looking like a trick or magic
　　b) difficult; awkward

5 go out the window
　　a) get forgotten about
　　b) leave in a particular way

Vocabulary 1: adverbials expressing attitude and communication idioms
▶ *CB page 156*

1 Find seven adverbials expressing attitude in this grid. One of them is written diagonally!

B	A	S	F	R	A	C	L	Y	C	L	E	L	L	Y
A	C	T	U	A	L	L	Y	I	V	T	R	I	O	B
S	L	E	N	P	V	N	O	L	E	Y	S	T	B	A
I	E	R	M	P	F	R	A	N	K	L	Y	E	A	R
C	A	Y	T	A	L	L	F	R	O	C	L	Y	S	Y
A	R	P	E	R	S	O	N	A	L	L	Y	F	C	E
L	L	R	S	E	I	O	B	Q	U	E	P	S	I	L
L	Y	E	D	N	A	C	I	V	A	L	Y	O	L	A
Y	I	S	O	T	M	P	R	T	I	C	K	L	Y	T
O	P	L	A	L	Y	S	U	R	P	O	B	A	R	C
A	N	Y	D	Y	K	A	T	I	E	U	U	K	M	U
S	F	U	L	T	G	S	E	S	T	L	Y	S	O	L
C	L	E	L	Y	C	L	R	L	S	A	X	S	L	L
E	L	D	Y	S	E	Y	T	Y	V	E	W	E	K	Y

2 Put these adverbials into the correct columns according to what they express.

disappointingly	significantly	strangely	luckily
typically	interestingly	thankfully	
unsurprisingly	predictably	amazingly	
inevitably	remarkably	regrettably	

expected	surprising
important	**fortunate / unfortunate**

3 Choose the most appropriate adverbial to go in each sentence and in each case decide where (1 or 2) to put it.

| unsurprisingly | thankfully | interestingly |
| regrettably | typically | strangely |

1 I had arranged to see him but **1** when I got there **2** he wasn't in.
2 **1** They invited us months ago and I had to tell them that **2** we had a prior engagement.
3 **1** When I asked him to discuss the matter with me, he was **2** always rude to me.
4 She was getting so **1** fed up that **2** she asked to leave and I was quite glad she did.
5 We ran out of money but **1** we ran into my uncle who **2** lent us £100.
6 People do **1** use mobiles more nowadays and **2** not always in the ways you would expect.

4 Replace the underlined words in the sentences with the correct form of these communication idioms.

to make head nor tail	to talk at cross purposes
to get a word in edgeways	to get a real talking to
to get hold of the wrong end of the stick	
to speak one's mind	

1 I soon realised that <u>we weren't speaking about the same problem</u>.
2 <u>I was really told off</u> about being late with my homework.
3 She got cross with me because <u>she'd misunderstood what I was talking about</u>.
4 I'm sorry but <u>I couldn't understand</u> his essay.
5 I tried to speak but <u>I couldn't stop her for long enough to say what I wanted to say</u>!
6 I like her because <u>she always says what she thinks</u>.

Reading: multiple matching (Part 4)
▶ CB pages 154–155

About the exam: In the exam you have 1 hour and 15 minutes to do the four Parts and complete your answer sheet. This allows you about 20 minutes per task.

Strategy
In Part 4 you have to find a lot of information quite quickly, so practise skimming and scanning the texts rather than reading every word.

1 Allow yourself 25 minutes for the task below.

- Skim through the questions underlining key words – 2 mins.
- Read through each text one at a time and mark the questions you think are answered in the text – (3 mins per text) 15 mins.
- Go back and scan through all the texts for the answers to any questions you are not sure about – 5 mins.
- Check you have completed the answer sheet correctly – 1 min.

Now do the task below and time yourself.

2 You are going to read five reviews of books on language written by the same author. For questions 1–15, choose the review (A–E). The reviews may be chosen more than once.

Which book:

encourages people to discuss communication differences	1
claims people use different methods to achieve the same goals	2
says one party has high expectations of the other	3
offers skills that may transfer to another area of your life	4
claims we misread the motivation for certain types of talk	5 6
suggests we use language for different purposes	7
claims one way of communicating is no better than another	8
says one person feels in a weaker position	9 10
suggests alternative methods should be used for communication	11
uses personal insights from the author's own life	12
offers a plan for improvement	13
regrets what gets missed because of bad communication	14
suggests our communication methods can have an impact on our success	15

A **You just don't understand**

Why is it that some women and men seem to talk at cross purposes? Why do so many women feel that men don't tell them anything but just lecture and criticise? Why do so many men feel that women nag them and never get to the point? In this pioneering book Deborah Tannen shows us how women and men talk in different ways, for profoundly different reasons. Some have claimed that conversations are the forum of male power games, but the author suggests that jockeying for attention is not the whole story and that even when domination is the result, it is not always the intention. She shows how many frictions may arise because girls and boys grow up in essentially different cultures. Where women use language to seek confirmation, make connections and reinforce intimacies, men use it to protect their independence and negotiate status. The result is that conversation becomes a cross-cultural communication, fraught with genuine confusion.

Reproduced by kind permission of Virago, an imprint of Little, Brown Book Group UK

B **You're wearing that!**

Mothers and daughters often misunderstand each other as they struggle to find the right balance between closeness and independence. They both want to be seen for who they really are, but tend to see the other as falling short of who she should be. Each overestimates the other's power and underestimates her own and Deborah Tannen examines every aspect of this complex dynamic. With groundbreaking insights, pitch-perfect dialogues, and deeply moving memories of her own mother, Tannen untangles the knots daughters and mothers can get tied up in. I have had a very difficult relationship with my mother. I perceived her as very controlling – now I am beginning to see that it was maybe her way of showing that she cared. Most of all though, I have had severe communication problems with my younger daughter and this book was like someone switching a light on in my head. Everything she said rang true!! It is already beginning to transform my communication skills in relation to both the 'difficult' women in my life.

C I only say this because I love you

In this outstanding book, conversational analyst Deborah Tannen captures the verbal essences of how to improve our family relationships. The book deals with situations which range from being praised for some menial accomplishment to 'I care, therefore I criticise' (usually from Mum) to sarcasm (usually from a spouse or teenager, suggesting you must be an idiot). The book addresses how to improve both your speech and your listening. On the listening side, you are encouraged to focus on the underlying message and to find the most positive one. Where you could hear criticism, focus on the fact that the other person is expressing caring. But you should confront direct criticism because there is usually another motive at work. Get it out in the open. The ventilation will improve the relationship. On the speaking side, you are encouraged to avoid sarcasm or getting the other person to think exactly like you do (especially if they are a different sex and much older or younger). After you have finished enjoying this set of methods for avoiding and mitigating those painful moments, I suggest that you think about where you could do the same things at work and with friends.

D The argument culture

Deborah Tannen is an expert on miscommunication. In The Argument Culture she posits that misunderstanding is endemic in our culture because we tend to believe that the best way to a common goal is by thrashing out all our differences as loudly as possible along the way. Thus we are treated to a whole array of confrontational public forums, from partisan politics to media circuses, all based on a metaphor of war. What gets lost in all the shouting, Tannen says, is thoughtful debate and real understanding. Perhaps it's time to consider other methods of communication, she suggests. In addition to outlining what she considers the worst excesses of our argument culture, she discusses the different ways in which young boys and girls express disagreement or aggression. Finally, she offers a survey of other, mostly non-Western ways of dealing with conflict, including the use of intermediaries and rituals. After reading The Argument Culture you may never again be able to view the evening news in the same way.

E Talking from 9 to 5

Deborah Tannen looks at the role played by talk 'from 9 to 5', focusing in particular on the differing conversational rituals that typify men and women. Those common among men involve opposition such as banter, joking and playful put-downs; common among women are ways of maintaining the appearance of equality, avoiding boasting and downplaying authority. Arguing that no one style is superior, Tannen shows that when conventions are taken literally, there are negative results for both sides. She illuminates the different ways men and women make decisions, ask for information and delegate. Then she shows how these styles affect how we are judged in the workplace. Talking from 9 to 5 is a brilliantly incisive book that offers powerful new ways of understanding what's really going on at work. I have read widely on the differences between men and women, but this gets right to the heart of the differences and provides clear, simple strategies for women to stop being put down by men and to develop their careers without having to become pseudo men.

3 Which book would be most likely to interest:

1 teenage girls?
2 women in love?
3 men with children?
4 a businessman about to travel to another country?
5 a woman who is responsible for a team of people?

4 Match the highlighted words and expressions from the texts with these meanings.

a) the unexpressed meaning in what you are saying
b) a problem that is always present among a group of people
c) disagreements or a lack of friendship
d) a large or impressive range of a particular thing
e) talking too proudly about your abilities and achievements
f) to be less than what you expected or hoped for
g) to keep complaining about someone's behaviour
h) the open expression of opinions or feelings about something
i) friendly conversation in which people make a lot of jokes
j) the way in which people behave, react and affect each other

Grammar 1: participle clauses
▶ *CB pages 156–158*

Participle clauses allow you to express yourself using very few words. Past participle clauses have a passive meaning. They are used in written more than spoken English.

1 Match the reasons why we use participle clauses with the example sentences.

a) to replace a relative pronoun or a verb
b) to replace words which give reasons, show results or indicate time

1 Having missed so many lectures, she struggled with the exams.
2 People applying early stand a better chance of getting a place.
3 Universities situated next to city centres attract more students.
4 Having been rejected several times, she decided to change her plans.

2 Rewrite these sentences using a participle clause.

1 People who choose to study medicine are very committed.
2 I applied early so I was disappointed not to be accepted.
3 I read the book quickly because it was so good.
4 Courses which are run this term will start on Tuesday.
5 The lecturer started to speak when he had got the students to be silent.
6 Anyone who wishes to join the book club should come along on Wednesday.

3 The following sentences all contain mistakes. Rewrite them, as participle clauses, correcting the mistakes.

1 Having crashed, they couldn't get home by car.
2 People learning languages who are offered more jobs.
3 Losing his job, so he went travelling abroad.
4 Closing early, she had to leave the library.
5 Having completed her course, once she decided to get a job.

Vocabulary 2: similes

1 Put these adjectives into the correct gaps to make similes.

strong	light	white	quick	cool	busy
cold	free				

a) as ...... as a cucumber
b) as ...... as a bee
c) as ...... as a feather
d) as ...... as an ox

e) as ...... as a flash
f) as ...... as ice
g) as ...... as a bird
h) as ...... as a sheet

2 Put these similes into the correct gaps.

like a bullet	like a red rag to a bull
like a fish out of water	like a log
like a tin of sardines	like cotton candy

1 We were all squashed together ....
2 He felt very uncomfortable, ...
3 He shot out of the house .... as if he was being chased.
4 He slept ....; nothing could wake him.
5 If you mention it to him he always argues; it's ....
6 It was a perfect day and the clouds were ....

3   For questions 1–12, read the article below and decide which answer (A, B, C or D) best fits each gap. There is an example at the beginning (0).

HITTING THE RIGHT BUTTON

With boys' exam results lagging behind those of girls in the UK, is greater **(0)** .....B...... on using ICT the way to raise their game?

Boys have a natural **(1)** .... with computers. It can often be hard to **(2)** .... them away from the little screen. And with ICT increasingly seen as a **(3)** .... of modern education, it's natural to assume that computers can play an important role in helping underachieving boys raise their standards.

There is growing research that **(4)** .... that ICT is motivating, and for boys in particular. Boys are more confident in ICT and use it more frequently, particularly at home, so it seems to be an obvious **(5)** .... to say 'Let's use ICT as a way of re-engaging boys in learning'. But is there any **(6)** .... that it works?'

Lots of boys don't like writing and find handwriting a **(7)** .... But they're more willing to try out different styles and **(8)** .... longer pieces, using computers. But computers are no panacea. People think boys and computers go together, but boys still need **(9)** .... on how to do it. Ask a boy to find out something on the Internet, for instance, and he will cut and paste something, stick it into Word, **(10)** .... it in and call it research. He probably hasn't even read it. If you simply give boys a whole load of **(11)** .... tasks, using a computer is not going to improve their attainment any more than anything else.

There is no substitute for good teaching. What **(12)** .... is the interaction between the teacher and the pupil with the materials.

0	**A** accent	**B** <u>emphasis</u>	**C** attention	**D** priority
1	**A** alliance	**B** relation	**C** affinity	**D** sympathy
2	**A** tear	**B** rip	**C** claw	**D** seize
3	**A** pier	**B** pillar	**C** column	**D** post
4	**A** approves	**B** exhibits	**C** certifies	**D** establishes
5	**A** hop	**B** spring	**C** leap	**D** skip
6	**A** declaration	**B** testimony	**C** evidence	**D** manifestation
7	**A** chore	**B** duty	**C** job	**D** task
8	**A** build	**B** compose	**C** frame	**D** contrive
9	**A** conduct	**B** government	**C** guidance	**D** control
10	**A** deliver	**B** hand	**C** pass	**D** present
11	**A** meaningless	**B** worthless	**C** senseless	**D** aimless
12	**A** signifies	**B** values	**C** registers	**D** counts

Speaking: (Part 4)

About the exam: In Parts 3 and 4 of the Speaking exam you have a discussion first with your partner and then with your partner and the examiner. You may want to disagree with something somebody says.

Listen to the recording of a Part 4 discussion and tick the expressions you hear.

I agree up to a point, but …   *You could be right, but …*

I completely disagree.   *I'm afraid I don't agree.*

I'm not sure if I agree.   *That's an interesting idea, but …*

Actually, as a matter of fact, I think …

Which of the above is the strongest expression of disagreement and which are the weakest?

Grammar 2: passives 2 (usage)
▶ *CB page 161*

1   Match the uses of the passive (a–d) to the sentences (i–vii) in the text below. In some sentences there are two possible reasons for using the passive. The first one has been done for you as an example.

Uses of the passive

a) We use the passive when the active form would require the use of an indefinite or vague pronoun, e.g. *someone, they, people*.

b) We often use the passive with verbs such as *think, believe, say, know* to give a general opinion.

c) Using the passive means we can make a statement sound more impersonal and less connected to the speaker or writer.

d) Using the passive means we can avoid an awkward change of subject in the middle of a sentence.

SKELETON CONFIRMS EXISTENCE OF PORTERING TRIBE

The skeleton of an ancient man was found in the foothills of the Himalayas in 1986. [i *a/d*] It was thought that he belonged to an ancient tribe that were mountain porters. [ii ......] The theory was confirmed when climbing tools were found nearby. [iii ......] It now seems extraordinary that the idea that people lived so high up was treated with contempt in the last century. [iv ......] Today, much more work <u>has been done</u> around the theory which states that the Himalayas were heavily populated by these 'portering' tribes at one time. [v ......] In addition, sightings of the so-called yeti have been reported every decade or so for 150 years. [vi ......] However, the existence of this more elusive 'tribe' is still generally ascribed to legend. [vii ......]

What kind of text do you think this is?

a) a formal text in an academic paper or journal

b) a general article in a magazine

2   Rewrite the following sentences so that the underlined part is in the passive.

1 People frequently <u>ask me</u> if parapsychology is recognised by universities.

2 <u>He had warned me</u> that revisiting the past may bring back some painful memories.

3 <u>You must list</u> references at the end of an essay.

4 <u>Someone questioned</u> his sources.

5 Everyone <u>often says</u> that things were better in the 'good old days'.

6 Scientists <u>have thought</u> for some time that life on other planets may be possible.

Use of English: key word transformations (Part 5)

1   Complete the second sentence so that it has a similar meaning to the first sentence, using the word given. Do not change the word given. You must use between three and six words, including the word given.

NB: All of the following questions focus on the passive. In the exam this task will contain a variety of structures.

1 They have decided they will publish the book this summer.
   PUBLISHED
   It has been decided .... this summer.

2 They said the principal was resigning in the summer.
   BE
   The principal .... in the summer.

3 The lectures gave the students an insight into modern history.
   GIVEN
   The .... modern history by the lectures.

4 The school issued a leaflet telling students how to apply.
   BY
   .... the school telling students how to apply.

5 The school is setting the exams in June.
   BEING
   The exams .... in June.

6 People think that bilingual children were disadvantaged in the past.
   THOUGHT
   Bilingual children .... in the past.

7 Nobody notices children who fail at school.
   ATTENTION
   No .... children who fail at school.

8 Everybody should learn how to speak a second language.
   TAUGHT
   A second language .... everybody.

Writing: proposal (Part 2)
▶ *CB pages 163–164*

About the exam: In Paper 2, Part 2, you may have the choice of writing a proposal. You will be assessed on organisation and appropriacy as well as accuracy.

Strategy
1 Plan carefully to make sure you answer all the points in the question.
2 Make sure your proposal is persuasive. Use persuasive language and give reasons for your suggestions. Look at the writing sections in Units 4 and 9 if you need help with this.

1 Read this task.

You see this announcement on a mobile phone company's website.

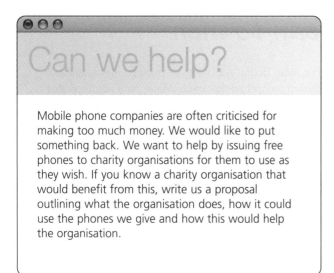

Can we help?

Mobile phone companies are often criticised for making too much money. We would like to put something back. We want to help by issuing free phones to charity organisations for them to use as they wish. If you know a charity organisation that would benefit from this, write us a proposal outlining what the organisation does, how it could use the phones we give and how this would help the organisation.

2 Read this sample answer and complete the gaps with appropriate headings. Use the points in the question to help you decide.

1 ....
The aim of this proposal is to suggest a charity organisation which would benefit from having free mobile phones.

2 ....
A very worthy charity organisation is KidsHelp. This is an organisation in my local school which looks after and helps kids who do not have the opportunity to do many things. It may be that their parents do not have much money or maybe they have a lot of other children in their family. KidsHelp provides them with time in the gymnasium where they can practise sports or get together to do other activities and it also takes the children out for the day during the holidays to local museums or beaches.

3 ....
If we had some mobile phones this would help us enormously as we have no official office we can use on the school premises. We could use the phones to check up on children in their own homes and to find out where they are if they miss a session. Additionally, the phones would be very important when we are travelling for the day, both to stay in touch with the whole group and to allow children to speak to their parents while they are away, for example if we are delayed getting back.

4 ....
I would strongly recommend that our organisation be given the free phones as it would improve our safety and security and make the parents feel more confident about letting the children come to us for activities and so on. Also it would allow us to make a range of calls seeking sponsorship for our charity, without having to use our private numbers for this.

1 a) Introduction
   b) A proposal
2 a) Who are the kids?
   b) The charity organisation
3 a) Why the phones are important
   b) How the organisation would use the phones
4 a) How the organisation would benefit
   b) Why we need the phones

3 A proposal is usually written in quite formal or very formal language. Match the informal language below to more formal language in the sample answer.

a) gives
b) because
c) I think you should give …
d) I'm going to suggest …
e) so we can stay
f) possibly
g) so we don't have to

┌ Improve! ◀───
│ When you write a report or proposal, make sure
│ that you use a range of formal and objective
│ language.
└──

4 Write your own answer to the task in Exercise 1. Remember to use both content and language to persuade the reader. Write your answer in 220–260 words.

Reading: gapped text (Part 2)

Strategy
1 Skim through the gapped text to understand the story or argument.
2 Look carefully for linking words, referring pronouns, determiners and abstract nouns in the gapped text and the missing paragraphs.
3 Make sure you check your chosen paragraph fits with what comes before *and* after the gap.

1 Skim through the text quickly and answer these questions.

1 What type of books do men like reading?
2 How did the writers find out about men's reading habits?

2 You are going to read an article about what men read. Six paragraphs have been removed from the article. Choose from the paragraphs A–G the one which fits each gap (1–6). There is one extra paragraph which you do not need to use.

What books mean to men

When we asked women which book had helped them most during their lives, the clear winner was *Jane Eyre*, with *Pride and Prejudice* not too far behind. When we repeated the exercise with men, a very different reading list emerged.

1

This year, we tackled the obvious next question: what do men read to get them through life? Women had described a number of key moments in their life at which they unselfconsciously acknowledged that fiction had offered them guidance or solace. But many men we approached did not seem to associate reading fiction with life choices. One told us: 'I guess that if you admit to having a watershed novel, then you're admitting to having a watershed moment, which is something that a lot of men don't necessarily want to divulge.'

2

Still, in spite of a certain anxiety about revealing that fiction had any impact on their day-to-day lives, the great majority of our respondents were intrigued by our inquiry and happily offered us time, leading to some fascinating results. Men's formative reading does indeed differ markedly from women's.

3

Part of the reason this type of theme resonated with them was that, to a far larger degree than women, men's formative reading was done between the ages of 12 and 20 – indeed, specifically around the ages of 15 and 16.

For men, fiction was a rite of passage into manhood during painful adolescence. Many men admitted that they had read little fiction since, though mature men returned to fiction reading in later life and expressed increasing enjoyment in reading for 'self-reflection'.

4

We found a strong sense of nostalgia among male readers as they looked back to their formative years; many had tended to lose interest in fiction in favour of non-fiction on entering into adulthood. One consequence of this was that several men admitted that they were reluctant to re-read a book which had been almost painfully important to them at puberty. 'I'm afraid I might find it too mawkish now', 'It might not live up to my memories', 'It might seem dated now' became familiar responses.

5

A further difference was that men were much more specific and literal about the kind of plot and character they were interested in reading about. This may have produced an accidental concentration on male authors, for 'adventure' and 'triumphing over adversity' fiction.

6

This did not seem ever to be the case for men, though some men admitted to having made a sound investment in an author – such as Orwell – whom they used as a guide throughout their adult life on the basis of a first encounter in adolescence.

A

Men's reading clearly shows a majority of books with strong active narrative themes – books that might traditionally be described as quintessential boys' books. No surprise there, perhaps. Except these choices were made on the basis of a conscious commitment to novels that take the reader in a direction of personal development. Men's reading choices focus on novels that include intellectual struggle. Personal vulnerability is represented as an angst-ridden struggle against convention, a sense of isolation from social normality.

B

Many adult men we talked to openly showed an almost complete lack of interest in reading which drew them into personal introspection, or asked them to engage with the family and the domestic sphere. On the other hand, those who had remained avid readers could see distinct patterns emerging in their choices which differed from those selected by women.

C

A little over a year ago, we conducted a survey of women readers to find a 'watershed' women's novel – the book which, above all others, had sustained individual women through key moments of transition or crisis in their lives. The top titles that emerged were surprisingly varied. They ranged from *The Lord of the Rings* to *Gone with the Wind*.

D

However, looking back, men also recalled a kind of 'mentoring' by authors encountered as a teenager – the same word was used by a surprising number of those we interviewed. Having found an author who 'spoke' to them, a man would have trusted them as a literary guide, reading all of their works, and also works quoted from or cited by them. Orwell, in particular, was cited frequently as having guided our male reader in his choices of author. This idea of mentoring had never cropped up in our survey of women's reading.

E

So how do we interpret the men's list, and our outright winner – Camus's *The Outsider*? Men use fiction almost physically as a guide to negotiate a difficult journey. They use fiction almost topographically, as a map. Many of our women respondents explained that they used novels metaphorically – the build-up to an emotional crisis and subsequent resolution might have helped negotiate an emotional progress through a difficult divorce, or provided support during a difficult period at work, or provided solace when things seemed generally dull.

F

In an effort to explain this rediscovery of reading, Professor Rob Dickins, a record-industry impresario with boundless energy for reading, whom we had interviewed early on in our survey, pointed out this reading in later life was bound to be influenced by that emotionally shaping early reading. He felt that women and men would surely arrive in maturity at different patterns of reading based on adolescent choices.

G

Amongst those who were prepared to acknowledge this 'weakness', men's reading did not show the same range as the women's had done. The choices clustered around a set of out-and-out favourites, such as Camus's *The Outsider* and Salinger's *The Catcher in the Rye*. These titles remained consistently popular, which was something that failed to happen with the women's titles, which changed daily, throwing up little-known books alongside familiar classics.

3 Practise transferring your answers to the answer sheet (see Key).

Vocabulary 1: books and stories
▶ *CB page 169*

1 Complete the crossword.

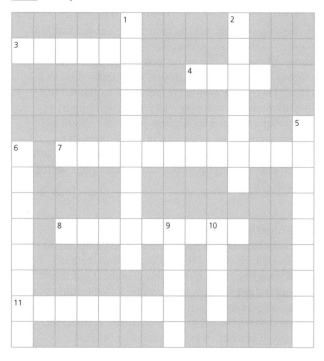

Across

3 one book in a series of books, e.g. an encyclopedia

4 to read quickly to find the main facts or ideas

7 to read or deal with a lot of boring written work

8 the soft-cover version of a book

11 an exciting story about a murder or crime

Down

1 a popular book which many people buy

2 copies of a book that are produced and printed at the same time

5 a detective story where you don't find out who committed the crime until the end

6 to read short parts of a book but not the whole thing

9 the summary on the back cover

10 one of many books that are all exactly the same

2 Match the words and expressions that we can use when we talk about books below to their meanings. Use a good dictionary, such as *The Longman Exams Dictionary*, to help you.

1	opens with	i)	an idea or phrase that's been used so much that it is not effective
2	derivative	ii)	making you believe it is true or right
3	brims with	iii)	the scene described at the beginning of a book
4	cliches	iv)	describes something in a particular way
5	flashbacks	v)	to have a lot of a particular thing, quality or emotion
6	densely (written)	vi)	scenes that show something that happened before that point in the book
7	convincing	vii)	copied or taken from another source (derogatory)
8	paints a picture	viii)	containing a lot of information; difficult to understand

3 Use the words and expressions in Exercise 2 to complete the review below.

SIGN OF THE TIMES

This historical novel **(1)** .... of how life was lived during the war. The novel **(2)** .... the central character, Elise, arriving at a party at the end of the war and the rest of the story is told in a series of **(3)** .... The plot is, at times, complicated and some parts are **(4)** .... but the writing is fresh and devoid of the usual **(5)** .... used to describe the war. It **(6)** .... energy and vitality as it tells the tale of a young girl coming of age at a time of turmoil. The emotions and concerns that Elise feels are entirely **(7)** .... and we can almost imagine ourselves there with her. How welcome this novel is after so many unoriginal and **(8)** .... novels on the subject.

Speaking

Put the following advice into the correct column:

use a range of vocabulary and structures

repeat your points

listen to your partner

ask the examiner to repeat anything you don't understand

speak as quickly as possible

go back and correct yourself if you make a mistake

disagree with something said if you have a different view

DO	DON'T

Listening: short texts (Part 1)

Strategy

1 You will be given a short time to read through the questions before you listen.

2 Use the information in the questions to predict the vocabulary and structures you expect to hear.

1 You will hear three different extracts. For questions 1–6, choose the answer (A, B or C) which fits best according to what you hear.

Extract One

You hear two people on a radio programme talking about the book *The Pelican Brief*.

1 What did the man particularly enjoy about *The Pelican Brief*?

  A its pace

  B its ending

  C its subject matter

2 According to the woman, how does *The Pelican Brief* compare with other novels by the same author?

  A The plot is more convincing.

  B The characters are more likeable.

  C The themes are more interesting.

Extract Two

You hear part of a conversation in a bookshop between a mother and her son.

3 Why does the woman think that boys read so little?

  A They lack the necessary concentration.

  B They play too much sport and too many computer games.

  C They think their friends are more important than reading.

4 How does the boy feel about reading books?

  A irritated that he cannot finish a book quickly

  B worried that he will not understand some words

  C frustrated that he cannot see the point of reading books

Extract Three

You hear part of an interview with a newspaper editor, Sally Hughes.

5 According to Sally, books will be less available in the future because

  A books will only be published on the internet.

  B publishers will invest less in paper books.

  C bookshops will decrease in number.

6 When talking about writing in the future, what do the two speakers agree about?

  A Authors will need to change their style.

  B The type of novels available will alter.

  C The quality of writing will remain unchanged.

2 Practise transferring your answers to the answer sheet (see Key).

Part 1			
1	A	B	C
2	A	B	C
3	A	B	C
4	A	B	C
5	A	B	C
6	A	B	C

3 Check you know the meanings of these words and expressions from the listening extracts. Complete each of the sentences below with the correct form of one of the words or expressions.

prolific	hang out	put somebody off	mores
throw up			

1 The book .... some interesting questions.

2 I thought the film was so bad that it .... reading the book.

3 She's very .... and has written 60 books altogether.

4 The social .... of the time meant she had to write under a man's name.

5 The café was a place where authors met and .... together.

Grammar 1: expressions with *get* and *have*

1   Match the sentences below to the use of the structure.

a) Get the kitchen cleared up before I come home!

b) I must get the television fixed before the cup final!

c) I got my science project done this weekend.

d) Can you get your boss to speak to your colleague about the problem?

e) She had her MP3 player stolen this afternoon.

1   finish something

2   used in orders or with imperatives

3   something unfortunate that happens to someone

4   ask someone else to perform an action on our behalf

5   something we don't do ourselves, but someone does for us

2   Complete these sentences using *get* or *have* and the correct form of the words in brackets.

1   I .... in a salon down the road. (*hair / cut*)

2   I must .... written by Monday. (*letter / write*)

3   .... or I'll throw everything out. (*room / tidy*)

4   I need to .... – I never know the time! (*watch / repair*)

5   Why don't you .... the decorating for you? (*him / do*)

6   We're going to .... in the summer. (*house / paint*)

7   I'm going to .... for my new computer. (*father / pay*)

Use of English: gapped sentences (Part 4)

1   Think of one word only which can be used appropriately in all three sentences.

1

He's just .... his job in so I don't know what he'll do now!

It was rush hour so the trains were absolutely ....

Please make sure you get your suitcase .... and ready to take downstairs by 1pm.

2

The country was .... into chaos by the transport strike.

The restaurant is now closed so if you don't leave I will have you .... out.

After he spoke the debate was .... open to the audience.

3

In this lecture, I'll will be examining where the .... of the English language took place.

She speaks Hindi well but she's British by ....

I was so excited about the .... of my child that I couldn't wait.

4

I gave the ball such a hard .... that it went out of play.

Why do you always .... up such a fuss about going to the dentist?

If he doesn't study harder I think they will .... him out!

5

I know the song but I can't put a .... to it.

People often commit very selfless acts in the .... of love.

I would have had a lot of tax to pay so I registered the business in my son's ....

2   Practise transferring your answers to the answer sheet. Remember to use capital letters.

1															¹ 1 0 u
2															² 1 0 u
3															³ 1 0 u
4															⁴ 1 0 u
5															⁵ 1 0 u

Vocabulary 2: synonyms

1   Match each of these words to their definitions. Use a good dictionary, such as *The Longmans Exams Dictionary*, to help you.

1   boost   increase   maximise

   a) become larger in amount, number or degree

   b) increase something to the greatest possible size

   c) get more of; improve something

2   far-fetched   unlikely   inconceivable

   a) not probable or expected

   b) very unlikely to be true

   c) too strange or unusual to be real or possible

3   typically   generally   normally

   a) in a way that a person or group is usually believed to behave

   b) by or to most people; considering something as a whole

   c) in the usual or expected way

4　countless　　numerous
　　a) too many to calculate the total number
　　b) very many

5　coincidence　　luck　　chance
　　a) the force that seems to make good things happen without cause or reason
　　b) when events happen at the same time in the same place or to the same people in a way that seems surprising or unusual
　　c) the way some things happen without being planned

2　Use words from Exercise 1 to complete these sentences. The words in bold are words that go with the missing word. Use your dictionary to help you.

1　I'm hoping to .... my **confidence** by buying a new suit for the interview.

2　Her **story** was pretty ....! I wonder if she made it up.

　　It's .... that he would **behave** like that. I don't believe you.

3　It is .... **accepted** that the story is true.

　　Pasta is a .... **Italian** dish.

4　The vaccination has saved .... **lives**.

5　It was **pure** .... that we were on the same train!

Use of English: word formation (Part 3)

1　Read the text. Use the word given in capitals to form a word that fits the space. There is an example at the beginning (0).

How to talk about books that you haven't read

A **(0)** *distinguished*. French professor has become a surprise bestselling author by writing a book explaining how to wax **(1)** .... about tomes that you have never actually read. Pierre Baynard, a **(2)** .... in the link between literature and psychoanalysis, says it is perfectly possible to bluff your way through a book that you have never read, most **(3)** .... if that conversation is with someone else who also hasn't read it.

Obviously I haven't read Mr Baynard's book, but it is in the spirit of his **(4)** .... that I shall proceed to write about it anyway. The first thing to say about *How to Talk About Books that You Haven't Read* is what a **(5)** .... concept this is. In many circles, it is crucial to be able to hold your own in a **(6)** .... conversation, but the trouble is, in these hurried times, who has the **(7)** .... to really get to the bottom of Proust?

Baynard himself confesses to never having finished *Ulysses*, by James Joyce.

Personally, I have a theory that there is every **(8)** .... that Joyce himself didn't even finish writing the book, since I have never actually met anyone who has read the thing cover to cover. Perhaps *Ulysses* is a book made **(9)** .... by the author just to expose frauds. Perhaps Joyce was **(10)** .... having a laugh.

DISTINGUISH

INTELLECT
SPECIAL

REWARD

BELIEVE

MASTER

LITERATURE
PERSEVERE

LIKELY

READ

PURPOSE

2　Practise transferring your answers to the answer sheet. Remember to use capital letters.

1		1　1　0　u
2		2　1　0　u
3		3　1　0　u
4		4　1　0　u
5	SAMPLE	5　1　0　u
6		6　1　0　u
7		7　1　0　u
8		8　1　0　u
9		9　1　0　u
10		10　1　0　u

Grammar 2: mistakes
▶ *CB pages 173–174*

1   Correct the spelling of these words. One of them is correct.

wether (if)

neccessary

recieve

dissappointing

choise

intresting

reccommendation

beleive

comfortable

recquire

2   Put the correct punctuation in this article and decide where it should be paragraphed.

HARRY POTTER AND THE HALF-BLOOD PRINCE

the story in this book is a lot darker than the previous ones and opens up more possibilities for the storyline relationships are made so we understand the characters more there are a few surprises and we learn a few things about Voldemorte we also learn more about the characters feelings towards each other not that these werent fairly clear through the previous few books however the story isnt quite as enjoyable as the others the humour seems to be a little darker and there is less action in this but this doesnt affect the book much overall I loved it although it seems to be orientated more towards older readers this time I cant wait for the next book to come out next year the questions and possibilities for the next book at the end of this one leave you waiting for more overall this is well worth reading

3a   In which sections of the exam is spelling important?

Reading: Part 1 ☐ Part 2 ☐ Part 3 ☐ Part 4 ☐
Writing: Part 1 ☐ Part 2 ☐ Part 3 ☐ Part 4 ☐
English in Use: Part 1 ☐ Part 2 ☐ Part 3 ☐ Part 4 ☐
Listening: Part 1 ☐ Part 2 ☐ Part 3 ☐ Part 4 ☐

3b   In which sections of the exam is punctuation important?

Reading: Part 1 ☐ Part 2 ☐ Part 3 ☐ Part 4 ☐
Writing: Part 1 ☐ Part 2 ☐ Part 3 ☐ Part 4 ☐
English in Use: Part 1 ☐ Part 2 ☐ Part 3 ☐ Part 4 ☐
Listening: Part 1 ☐ Part 2 ☐ Part 3 ☐ Part 4 ☐

Writing 1: Part 2 questions

Choosing a Part 2 question

In Part 2 you have a choice of three questions on general topics and two set text questions (see below). You should choose the question where you are familiar and comfortable with what is required. You should NOT choose the set text question unless you are familiar with one of the set texts.

1   Look at these possible Part 2 general questions.

1   Many people collect things. Write an article for a magazine describing what you collect, explaining how you became interested in collecting and persuading other people to start a collection of something.

2   Your teacher asks you to write an essay on the following subject:

Large shops are ruining our towns. Small, interesting shops struggle to survive and the big shops all sell the same things!

How far do you agree with this statement?

3   You have been asked to write a report on a sports course you attended. In your report briefly describe your experience, suggest how the course could be improved in the future and say whether or not you would recommend the course to others.

2   Complete the table with the type of language required for each question.

	topic vocabulary	grammar	functional language	task type
Question 2		*past and present tenses, modals*		*article; informal, title*
Question 3	*shopping, buildings*			
Question 4			*describing, suggesting, recommending*	

3 Which two features – vocabulary, grammar, functional language, genre – are the most important in making your decision?

Check your answer in the Key to see if you made the right choice.

Writing 2: the set text question (Part 2)

About the exam: In Paper 2, Part 2, Question 5, you will have the choice of writing about a set text. You will have a choice of two set texts. There will be one question for each set text. You may be asked to write an essay, a review, an article or a report.

Strategy

1 Do NOT attempt this question if you do not know the book, even if the title sounds familiar.
2 Make sure you are familiar with the part of the book that the question asks you to focus on e.g. the characters or a particular scene or event.
3 Don't write too much on describing the plot. Look at the question carefully and make sure you cover all the points equally.

1 Focus.

Below are some points you may be asked on a question on a set text. Think of a book you know and see if you can do any of these tasks:

- Compare two of the characters
- Evaluate the beginning (did it get you interested immediately?)
- Evaluate the ending of the book (could it have been different?)
- Describe what creates the tension or the comedy in the book
- Describe who was the most likeable and the least likeable character (why?)
- Describe the setting (location or time period) of the book

2 Planning.

Questions on the set texts will usually ask for your evaluation and views. You will not be expected to describe the plot in detail or quote from the book. Only a part of the question will ask you to describe something from the book. You must plan your answer carefully to cover all the points and give a balanced response.

Look at this example question and plan:

Your teacher has asked you to write an essay comparing two characters in a book you have read, saying which you prefer and why. Write your answer in 220–260 words.

Plan	Approx number of words
paragraph 1: introduction	20–30
paragraph 2: brief description of the two characters (e.g. names and role in the novel)	50
paragraph 3: comparison of personality	70
paragraph 4: which I prefer and why	70
paragraph 5: conclusion	20–30 230–250

Make a similar plan for the question below.

You are asked to write an article for your college English language magazine on a book you have read recently. Describe the most important event in the book, explain why it was important and what you think would have happened if this event had not taken place. Write your answer in 220–260 words.

Plan	Approx number of words

▬ Improve! ◄

How can you make your answer to the set text question better?

- Don't just describe the plot of the book
- Make sure you give your opinion with reasons
- Use a range of language, especially adjectives

Practice exam

Paper 1 Reading

You have 1 hour and 15 minutes to complete this paper.

Part 1

You are going to read three extracts which are all concerned in some way with sleep problems. For questions **1–6**, choose the answer (**A, B, C or D**) which you think fits best according to the text.

Mark your answers **on the separate answer sheet**.

Night owl or early riser?

Scientists nickname early risers 'larks' and people who like to stay up late 'owls'. While about 80 percent of people fall into the middle of the spectrum, only slightly favouring the morning or the night, it is now believed that about 10 percent of the population are extreme larks and a further 10 percent are extreme owls. Larks are most alert around noon, are at their best in the late morning, and are talkative, friendly, and pleasant from around 9 a.m. to 4 p.m. Owls, meanwhile, are not really up and running until the afternoon, are at their most productive later in the day, and most alert around 6 p.m. Research has also shown that children tend to sleep later and later in the morning until they reach about age twenty. At that point, there is an abrupt change in sleeping habits and the mid-point starts getting earlier and earlier again. Scientists believe such a sudden shift suggests a biological cause and serves as the first marker for the end of adolescence. The study also reflects the trend for girls to mature faster than boys: the women in the study who slept the latest were 19.5 years of age compared with 20.9 years of age for the men. The research involving teenagers has highlighted the unique sleep needs required by this age group: adolescents sleeping late should no longer be considered lazy, but as exhibiting normal biological traits for their age. This study has also sparked a debate about the early start of the school day and whether it should be adjusted to account for teenagers' need for more sleep.

1   The writer states that research shows that in the middle of the day

   A   early and late risers both function best.
   B   early risers begin to feel tired.
   C   late risers begin to be more talkative.
   D   early and late risers are at different stages.

2   The writer suggests that the research on people under the age of twenty

   A   has proved that girls mature faster than boys.
   B   has demonstrated that boys need more sleep than girls.
   C   has prompted a change in school start times.
   D   has confirmed that teenagers can be lazy.

What to do if you're not sleeping

The key to feeling refreshed is having a regular pattern, not how many hours of sleep you get. If you go to bed before you're really tired and then sleep badly, you'll tend to stay in bed later in the morning, which will affect the next night's sleep, and so on. The following steps can help you establish a good pattern. Set yourself a routine. For example, go to bed only when you really feel tired enough to sleep. If you read, watch television or use your computer in bed, you'll find that although these are restful, they are waking activities. So if you don't fall asleep within twenty minutes, get up and relax in another room. Do something soothing, such as listening to music, until you're tired enough to go back to bed. You should repeat this process if you are awake for long periods. Set the alarm at the same time each morning. Don't sleep in late to make up for a bad night. This will only make it harder to sleep the following night. You may feel the effects of this for several weeks, making it hard to get back to a regular pattern. Avoid taking a nap during the day. But if you really are overtired, taking a short nap after lunch can be beneficial. After a long flight, you need to get your body clock in tune with local time. However tired you feel, avoid going to bed until the local bedtime and get up reasonably early the next morning. You should then quickly adjust to a new pattern.

line 8

3 According to the writer, sleep patterns can be disturbed by

    A not napping during the day.
    B not sleeping after long-distance travel.
    C not getting up early enough after a late night.
    D not setting the alarm at a regular time.

4 The writer mentions leisure activities in lines 8 and 9 to illustrate

    A the kinds of activities you can do to relax.
    B things you should avoid doing in bed.
    C ways to take your mind off not sleeping.
    D methods of winding down before bedtime.

BOOK REVIEW

When your child isn't sleeping, chances are that you aren't either. *Solve Your Child's Sleep Problems* – the tired parent's essential reading for more than ten years – offers valuable advice and concrete help when lullabies aren't enough to lull your child into dreamland. This book is a practical, easy-to-understand guide to common sleeping problems for children aged one to six. Detailed case histories on night waking, difficulty sleeping and more serious disorders such as sleep apnea and sleepwalking help illustrate a wide variety of problems and their solutions. New parents will benefit from the approach taken, which is proactive advice on developing good sleeping patterns and daily schedules to ensure that sleeping problems don't develop in the first place.

This book is brilliant. It not only explains how and why the suggested techniques work but also gives case studies of children that the techniques have been used on. I am the envy of many of my friends with children because mine now sleep through the night unless they're ill. I'd recommend this book to anyone with young children who is having problems with them sleeping. It even covers helping older children to sleep and dealing with the transition to sleeping alone as well. The techniques really do work in a short space of time with very little distress to all. You'll also find a bibliography of children's books on bedtime, sleep and dreaming, as well as a list of helpful organisations. Here's a book that is sure to put you and your whole family to sleep – in this case, that's a good thing!

5 In the first paragraph, which aspect of the book does the writer recommend?
    A the length of time it has been published
    B the authority of its advice
    C the usefulness of the examples given
    D the section for new parents

6 In the second paragraph, the result the writer mentions is
    A her pleasure that her children sleep better than others.
    B her gratitude that her children sleep in their own rooms.
    C her enjoyment of the recommended children's books.
    D her relief that her children are no longer distressed.

Turn over ▶

Part 2

You are going to read a magazine article. Six paragraphs have been removed from the article. Choose from paragraphs **A–G** the one which fits each gap (**7–12**). There is one extra paragraph which you do not need to use.

Mark your answers **on the separate answer sheet**.

Think about what animals feel!

The organisation Compassion in World Farming (CIWF) works to advance animal well being worldwide

We have to recognise that humans share the planet with as many as 4700 species of mammals, 9700 species of birds, 4800 species of amphibians, over 23,000 species of fish and around 6000 species of reptiles (as far as we know up to now), not to mention the countless species of invertebrate animals. We interact with and use animals in a multitude of ways in our daily lives.

7 _____

The most basic way of experiencing the world is through feeling or sensation. 'Sentience' is defined as the ability to have perceptions and sensations. A 'sentient animal' is an animal that is aware of its surroundings and of what happens to it and is capable of feeling pain and pleasure, at the least. The current scientific consensus is that all vertebrate animals, at least, are capable of feeling pain and experiencing distress.

8 _____

Questions like these may seem simple, even simple-minded, but in fact they are very complex and important to our understanding of the place of humans in the natural world. We need to know how animals experience the world – what they feel, why they behave in the ways they do, how they understand their environment, how and what they communicate.

9 _____

Modern research is proving these are founded in fact – it turns out that many of the animals we interact with also have more complex mental and emotional lives than people have understood in the past. New

scientific research is constantly revealing new evidence of animals' cognitive abilities and their emotions. It has shown, for example, that some animals can both remember and anticipate events and some can foresee their future needs and plan ahead.

10 _____

Further evidence of this sophistication is that they can maintain complex social relationships in their groups. Some animals can understand what another animal is going to do and attempt to deceive that animal in order to gain an advantage. Some animals enjoy learning a new skill. Some animals react to other animals in ways resembling human empathy. On the negative side, animals can experience the unpleasant emotions of pain, fear, frustration and probably boredom as well.

11 _____

Perhaps more importantly, we cannot assume that if an animal behaves in ways that look familiar to us, the animal has the same mental experiences as a human would have in similar circumstances. But it is equally important not to underestimate animals' feelings and the sophistication of their mental processes, because this may well affect how we behave towards animals.

12 _____

What is exciting about the present time is that scientists are once again interested in studying animals' emotions and mental processes and that huge progress in understanding animals is being made.

Compassion in World Farming

A   But how can we guess what these feelings may be? From the point of view of evolutionary biology, it makes sense that humans should share many of our emotional and cognitive abilities with some of the other animal species. Throughout history people have known that animals do very 'clever' and impressive things – such as a bird building an intricate nest or a mother animal teaching her young. Folk stories all over the world attribute intelligence and cunning to animals.

B   So a huge increase in scientific research on animal sentience is beginning to answer some of the questions about animal sentience and animal consciousness. However, we have to remember that abilities will vary between species.

C   This means that we have to think about how we treat these animals that are so important to us. The work that CIWF does on farm animal welfare is based on the recognition that animals are sentient beings. In other words, they are capable of being aware of sensations and emotions, of feeling pain and suffering, and of experiencing a state of well being. CIWF believes that our own behaviour towards animals should be guided by recognition of their sentience.

D   The facts and theories of animal sentience are still hotly debated among scientists and philosophers. But most people over history have assumed that many animals feel pain, hunger, thirst, heat, cold, fear, anger and other basic emotions, because we have everyday evidence that they do.

E   Certainly there are many unsolved mysteries and questions remaining for future study and debate and this will be one of the most exciting areas of biology in the coming decades. For example, we may eventually be able to prove beyond doubt what an animal is feeling, or perhaps thinking.

F   However, many of us are aware that animals may experience more than just these physical feelings. At some time we must all have watched another animal – a dog, a cat, a horse, a bird, a flock of sheep – and wondered, 'What is she feeling now?' or 'Why is he behaving like that?' or 'What do they want?'. Yet although most of us use animal products every day, we make little effort to find out about the animals' needs and wants, or about their emotional lives.

G   Importantly, it has also demonstrated that several of the abilities that in the past have been thought to be uniquely human – for example, the use of tools, the ability to plan ahead, the ability to empathise with another or to deceive another, the transmission of skills in ways that can be classified as 'culture', behaviour that can be classified as 'morality' – are now known to exist to some extent among non-human animals too.

Part 3

You are going to read a newspaper article. For questions **13–19**, choose the answer (**A, B, C or D**) which you think fits best according to the text.

Mark your answers **on the separate answer sheet**.

What Ellen did next

The round-the-world sailor talks about money, boyfriends and her latest challenge. But will she ever race round the world again?

When Ellen MacArthur sailed into Falmouth Harbour in February 2005, the tiny twenty-eight-year-old had battled against huge seas to shave thirty-two hours off the round-the-world record. But the trouble with extraordinary feats is that everyone wants an encore. Since February 2005, she has kept us waiting. Has she lost her nerve?

Ellen has been far from idle. She's taken part in an exhausting series of races and challenges but compared with the sailing equivalent of conquering Everest several times, such adventures seem tame. That's deliberate, she says. 'Setting the world record was hugely exhausting. It takes six months to a year to get over it because you are living on adrenaline and acute levels of stress. In the Southern Ocean I had twenty minutes' sleep in three days: the seas were so huge that I had to keep changing the sails or else I would capsize. In a race you can't stop and take the sails down. Everything is full-on all the time. You reach the point of exhaustion where you can't stop.'

But surely, once she was back, she could relax? Catching up on sleep wasn't the problem, she says, learning to eat normally was. 'You know the feeling when you go to an exam and the last thing you want to do is eat? It's like that all the time. On the boat you eat because you know you have to, to keep your strength up. You'd think that when you get back you'd be desperate for fresh food or ice cream but you don't feel hungry and you don't bother to eat because you know it doesn't matter, because nothing is happening.' It sounds as if she felt depressed, but she denies it. Like a true motivational speaker, she is relentlessly upbeat.

She has no qualms about admitting, however, that during the races she often had to 'dig deep' into herself – by which she seems to mean overriding feelings of panic with grim determination. She can, for example, say precisely how many times she has had to ascend the mast, a lone sailor's most terrifying ordeal. 'It's horrendous as you really get a battering, especially on a multi-hull because the two outer hulls slap down on the water alternately, causing the mast to shake violently. You are more likely to break your back or your leg or your arm than to fall off. You have to go into mechanical mode, thinking, 'This is what I have to do.' If you think, "I'm going to die", you shouldn't be on the boat at all. Training is crucial but, physically and mentally, you can't keep putting yourself through that.'

Despite her ease with words and friendly demeanour, she must be a loner. 'Not at all,' she says. 'Even if I am sailing solo I'm in constant touch with the team. I felt nothing after I broke the round-the-world record until forty-five minutes later, when the shore team arrived. Afterwards, sailing with others again was fantastic.' On her own she says she's never bored, she travels somewhere in her head, but she doesn't seem to be so much in a world of her own that she's insensitive to other people. When she looked back over pre-race photographs and saw the strain on her parents' faces as they said goodbye, she felt terribly guilty, but at the time she was so busy steeling herself for the ordeal ahead that she didn't notice.

She's been like that, she says, ever since she fell passionately in love with sailing, aged four, while staying with an aunt who owned a boat. From then on, she saved up all her time and pocket money to go sailing. Aged seventeen, she had already qualified as a Yachtmaster before she sailed around Britain. 'For my parents, as non-sailors, it was very hard. But they never said, "Why don't you get a proper job?"' Her exceptional will to win impressed Mark Thompson, against whom she competed in a transatlantic race two years later in 1996. Although he beat her, she was so eager to continue sailing that he decided to quit in order to go into business, finding sponsorship for her. Their company, Offshore Challenges, now employs thirty-five people.

What drives her, she says, is learning new things: whether becoming fluent in French, an expert on meteorology, or learning to film her own exploits. Part of what makes her instantly likeable and a sponsor's dream is her ability to convey the extraordinary experiences she's had, both through words (she's written two autobiographies) and pictures. She talks fluently and vividly about the albatrosses that swoop like low-flying planes over the deserted whaling stations on South Georgia, or the flotillas of fishing boats she saw when she sailed up the Yangtse river at night.

But it's more than just the nautical equivalent of trainspotting because Ellen is genuinely moved by her encounters. Visiting South Georgia, where 175,000 whales were slaughtered with no thought for the future of the species, has inspired her to learn more about sustainability. She doesn't yet know what she will do with her knowledge but she would make a good figurehead for any turn-off-the-lights campaign.

13   Ellen says that the experience of sailing round the world

    A   has left her feeling very lazy.

    B   has made her scared of repeating it.

    C   has enabled her to tolerate high levels of stress.

    D   has limited her to less challenging activities.

14   What did Ellen find difficult after completing the round-the-world race?

    A   having to eat when she lacked an appetite

    B   controlling cravings for certain types of food

    C   recognising the importance of eating regularly

    D   allowing depression to affect her eating habits

15   How does Ellen say she coped with a frightening experience on the boat?

    A   by having special training

    B   by thinking about what could go wrong

    C   by conquering her fears

    D   by practising the task many times

16   In the fifth paragraph, what does Ellen say about sailing alone?

    A   She uses her imagination to divert herself.

    B   She can cope only if she has a team to help her.

    C   She is aware of how much it upsets her parents.

    D   She prefers sailing with a group of people.

17   Ellen was given the opportunity to become a professional sailor because of

    A   her youth.

    B   her enthusiasm.

    C   her ability.

    D   her experience.

18   According to the writer, why is Ellen so popular with sponsors?

    A   because she is willing to try new experiences

    B   because she has done things that are unusual

    C   because she likes describing what she's done

    D   because she is a good communicator

19   In the final paragraph, the writer says that in the future Ellen could

    A   become a student.

    B   become a figurehead.

    C   work with whales.

    D   move to another country.

Part 4

You are going to read an article in which an author gives advice about writing books. For questions **20–34**, choose from the sections **A–E**. The sections may be chosen more than once.

Mark your answers **on the separate answer sheet**.

In which section does the writer mention

the advantage of planning rest periods into her work	20
the distractions of the non-creative aspects of a book	21
doing something different from her intentions	22
taking somebody up on their suggestion	23
being forced to acquire a skill	24
having to do a job and write at the same time	25
being grateful for some outside input	26
alternating the type of work she is doing	27
doing a task which used up a lot of time	28
the stage at which she prefers to review her work	29
her methods for resolving difficulties	30
worrying about the quality of her work	31
being prepared to change her plans	32
being surprised at having become a writer	33
recognising that people work differently	34

Working on the book: lessons learned so far

I am currently writing a book on libraries and technology and thought I would share some of the things I've learned so far about writing a book

A It's really important to manage the project well. Write down all of the tasks that need to be done by your deadline and give yourself deadlines for each task. Mentally, I just can't handle doing things at the last minute, so I've had to become very good at planning and following through with my plans. Structure things the way that works best for you. There is no right way to write a book. I got advice early on that I should do research for a few months and then spend the rest of the time writing. But because each of my chapters is on a different subject, I find it better to spend a week researching a chapter and a week writing the chapter (sometimes less and sometimes more depending on the topic). This is what works best for me for this particular project. Figure out what works best for you and do it that way.

B I went through a period when I was about halfway done with the writing part of the book when I really didn't want to write. I just felt worn out and unmotivated. So I restructured my deadlines in light of how I was feeling. It's important that you put some padding into your project plan for such malaises. You can't force yourself to write or your writing may end up being awful. Also a book is a lot more than research and writing. There are so many other things, like figures, graphics, citations, etc., that you have to think about. I decided to save most of this stuff until the end, because I don't want to lose focus on my writing. At first, I was trying to create correct citations while I was writing and it was taking up too many hours and too much mental energy. I decided to just write and put all of the citation information down in whatever form I happened to put it in for now. I'll fix them when I edit the chapters.

C It's a good idea not to edit anything until you've written everything. Maybe it's just me, but I will totally lose focus if I start editing any of my writing before I've finished writing. Also, it's better to edit when you know what the whole book looks like and you know better what needs to be restructured. You will need to lay out the chapters in your book for your proposal, but don't

be surprised if it doesn't work out when you start writing. You need to be flexible. I've been writing more than I'd projected for nearly every chapter, but I made a conscious decision not to worry about it until I edit the book so that I don't lose focus on writing. I'm sure there are plenty of things I can cut later on, but I don't want to obsess over it while I'm writing. The more I think about things other than writing, the more difficult I find it to write.

D If you're having trouble, talk to your editor. My editor has given me a lot of good advice. An editor is a good support since they deal with crazy writers all the time. My husband has also been a big help in keeping me sane. It's important to have someone (significant other, parent, friend, etc.) you can talk to about all of your irrational fears about whether the book and your writing are good enough and who will tell you that you are being ridiculous. I don't know if I could have done this without Adam's support. When I freak out about stuff, he's always there to encourage me and to help me come up with a concrete plan to get things done.

E Books are really hard to write when you are working full-time – but totally worth it. I hadn't actually planned on writing a book. I was approached by my editor who asked me if I'd ever considered writing a book. And while I honestly hadn't thought of it since school, I was certainly interested. This is an amazing opportunity and I probably would have regretted it for ever if I'd said no. Don't underestimate yourself! You may think that you couldn't ever write a book. You may love to write but think that you're not good enough. You may not think you have anything interesting or worthwhile to say. Consider for a moment that maybe you are wrong. Maybe you are underestimating yourself and are looking at yourself through a funhouse mirror. I have spent most of my life thinking that I'm not good enough for things and have let plenty of opportunities pass me by. So whether someone emails you and asks you to write a book or not, if you want to do it, go for it!

http://meredith.wolfwater.com

Paper 2 Writing

You have 1 hour and 30 minutes to complete this paper.

Part 1

You **must** answer this question. Write your answer in **180–220** words in an appropriate style.

---

1   You are on the student committee of a college where you are studying in Ireland. Every year the committee organises a school trip for students. This year the Principal, Mr Gavin, has given the committee two suggestions to consider.

Read the two suggestions for school trips below together with your notes on what the students would like. Then, **using the information appropriately**, write a proposal to Mr Gavin saying which trip you would prefer and why, explaining why the other trip is unsuitable and persuading the principal to contribute towards the cost of the trip.

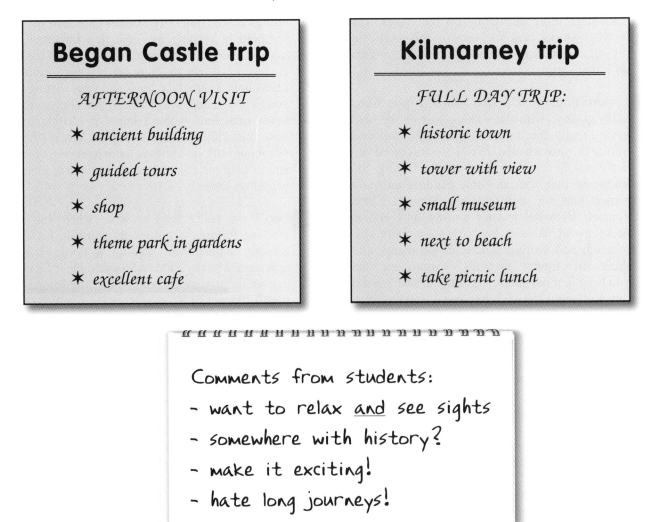

Began Castle trip

AFTERNOON VISIT

* ancient building
* guided tours
* shop
* theme park in gardens
* excellent cafe

Kilmarney trip

FULL DAY TRIP:

* historic town
* tower with view
* small museum
* next to beach
* take picnic lunch

Comments from students:
- want to relax <u>and</u> see sights
- somewhere with history?
- make it exciting!
- hate long journeys!

Write your **proposal**. You should use your own words as far as possible.

Part 2

Write an answer to **one** of the questions **2–5** in this part. Write your answer in **220–260** words in an appropriate style.

---

2 You see this announcement on a music website.

> **Music Events**
>
> Every year there are hundreds of music events and festivals. Some are good and some are not good. We want you to write a report to put on our website about a music event you have attended. Tell us about the event and whether or not you enjoyed it and why, and say how the event could have been improved.

Write your **report**.

3 In class you have been discussing problems caused by damage to the environment. Your teacher has asked you to write an essay on the following topic:

Environmental problems are now so huge that governments, not individuals, should be responsible for solving them.

To what extent do you agree?

Write your **essay**.

4 A friend of yours is writing a book on traditions in other countries and has asked you for a contribution about your country. Write a contribution to the book explaining which tradition is most important in your country and why and saying whether or not you think this tradition will change in any way in the future, giving your reasons.

Write your **contribution** to the book.

5 Answer **one** of the following two questions based on one of the titles below.

a) *The Pelican Brief* by John Grisham

Your college magazine has asked you to write a review of a book that is really exciting. You decide to write a review of *The Pelican Brief*, describing which parts of the story were the most exciting and why and saying why you would recommend the book to other readers.

Write your **review**.

b) *Lucky Jim* by Kingsley Amis

You decide to write an article for your college magazine about *Lucky Jim*, saying why you think Jim is a typical academic person and whether or not you would like to be like him, giving reasons for your views.

Write your **article**.

Paper 3 Use of English

You have 1 hour to complete this paper. The paper contains five parts.

Part 1

For questions **1–12**, read the text below and decide which answer (**A, B, C or D**) best fits each gap. There is an example at the beginning **(0)**.

Write your answers **on the separate answer sheet**.

Example:

| 0 | **A** left | **B** wasted | **C** exhausted | **D** thrown |

Why laughter is good for you

'A day without laughter is a day **(0)** ....', said the comedian Charlie Chaplin and scientists are starting to agree. Every couple of months there are news stories **(1)** .... that chuckling is good for your health and scientists are only **(2)** .... beginning to understand what happens in the brain when we laugh. We don't laugh only because something is funny but also for a range of social reasons **(3)** .... when we feel awkward or surprised. But laughing is a pleasurable **(4)** .... for most of us and so researchers are looking at the health benefits it could have. A doctor in India has even developed 'laughter clubs', an idea which has **(5)** .... all over the world and which allows stressed-out executives to laugh their way **(6)** .... to good health. A giggling fit will certainly **(7)** .... out your abdominal muscles, but is there scientific evidence for any other health benefit?

Until there is good scientific evidence that regular laughter **(8)** .... life, the health benefits of laughter will remain controversial. In social situations, however, laughter is a natural **(9)** .... we use to help interactions go smoothly. For social reasons, we feel that we have to keep a conversation **(10)** .... and laughter is one method we use. It does seem **(11)** .... that laughter is a good thing and everyone feels better after a good chortle. It may not be the magic treatment for all **(12)** .... but it does no harm and improves quality of life. So perhaps laughter is no joke after all.

1	**A** detailing	**B** charging	**C** notifying	**D** claiming
2	**A** perfectly	**B** just	**C** simply	**D** so
3	**A** such	**B** example	**C** like	**D** instance
4	**A** experience	**B** episode	**C** incident	**D** happening
5	**A** covered	**B** spread	**C** distributed	**D** issued
6	**A** over	**B** back	**C** down	**D** up
7	**A** find	**B** try	**C** work	**D** make
8	**A** lasts	**B** stretches	**C** continues	**D** prolongs
9	**A** apparatus	**B** structure	**C** appliance	**D** mechanism
10	**A** going	**B** performing	**C** operating	**D** running
11	**A** spontaneous	**B** intuitive	**C** involuntary	**D** native
12	**A** miseries	**B** hurts	**C** ills	**D** trials

Part 2

For questions **13–27**, read the text below and think of the word which best fits each gap. Use only **one** word in each gap. There is an example at the beginning **(0)**.

Write your answers **IN CAPITAL LETTERS on the separate answer sheet.**

Example: | 0 | T | O | | | | | | | | | | | | | | | | | | | |

Virtual rock star

Have you ever pretended **(0)** .... play the guitar, strumming the air while listening to imaginary music? This activity is called 'air guitar' and music inventors have just **(13)** .... responsible for taking it to a whole new level! Computer technology can now enable you to become the rock star of **(14)** .... dreams. Just **(15)** .... anyone can become a rock star by putting on a pair of gloves and playing a virtual guitar, even you! Researchers from Finland have made **(16)** .... possible for aspiring performers to play an invisible guitar and have their movements turned into music, **(17)** .... to technology such as a webcam and some software. Apparently, though, it'll cost you over £200 **(18)** .... it's on the shelves. The virtual air guitar uses a process **(19)** .... 'reads' the hand movements of the air guitarist and records **(20)** .... on a machine which translates the movements **(21)** .... music. Orange gardening gloves are worn **(22)** .... the performer and a webcam is connected to software which can detect movement. A researcher showed me **(23)** .... it works by explaining that you have to imagine that you are holding a guitar and then swing your right hand over the strings as **(24)** .... you were playing a note. The distance between your hands alters the sound. The idea of this clever invention is **(25)** .... to play songs but to give an explosive audio show.

A researcher said, 'Our vision is that the virtual air guitar **(26)** .... become known as the new karaoke.' So, if you had the money, you **(27)** .... start a virtual band with your friends and be headed for instant stardom.

Part 3

For questions **28–37**, read the text below. Use the word given in capitals at the end of some of the lines to form a word that fits in the gap in the same line. There is an example at the beginning **(0)**.

Write your answers **IN CAPITAL LETTERS on the separate answer sheet**.

Example: | 0 | C | R | I | T | I | C | A | L | | | | | | | | | | |

Accentuate the positive

We all have **(0)** .... thoughts about ourselves and often our   **CRITIC**

(28) .... lives can seem full of negative attitudes towards us, whether   **DAY**

it's a hostile look or a bald **(29)** .... Learn to focus on the positives   **REJECT**

and develop an inner monitor that sorts out the difference between useful

advice and **(30)** .... criticism or opinions. If you feel overwhelmed   **HELP**

by someone's negative opinion of you, think three positive thoughts that,

(31) ...., they could be having about you. Imagine them telling you this   **IDEAL**

in an **(32)** .... fashion. Also, as soon as you have a negative thought,   **ENCOURAGE**

change your body **(33)** .... to the way you would sit or stand if you were   **POSE**

feeling **(34)** .... of yourself. If you can't imagine someone's positive   **PRIDE**

opinion of you, then deflect your attention to, for example, the **(35)** ....   **WARM**

of the room. It can be very **(36)** .... when we realise we have a choice   **POWER**

about where to invest our thoughts and we can start to **(37)** .... that   **STRONG**

ability through committed practice.

Part 4

For questions **38–42**, think of one word only which can be used appropriately in all three sentences. Here is an example **(0)**.

Example:

0   The computer was delivered late so they agreed not to .... me for delivery.

He's been put in .... of accounts while the boss is away!

The director shouted '.........................!' and all the soldiers ran into battle.

Example: | 0 | C | H | A | R | G | E | | | | | | | | | | | |

Write only the missing word **IN CAPITAL LETTERS on the separate answer sheet**.

---

38   It is a good idea but in .... of cost, I'm not sure we can afford it.

By signing this you agree that you have read and understood the .... of agreement.

The school year is usually divided into three .... in the UK.

39   I think finally getting him to sit down to do some work is a major .... forward.

If he's agreed to improve his time-keeping then that is at least a .... in the right direction.

I fell because I didn't see the ...... as I was coming out of the cathedral.

40   The business eventually plans to expand into every .... of the globe.

He was very unhappy but since his holiday I think he's really turned a .... and is on the road to feeling better.

You can see the sign for the bank just on the .... before you turn into Glebe Road.

41   I don't think he realised he'd said anything wrong but I knew he was walking on thin ....!

My gloves were useless so my hands were as cold as .... when I was skiing.

The expedition members were in great danger when they crossed the .... as it was spring and it was starting to melt.

42   I'm not at all ambitious – I want to travel and get out of the rat ....

She ran the .... so fast that she broke the record.

Saving the planet is a .... against time and one I'm not sure we'll win.

Part 5

For questions **43–50**, complete the second sentence so that it has a similar meaning to the first sentence, using the word given. **Do not change the word given**. You must use between **three** and **six** words, including the word given. Here is an example **(0)**.

Example:

0 'Where do you think he is?' she said.

WONDERED

She ....

The gap can be filled with the words 'wondered where he was', so you write:

Example: | 0 | | *WONDERED WHERE HE WAS* |

Write only the missing words **IN CAPITAL LETTERS on the separate answer sheet.**

---

43 It wasn't until I finished going out with him that I realised I missed him.
BROKEN
I realised .... him that I missed him.

44 I hadn't seen such a wonderful painting before.
NEVER
.... such a wonderful painting.

45 I'm sorry but we are unable to help.
REGRET
I .... we are unable to help.

46 I lost my keys so I was late.
IF
I .... I hadn't lost my keys.

47 She was beginning to change her mind about taking the job.
SECOND
She was .... the job.

48 The problem is not my fault.
BLAME
I .... the problem.

49 The police thought he had been living in Canada.
HAVE
He .... in Canada.

50 His wallet isn't here so I'm sure it was stolen.
MUST
His wallet ....

Paper 4 Listening

Part 1

You will hear three different extracts. For questions **1–6**, choose the answer (**A, B or C**) which fits best according to what you hear. There are two questions for each extract.

Extract One

You hear part of an interview with a biologist who has just returned from Chile.

1   What aspect of the desert did the biologist find surprising?

    A   the diverse landscape
    B   the unvarying temperature
    C   the range of plants

2   Why does the biologist say he would like to return?

    A   to continue his research
    B   to explore new areas
    C   to investigate a problem

Extract Two

You hear two people talking about a problem with a bank.

3   Why did the man decide to close his bank account?

    A   The service at the bank was inefficient.
    B   The location of the bank was inconvenient.
    C   The rates offered by the bank were inadequate.

4   How does the woman feel about his decision?

    A   angry
    B   worried
    C   confused

Extract Three

You hear part of an interview with a champion tennis player called Mark Bevan.

5   How did Mark get involved in professional tennis?

    A   by attending a special training academy
    B   by entering competitions from a young age
    C   by receiving sponsorship from a university

6   What is Mark's view of children playing tennis?

    A   They should receive better supervision.
    B   They should continue studying for longer.
    C   They should be protected by stricter regulations.

Part 2

You will hear a photojournalist called Angus MacDonald talking about a trip he made recently. For questions **7–14**, complete the sentences.

TRAVELLING THE SILK ROAD

Angus had his trip paid for by a [_____ **7**] at a charitable organisation.

The purpose of Angus's trip was to produce a [_____ **8**] to encourage grant applications.

His trip involved recording information on several [_____ **9**] over a period of eight weeks.

On the journey, Angus travelled with [_____ **10**] , who could explain the work that was being done.

As well as looking at art treasures he saw a performance by specialist [_____ **11**] in the open air.

Angus particularly enjoyed photographing the collection of [_____ **12**] in Kyrgyzstan.

He was also shown hidden murals that had been ruined by [_____ **13**] .

Money invested in the project will allow precious objects to be displayed in special [_____ **14**] , which will help preserve them.

Part 3

You will hear part of a radio interview in which John Tulsa, a lecturer in business studies, is talking about motivation. For questions **15–20**, choose the answer (**A, B, C or D**) which fits best according to what you hear.

___

15 According to John, what can being distracted result in?

    A   an inability to solve problems

    B   a lack of control over tasks

    C   a focus on unimportant tasks

    D   a failure to work hard

16 John says that hard work may involve

    A   ignoring other aspects of your life.

    B   forcing yourself to do unpleasant tasks.

    C   doing one task without a break.

    D   achieving very little initially.

17 What is John's criticism of some business experts?

    A   They fail to mention how hard they work.

    B   They are paid too much for what they do.

    C   They claim that achieving success is easy.

    D   They focus on the rewards they receive.

18 Why does John say it is important to be relaxed?

    A   You will be able to see solutions more clearly.

    B   It will allow you to become more productive.

    C   It will enable you to be more creative.

    D   You will be more effective at guiding others.

19 According to John, how can you change your self-image?

    A   by doing one project at a time

    B   by asking others what they think

    C   by working harder than anyone else

    D   by measuring your successes

20 Why does John say you need less motivation as you become more successful?

    A   because you will find it easier to concentrate

    B   because you will be able to delegate work

    C   because you will be familiar with the work

    D   because you will want to avoid failure

Part 4

You will hear five short extracts in which people are talking about aspects of their work in a museum.

While you listen you must complete both tasks.

TASK ONE

For questions **21–25**, choose from the list **(A–H)** the person who is speaking.

A guide

B receptionist

C cloakroom attendant

D shop assistant

E café worker

F exhibits technician

G lecturer

H publicity assistant

Speaker 1 | 21

Speaker 2 | 22

Speaker 3 | 23

Speaker 4 | 24

Speaker 5 | 25

TASK TWO

For questions **26–30**, choose from the list **(A–H)** the opinion each speaker expresses.

A I hate working at fixed times

B I don't like dealing with children

C I'd like to apply for a promotion

D I find the work rather boring

E I have too much to do

F I enjoy helping visitors

G I can't stand it when it's quiet

H I'm not keen on the paperwork

Speaker 1 | 26

Speaker 2 | 27

Speaker 3 | 28

Speaker 4 | 29

Speaker 5 | 30

Paper 5 Speaking

Part 1 (3 or 5 minutes)

The interlocutor will ask you and the other candidate some questions about yourselves.

🎧 Listen to the recording and answer the questions. Pause the recording after each bleep and give your answer.

Part 2 (4 or 6 minutes)

The interlocutor will ask you and the other candidate to talk on your own about some photographs.

🎧 Listen to the recording and answer the questions. When you hear the first bleep, pause the recording for one minute and answer the questions. Then start the recording again. When you hear the second bleep, pause the recording for 20 seconds and answer the question.

Candidate A

- What different aspects of seeing wild animals do they show?
- How are the people feeling?

Candidate B

- What different aspects of watching sport do they show?
- How might the people be feeling?

Parts 3 and 4 (8 or 12 minutes)

Part 3

The interlocutor will ask you and the other candidate to discuss something together.

Look at the pictures and listen to the interlocutor's instructions. When you hear two bleeps, pause the recording for three minutes and complete the task.

> - What different ways of living do they show?
> - Which picture shows the most difficult way to live?

Part 4

The interlocutor will ask you and the other candidate questions related to the topic in Part 3.

🎧 Listen to the recording and answer the interlocutor's questions. Pause the recording when you hear each bleep and discuss the question with the other candidate.

Answer key

UNIT *1*

Vocabulary 1 p.8

1

indie | rock | rap
punk | pop | hip hop | heavy metal

2 1 d   2 f   3 a   4 b   5 c   6 e

3 We played some really awful **gigs** on our way up the ladder. Eventually we managed to get **signed** to a really good record **label**, who also said they would pay for the **distribution** of our records. Anyway, they were as good as their word and our record got heavily **plugged** on the radio and so we managed to get to number 18 in the **charts.**

4 1 set up   2 shot up   3 gearing up
    4 lined up   5 put out

Grammar 1 p.9

1 1 As a singer, I was forced **to do / into doing** awful jobs before **hitting** the big time.
    2 Rock bands' wealth means that ~~the~~ people are very jealous of them.
    3 I suggested **he knock / knocking** at producers' doors to get a record deal.
    4 He wants **us to** practise the song again at the weekend.
    5 I've been desperate **to break** into singing for years – now's my chance.
    6 CORRECT
    7 They're very boring because, **like** most boy bands, they only sing in one style.
    8 He was paid millions for the copyright so he **must** have loads of money by now.

2 1 Bigger profits will definitely mean more companies taking risks.
    2 The group felt quite pleased with their success.
    3 Is that the group which was voted the best last year?
    4 You can even be a success without being able to sing!
    5 We must never download music without paying for it.
    6 The chance to be an overnight success is hardly ever offered.

3 1 d   2 a   3 e   4 b   5 c

Listening p.9

1 1 noun   2 noun   3 adjective / compound
    4 noun   5 noun   6 noun   7 noun   8 verb

2 1 movement   2 rock   3 singles   4 festival
    5 producers   6 technology   7 pace   8 experiment

4 1 filter down   4 catch on
    2 has grown out of / grew out of   5 get in on
    3 moves on / is moving on

Tapescript

Man: The urban scene – broadly covering hip-hop, rap and R&B – is today firmly at the heart of mainstream culture, with its music and imagery impossible to ignore. In little more than twenty-five years, this new style of music, that began as a fringe scene in inner-city America, has evolved into arguably the most popular and influential movement in global pop, reaching far beyond its North American roots. Producers like The Neptunes, who have worked with the likes of Britney Spears and Justin Timberlake, have shaped the modern pop sound, and urban music is officially the most popular style in the US – overtaking rock in 2002 and now accounting for 25 percent of sales. Toussaint Davy, editor of *Tense* magazine, has suggested that it's never going to stop and that the more people get involved with the dynamism of the music, the more the music will move on.

Another landmark was reached in October 2003 when, for the first time, all the top 10 artists in the singles chart in the US were black. Urban artists have dominated the charts, with hip-hop duo OutKast recently spending two months at numbers one and two in the charts and on top of the albums chart. And it is not just a US phenomenon – new urban stars have won the UK's Mercury Music Prize for the best album of the year for the last two years, while even Prince Charles is getting in on the act and has hosted an urban music festival.

Toussaint Davy says that Middle America has totally embraced urban music in the last 12 months. He claims that when you have people like Britney Spears and Christina Aguilera working with rappers and prominent producers, it's only a matter of time before it starts filtering down to everyone else. And he has also suggested that the thing about hip-hop is that it's a very dynamic form of expression, so therefore you can't really hold back progress. This pattern of evolution – with black music being adopted by the mainstream – has been around since jazz and blues spread in the early 20th century. But modern hip-hop music was born in the mid-1970s when the vibrant funk, disco and soul scenes collided – helped by rapidly developing technology that spawned synthesizers and drum machines. R&B music has taken a different path, growing out of the soul of the 1960s and 70s, with a more sleek and romantic sound. But the two styles have now come together, giving R&B a harder edge and in turn making hip-hop more polished and commercial.

Part of the reason for its rapid spread is that the music's pace suits today's fast consumer-led culture and it is now the musical heritage of all America, not just young black inner-cities. While more established styles like pop have few new ideas to explore, this young street music is still evolving and prepared to experiment. It has been suggested that this is because it's the most exciting thing out there. In other words, it's not just some guys with guitars moaning about their girlfriends. This is probably why it's caught on – precisely because it's fresh and innovative in a way that other types of music aren't.

Reading p.10

1 was <u>disillusioned</u> by a <u>record company</u>
    has <u>not yet made</u> a record
    has formed <u>a business deal outside the industry</u>
    <u>recognises</u> the importance of <u>publicity</u>
    has used the <u>Internet</u> to further their <u>pop career</u>

mentions putting a <u>time limit</u> on their pop <u>career</u>
is <u>likened</u> to <u>other acts</u>
feels they are in a <u>better situation than</u> some <u>other acts</u>
has <u>not been signed</u> <u>despite</u> making <u>good records</u>
has been doing <u>publicity</u> that is <u>ineffective</u>
has <u>lost a member</u>

2 1 + 2: A, C (in any order)   10 B
3 B   11 D
4 D   12 E
5 C   13 E
6 + 7 C, D (in any order)   14 A
8 + 9 C, E (in any order)   15 E

3 1 A   2 B   3 B   4 A   5 B

Vocabulary 2 p.12

1

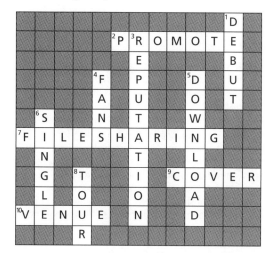

2a

-ity (noun)	-ation (noun)	-al (adjective)	-ent (adjective)
ability	alteration	central	confident
purity	demonstration	political	dependent
similarity	resignation	critical	prominent
	information	confidential	

2b able – <u>a</u>bility   similar – simila<u>r</u>ity   <u>al</u>ter – alte<u>r</u>ation
demon<u>s</u>trate – demonstra<u>t</u>ion   re<u>s</u>ign – resig<u>n</u>ation
in<u>f</u>orm – inform<u>a</u>tion   poli<u>t</u>ics – po<u>l</u>itical   <u>con</u>fidence –
confi<u>den</u>tial

Use of English p.12

1 1 comparative   2 regardless   3 scientific
4 increasing   5 influential   6 trial   7 distraction
8 fortunately   9 reasonable   10 technological

Speaking p.13

These are some example answers. Notice they include reasons
for opinions and also give examples.

Do you prefer staying at home to watch a DVD or going to the
cinema?

*I prefer staying at home actually because it means I can stop the
DVD when I want to eat and also I can talk to my friends so it's
more fun.*

Do you listen to American music or do you prefer music from your
country?

*I like music from my country, but most of the time I prefer listening
to American music. It's the music of our generation and it's more
varied than my country's music.*

Which film that you've seen has had the biggest impact on you?

*I think the Star Wars films are the films that have meant most to me
– they show a different life but they have a moral too and when
you watch them you are totally absorbed in the plots.*

Tapescript

Do you prefer staying at home to watch a DVD or going to the
cinema?

*I prefer staying at home actually because it means I can stop the
DVD when I want to eat and also I can talk to my friends so it's
more fun.*

Do you listen to American music or do you prefer music from your
country?

*I like music from my country, but most of the time I prefer listening
to American music. It's the music of our generation and it's more
varied than my country's music.*

Which film that you've seen has had the biggest impact on you?

*I think the Star Wars films are the films that have meant most to
me – they show a different life but they have a moral too and when
you watch them you are totally absorbed in the plots.*

Grammar 2 p.13

1 1 If you meet me at 6 p.m., I'll have got the tickets by then.
2 In my film career, I've had a variety of roles and have
enjoyed/enjoyed them all.
3 I got home that evening and discovered that my DVD
recorder had been stolen.
4 He's finally hanging up his guitar – next month he will have
been singing and recording for twenty years.
5 I've been trying to get a recording contract for months now.
6 They had only been building the film set for ten minutes
when the rain started.

2 1 verbs of feeling: like, love, hate, dislike, prefer
2 verbs of thinking or knowledge: believe, understand, know
3 verbs of possession: possess, belong, own, have, want
4 verbs of sensation: smell, taste, hear, care

Use of English p.13

1 1 have   2 one   3 get   4 how   5 without
6 what   7 having   8 been   9 Although
10 part   11 in   12 at   13 provided   14 worth
15 yourself

Writing p.14

3 2, 3, 5, 7
order: 2, 3 and 7 (may be interlinked), 5

4 2, 3 (all the others are too extreme)

5 1 there were no seats so we had to stand
2 were quite expensive
3 they were not very good
4 you did not deliver what was promised

5 I would like you to refund me.

6 I look forward to hearing from you/I look forward to your immediate response.

6

task	organisation	range	accuracy	register	effect on target reader
cover all the functions required	order the functions appropriately; balance the functions appropriately; use paragraphing and linking words	use a variety of vocabulary; use a variety of structures; use advanced level structures and vocabulary in places	check that structures, vocabulary and spelling are correct	use formal language and a polite tone	make sure the audience has enough information to respond; persuade the audience of your argument

UNIT 2

Reading p.16

1 Text 1: b; text 2: b; text 3: a

2 1 C   2 D   3 A   4 D   5 B   6 C

3 a – text 2; b – text 3; c – text 1

4 Text 1
 a) outstanding balance   d) a deal
 b) monthly repayment   e) staying power
 c) ripped off   f) frugally

 Text 2
 g) rub off   j) bygone era
 h) boost (sales)   k) emulate
 i) exploiting

 Text 3
 l) network   n) flashing
 m) pitfalls   o) develop a thick skin

Vocabulary 1 p.18

1 1 burnt-out   2 one-off   3 hard-up   4 fed-up
 5 run-down   6 built-up   7 well-off   8 worn-out

P	O	N	E	H	A	R	U	P	O
E	R	W	O	R	N	O	U	T	N
H	A	R	D	U	P	T	W	H	E
A	L	L	H	A	L	N	E	O	O
F	L	R	U	I	T	S	L	W	F
E	O	G	U	P	H	K	L	N	F
D	U	B	U	R	N	T	O	U	T
U	T	F	R	E	E	O	F	T	B
P	W	O	R	D	O	F	F	S	U
F	R	U	N	D	O	W	N	S	P

2 1 d   2 c   3 a   4 f   5 b   6 e

3 1 hard-hitting   6 self-made
 2 one-sided   7 mass-produced
 3 short-term   8 old-fashioned
 4 air-conditioned   9 so-called
 5 level-headed
 10 long-standing

Listening p.19

1 • students compared with older people
 • a comment on anti-branding
 • what brands students like
 • what type of products students buy
 • students' views on ethical brands
 • Channel 4's approach to students

2 1 b   2 b   3 a   4 a   5 c   6 d

4 1 b   2 b   3 a   4 b   5 a   6 b

Tapescript

F: Now, Martin, you're an experienced marketing consultant and you claim that students are a very different group of consumers from the rest of us. In what way? Is this because they have less money to spend?

M: (laughs) In fact, students are a lucrative market, with conservative estimates showing that spending for this group is well above £1 billion annually, which makes a whole raft of brands, products and services very keen to get up close and personal with them! And students are a group with a complex relationship to brands. My firm has done some research and has found a lot of similarities globally in behaviour in the typical student age range of eighteen to twenty-one. After university, by around twenty-two to twenty-four, they're getting into jobs and settling down; they're more self-confident and less taken in by brands. The eighteen to twenty-one category, on the other hand, is highly receptive to the presentation of new ideas, but can be critical of advertisers who talk down to them.

F: But there's a lot of talk nowadays about 'anti-branding', isn't there? Do you think that's an important influence?

M: The reality is that we still have those inner drives. When we first meet someone we weigh them up and brands are just a way of putting personality onto inanimate objects. In fact, Naomi Klein's much-hyped work on anti-branding, *No Logo*, has itself become a successful branded product, complete with logo. So maybe it's not so much the concepts of branding, advertising and marketing that offend as the techniques and mechanisms employed.

F: So how does this group of eighteen to twenty-one year olds choose a brand in the first place?

M: Well, clearly advertising plays some part, though less so for this student group than others. To be honest, I think that depends on how intelligent the message is. This age group is open to creating brand allegiances, which are likely to go on for the long term. But interestingly, it's not necessarily for the prestige music and fashion brands. Research on the fifteen to twenty-four age group found top brands for youth mixed up old and new, fashionable and more commonplace. This is because they typically seek out something that sets them apart from their peers and this is the principal motivation for brand selection.

F: So what kinds of products do they spend their money on? Jeans? Sports goods?

M: (laughs) It's not so much the specifics of what they need. This particular age group tends to be very conservative and only spend money on a very restricted set of products. For example, they need food but have no particular brand allegiances there. They spend money on clothes, drinks and music principally. And these are chosen according to what their peers are buying rather than the quality of the product or the cost. That's why companies invest so much in advertising to this group.

F: It's interesting that advertising is claimed as a more important factor than whether the brand is seen to be ethical. I thought students would be interested in supporting ethical products?

M: Yes, they do seem to be the most likely group to do this. The thing is, often ethical products can be hard to access – they're not always sold everywhere – and they can also be more expensive. So, I think the idea behind these products has the sympathy of the students, but they don't vote with their wallets.

F: And finally, Martin, are there any tips for attracting students to a brand?

M: Well, I can give you the example of Channel 4 television. They wanted to attract students and decided to sponsor several music festivals being held over the summer so they could get their name in front of students by aligning themselves to these big music stars. But students are notorious for wanting something for nothing and Channel 4 wanted to give them something to keep hold of which was useful and which was branded with the Channel 4 logo. To this end, they gave out magazines which listed events and had spin-offs like photo books and CD collections that have integrity and, thus, the oh-so-important credibility and authenticity.

F: So, that's … (fade) one way that …

Grammar 1 p.20

1 1 He consulted his bank manager, who told him it would be unwise to take out a loan.
2 Australian dollars and cents, which are completely different from the US notes and coins, were introduced in 1966. Australian dollars and cents, which were introduced in 1966, are completely different from the US notes and coins.
3 Even young children can open bank accounts, which they often maintain for the rest of their lives.
4 Banks carry out extensive market research which / that tends to show that students are attracted by special offers and free gifts.
5 Mortgages, which are special loans for the purchase of a property, are offered by most banks.
6 There are several similarities between the old and new Australian currencies, one of which is the size of some of the coins.
7 I am very impressed with my bank manager, who is always very friendly and helpful.
8 One day I had to do my banking with a new teller who I had never spoken to before.

2 1 Something that worries me is the high interest rate on that loan.
2 She is part of a business group, among whom she is the only woman.
3 I'm opening accounts at two banks whose interest rates are good.
4 It's worth investing in people whose businesses are doing well.

5 The advertising manager whose proposal I like is coming to see me tomorrow.
6 Companies use celebrities who have high profiles to sell their products.

Use of English p.20

1 1 can 2 up 3 about 4 one 5 no 6 with
7 that/which 8 who 9 a 10 where/because
11 never 12 in 13 your 14 despite 15 being

Vocabulary 2 p.21

1

types of ad	
full-page ad pop-ups	product placement flyers logo

audience	
target audience mass-market	consumer

features of an ad	
jingle logo	slogan

location	
hoarding full-page ad media	

2 1 d 2 f 3 a 4 c 5 b 6 e

Use of English p.21

1 1 location
2 graphics
3 increasingly
4 challenging
5 overpriced
6 uneconomical/uneconomic
7 investment
8 possibilities
9 resentful
10 intrusion

Speaking p.22

W: Ok, we have to decide first what method we think is most effective, don't we? Personally I think television is because its got colour, sound and the ads can be interesting.

M: I'm not sure I agree – I read magazines a lot and the ads do sink in even though I'm only reading the articles.

W: It seems a boring way to advertise, but I suppose a lot of people do read magazines so I'm happy to go along with that.

M: Now, what's the best way to advertise a CD? Well, I'd say radio again cos its' music!

W: Hmm … You may be right. But I'd go for instore promotions actually cos you've got the customers there.

M: Not sure I completely agree but I can see it might work well. (fade)

Grammar 2 p.22

1 1 We pay by direct debit three times the / a year.
2 I need to go to the / zero bank to close my account.
3 Apparently he's an / the excellent accountant and comes highly recommended.

4 Where's <u>the</u> / a cheque book that I gave you yesterday?
5 They said they would pay me for <u>an</u> / a hour's overtime.
6 When she went to the / <u>0</u> university, the fees were very expensive.

2 1 θ   2 a / the   3 θ   4 a   5 the
      6 a   7 the   8 the   9 the   10 the

3 1 goods   5 the means
      2 the information   6 the times
      3 the news   7 the power
      4 politics   8 a bank

Writing p.23

2 • reasons for choosing a holiday
      • reasons for choosing a car
      • what you think she should do
      • sympathy for your friend's problem
        order:
      • sympathy for your friend's problem
      • reasons for choosing a holiday and reasons for choosing a car
        (in either order; may be mixed together)
      • what you think she should do

3 sympathy for your friend's problem   20–30   1 point
      reasons for choosing a holiday   100   3 points with
                                                    reasons
      reasons for choosing a car   100   3 points with
                                                    reasons
      what you think she should do   30–40   2 points

4

Dear Sam,

<u>Lucky you</u>! I wish I had some money saved. I think you've done very well to save some money. I can understand you're confused about what to do.

If you have a holiday, <u>it'll be</u> a good idea because you say you <u>haven't</u> had one for ages and it will make you nice and relaxed before you start your hard studies at college. You've been working hard and everybody <u>needs a break</u>. At the same time, your life at college may be much easier if you've got a car and <u>you won't get</u> the chance to save the money again so <u>I can see why</u> you want to use the money for a car.

If I were you, <u>what I would do is</u> have a short break somewhere cheap, such as camping with some friends so you can relax, but then <u>I'd save</u> most of the money for a cheap car. <u>Why don't you</u> just buy something small and second-hand as you <u>won't</u> be driving long distances? <u>Actually</u>, you may want to think about whether or not you do really need a car. Isn't there a good bus or train service where you live? If you have a car at college, <u>you'll always be giving</u> your friends lifts and it could make <u>you fed up</u>.

I think a holiday is the most important thing and if you have enough for a car then <u>that'll</u> be good, but I don't think <u>it's</u> essential. <u>Write and let me know what you decide to do</u>!

Love
Mina

UNIT 3

Listening p.24

1a My friend <u>stopped talking</u> to me.
      My friend <u>stole</u> my <u>girlfriend</u>.
      My friend <u>became</u> very <u>jealous</u> of me.
      My friend <u>copied</u> everything I did.
      My friend got very <u>angry</u> with me.
      My friend <u>got me into trouble</u> at <u>work</u>.
      My friend always <u>asked</u> me for <u>money</u>.
      My friend <u>asked</u> me to <u>lie</u> for him.

1b stopped – no longer
      talking – speaking
      stole – took
      girlfriend – went out with
      became – started to be
      jealous – envious
      copied – did the same
      angry – cross
      got me into trouble – made a problem
      work – job
      money – cash

2 1 D   2 C   3 H   4 A   5 G   6 F   7 B
      8 A   9 H   10 D

Tapescript

Speaker one (female)
I hate having arguments and falling out with friends – it makes me really uncomfortable. I had a schoolfriend who was always in trouble, but I quite liked her until she suddenly changed and started wearing what I wore and taking up the same hobbies as me. It drove me mad. I didn't know what to do. I spoke to my sister who was a bit unsympathetic but my mother overheard me and told me to try talking to my friend about it. In the end I did and I asked another schoolfriend along for support and it was all sorted out. We're all still friends now.

Speaker two (male)
I don't think in general blokes have rows with their mates – it's never really happened to me. Except when I was younger – at school one of my mates always had loads of money and the girls loved him so I was surprised when he started saying nasty things about me. My other mates said it was because he resented me and envied me because I was better looking than him! It got quite bad, even the teachers noticed. But then he started going out with my sister and it was as if that made him feel he'd got his own back so it settled down after that.

Speaker three (female)
They always say you never really know people and I realised that when a very old friend of mine wanted some time off work. She got her boss to call me and I had to say I'd been ill and she was looking after me. I was quite angry that she'd put me in that position so I spoke to someone in my office about it. He seemed to think it was ok, but when I talked to my family, my uncle said it was my fault for agreeing to it and I shouldn't blame my friends for my weaknesses! He was right.

Speaker four (male)
Oh, once one of my mates went through a very funny period – sometimes you'd phone him and he was ok and other times he

wasn't. Eventually he gave up communicating with me completely. I assumed I'd done something to make him cross but later that year I got rather down and when I was talking to the doctor he said quite a lot of young people get depressed and do just want to be on their own. I realised then that must have been what my mate felt so I called him and he was really pleased to hear from me.

Speaker five (female)

It's awful falling out with friends. It's happened to me on more than one occasion, like when a mate of mine went through a strange period where she got very jealous of everybody else and it ended in her trying to keep up with all these rich types. She kept borrowing cash off me but couldn't pay it back. I had to confront her about it and when I met her, her uncle was with her. I didn't know him and I assumed he was there to support her but, in the end, he was the one who made her realise she had to pay me back.

Vocabulary 1 p.24

1

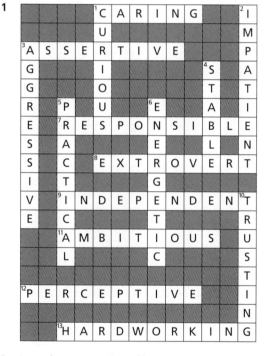

2 1 modest 3 stubborn 5 open-minded
2 frank 4 discerning 6 obstinate

Use of English p.25

1 1 D 2 A 3 B 4 A 5 C 6 D 7 A 8 B
9 C 10 D 11 A 12 B 13 C 14 A 15 B

Reading p.26

1 c

2 1 C 2 D 3 A 4 B 5 B 6 C 7 A

3 1 b 2 a 3 a 4 b 5 a 6 b 7 b

Grammar 1 p.28

1 1 f 2 c 3 a 4 b 5 e
6 i 7 d 8 g 9 h

2 1 might 5 should
2 wouldn't 6 can't
3 could 7 may
4 must 8 needn't

3 1 must 7 can't
2 should 8 might/may
3 should 9 can
4 can't 10 must
5 must 11 might/may
6 can't 12 must

Vocabulary 2 p.29

1 1 d 2 f 3 b 4 h 5 a 6 g 7 c 8 e

2 1 fell for 5 falling out with
2 broken up with 6 stand up to
3 getting fed up with 7 taken to
4 go for 8 get on with

Speaking p.29

In the first picture <u>it looks as if</u> the couple are very much in love. <u>It's possible that</u> they've only just met as <u>it seems</u> they are quite fascinated with each other. <u>Maybe</u> they are thinking of getting married and of their life in front of them. The other couple also look happy – <u>they must feel</u> very comfortable with each other. <u>I would think</u> they've been married a very long time and <u>I guess</u> that must make them fond of each other. <u>I suppose</u> it's normal that in the early days of a relationship people are very happy and excited, but then, as time goes on, if they stay together <u>I imagine</u> that feeling of excitement gets replaced by affection for each other and the feeling that you know each other very well.

Tapescript

(female)

In the first picture it looks as if the couple are very much in love. It's possible that they've only just met as it seems they are quite fascinated with each other. Maybe they're thinking of getting married and of their life in front of them. The older couple also look happy – they must feel very comfortable with each other. I would think they've been married a very long time and I guess that that must make them fond of each other. I suppose it's normal that in the early days of a relationship people are very happy and excited, but then, as time goes on, if they stay together I imagine that that feeling of excitement gets replaced by affection for each other and the feeling that you know each other very well. The couple with children must be close but perhaps they are very distracted by the children.

(60 seconds at slightly slower than native speed)

Grammar 2 p.30

1

followed by *to*	followed by *-ing*	followed by *to* or *-ing* with little or no change in meaning
manage want cause agree allow plan expect design decide attempt able use hope	enjoy suggest avoid	start prefer like

2 1 staying
  2 to become
  3 decorating
  4 seeing
  5 meeting
  6 dancing
  7 to speak
  8 writing

Use of English p.30

1 1 She said she'd come round so **she must be** on her way now.
  2 I **wish he had been able to** come / I **wish he could have** come.
  3 I **succeeded in finishing** the preparations in time.
  4 You **don't have to** call him as he already knows about it.
  5 When he spoke to me he agreed that **it wasn't my fault**.
  6 She didn't want **to take part in** the singing.
  7 Anya didn't come to the dinner yesterday evening, so **she must have been** ill.
  8 The **chances are she'll** end up marrying him.

Writing p.31

2 3 a lot of people you don't know – the contribution will be for the book, which will be read by lots of people

3 3 a section of a book

4 • what you think is the general or typical opinion
  • supporting reasons for a general or typical opinion
  • the name of the country you are referring to
  • your opinion supported by general facts

5 In the UK attitudes to older people are not very positive, and this has been the case for a while, but these attitudes may change in the future as the population gets older.

It is clear that not everybody thinks the same, but there are certainly many negative attitudes to older people in the UK. This can be seen in the way that people are cared for when they are older in that they are often put into homes or left on their own rather than living with their families. Many families do not seem to consider that older people have any wisdom or anything to offer them and think that visiting the older members of their family is a duty rather than a pleasure. At the same time, many older people also find it harder to get jobs because companies are less willing to employ them.

However, in the future I think attitudes to older people will begin to change. The population in the UK is getting older, so younger people will be in the minority and will become more dependent on older people. Also many older people in the UK are very active and even do extreme sports or travel to faraway places, so this will make younger people think differently about them.

Overall, I would say there are negative attitudes to older people in the UK, but there are signs that this is changing and that attitudes in the future will be more positive.

UNIT 4

Reading p.32

1 a G   b A   c D   d B   e E   f C   g F
2 1 F   2 B   3 G   4 C   5 A   6 D
3 b
4 1 complex   4 kidney
  2 widespread   5 fixed
  3 received
5 It seems that the older we get as a society, the harder we are all trying to look youthful.

Cosmetic surgery and other anti-ageing **procedures** like Botox are booming. Even at a very conservative estimate, Britons are spending £225 million a year on such procedures, about half of which are concerned with trying to look younger.

Wendy Lewis, a beauty consultant, explains this by saying, 'Cosmetic surgery is an **epidemic** today. It is exploding [and] the desire for youth, beauty and perfection shows no signs of slowing down.' Simon Withey of the British Association of Aesthetic Plastic Surgeons says all aspects of cosmetic surgery are becoming more popular, for various reasons – among them that people are feeling an intense social pressure to look younger, especially in certain types of work.

'We get quite a lot of people who are in the media or very competitive jobs in the City, and they just feel as soon as they look a bit tired, that these younger guys and younger women are snapping at their heels, trying to chase them out of their jobs. There still is this feeling that youth and beauty is rewarded in some way in society, and I think it actually is.'

But is this situation going to change? Surely as the population ages further over coming decades, we are going to start accepting our looks and seeing old as beautiful? Angus McGrouther, Professor of Plastic and Reconstructive Surgery at Manchester University and the UK's first professor of plastic surgery, thinks that fundamental changes in society means the cosmetic surgery genie will never be put back in the bottle.

'The respect for the **wisdom** of ages has gone. What people have got to do is look competitive with other people in the marketplace. People will change their jobs several times in their lifetime, and move to a new local area when they retire. So to be accepted into all these new groups, judgements are made on appearance. All these pressures fit together.'

However, the number of people 'having things done' to look younger remains small.

A recent survey by TGI, published by Keynote Research, found that only 7 percent of all women would even consider having a facelift, and 4 percent of men a hair **transplant**, while only 11 percent of women would consider having Botox, and 4 percent of men.

Tim Westall of marketing consultancy April Strategy doesn't see <u>this</u> changing, but he thinks it is possible that society will start projecting a 'more mature expression of beauty' as we get older, although it is more likely it will express <u>contradictory attitudes</u> to age.

'There are <u>two</u> **mindsets** that operate, two attitudinal camps,' he says. 'One is about seeking physical perfection – 'the L'Oreal woman'. There's another which is about beauty from within, about your radiance being the **embodiment of** your life and your spirit and your character – don't over-adorn, and don't mask.'

Robert Diamond of the Diametric marketing consultancy <u>concurs</u> that we will probably see contradictory images of beauty and maturity in future, as advertisers **wake up to** the potential value of the over-50s' market.

'Expect the beauty industry to continue to focus on youth,' <u>he</u> says. 'But expect smart marketers to talk about "making the best of who you are" rather than trying to make you become someone different. **Take-up of** cosmetic surgery falls after 45 – older women are more interested in looking good for their age than trying to look a different age,' he says.

Continuing innovation in techniques and products available <u>also appears likely to have an impact</u>, with procedures becoming ever more simple, cheap – and therefore appealing. 'Treatments have become less risky, easier, in many cases more affordable and **accessible to** everyone,' says Wendy Lewis. 'People are looking to start early, have smaller things done in bundles, and ease into the ageing process without necessarily looking like they have had work done.'

Even if we do still see youth as the main **indicator of** beauty, and continue nipping, tucking, abrading and filling, is that necessarily a bad thing? Professor McGrouther wonders if <u>it may be a positive sign</u>.

'If people are living longer, healthier, happier lives, and their concerns are being spread to things like controlling weight, exercise, smoking, etc. – if it's making people happy at the end of the day, and it's not harming anybody else, <u>then that seems good</u>,' he said. 'In fact, I think some of the things we accepted in the past were probably wrong, such as that people should sit down in their carpet slippers when they reach a certain age.'

Vocabulary 1 p.34

1 1a) breakthrough
2a) diagnosis
2b) symptoms
3 advances
4 scans

If you answered 1a, 2b, 3b, 4b you are suspicious about the benefits of science.

If you answered 1b, 2a, 3a, 4a you are very sympathetic to science and approve of research.

If your answers were mixed then you feel ambivalent about science.

2 1 truth
2 reality
3 reflection
4 powerful
5 likely
6 powered
7 weight
8 trainer
9 director

3 1 assembly   2 monitor   3 revelation
4 contemplation   5 device

4 1 delivered a warning
2 go one better
3 ravages of time
4 take its toll

5 homeopathy   acupuncture   chiropractic   aromatherapy

Listening p.35

1 a explaining   b complaining

2 1 B   2 C   3 B   4 C   5 A   6 A

3 1 a   2 a   3 b   4 a   5 b   6 b

Tapescript

M = Male   F = Female

Extract One

You hear two people talking about an old television programme.

M: Do you remember that old TV programme, *The Six Million Dollar Man*?

F: Oh yeah, where the bloke had loads of himself replaced with bionic limbs and things that could do anything. Brilliant idea!

M: I saw they were thinking of remaking it but I hope they don't. It always had the same plots and I thought it was all too far-fetched myself. The bloke who acted the main part never did anything else, did he?

F: Dunno. You know that programme was very like that new one about the man who's got robotic arms and legs.

M: Is it?

F: The same old science stuff – you'd think things would have moved on a bit in the TV world. But I suppose what it shows is that we like familiarity so the old ideas sell best. I get really fed up with stuff on television – there's nothing really creative any more. I watch DVDs instead!

Extract Two

You hear part of a radio interview with a woman who is attending a science conference.

M: I'm now speaking to Marlene Sharp who's attending the conference as an ordinary business woman. Marlene, are you happy with the conference?

F: Yes, I think so. I've never been to this one before so I wasn't sure what it'd be like – I had heard that the speakers can be very variable, with some being excellent and others mediocre. I have to say I'm very impressed with how smoothly it's running and the information we've been given. There's a huge programme. Normally conferences tend to have a theme or focus, so this one is unique because it does cover so much ground.

M: And why did you come? To meet other people?

F: Well, that's a side benefit, I have to say, though they're often in a different sector from me, but I have now got an impressive list of contacts! I think it's very useful when you're in marketing, which I am, to see the various ways in which you can go about doing a talk and engaging people. I'm hoping to pick up some tips! Must dash now.

Extract Three

You hear two people on a science programme talking abut genetics.

F: So are you saying that you now approve of genetic research whereas you didn't before?

M: Yes, I am. You see, I used to be concerned about the way projects were organised and controlled, but I had to write an article about one for a paper a few months ago – I did quite an in-depth study – and I realised, however chaotic the funding is, the work is good and useful and could have enormously beneficial results. And there are more and more programmes now and I think that's good.

F: Hmm, not sure I completely agree with you. I know there's a lot of public funding for the programmes so the scientists *are* accountable to the government, but I'm not sure that'll always be the case. The big companies will get more and more involved if they think it will add to their profits in the long run. If you look back, the pace of change is increasing, so we do need to sort out some much more detailed guidelines for any new projects.

Grammar 1 p.36

1 a) ii   b) iv   c) iii   d) i

2 a) 7   b) 2   c) 5   d) 6   e) 4   f) 3   g) 1

3 1a   2a   3a   4b   5b

Use of English p.36

1 1 lift   2 conduct   3 living   4 stick   5 pack

Vocabulary 2 p.37

1

2 1 eye   2 ears   3 nose   4 fingers   5 eye
6 ear   7 finger

1 b   2 d   3 f   4 e   5 g   6 a   7 c

Grammar 2 p.38

1 1 Provided that   4 Even if
2 Were   5 Supposing that
3 As long as   6 Only if

2 1 **Imagine you had never studied** to be a doctor, what would you have been?

2 **Supposing you won the lottery, would** you give up working?

3 **Had I / If I had realised I could** catch malaria, I would have taken some tablets.

4 **Were I / If I were to have** a facelift, what would you think?

5 **Should you / If you should need any help**, do not hesitate to call.

Use of English p.38

1 1 He **might have been late** because he got stuck in traffic.

2 I'll **do the analysis as long as** you clear up the lab.

3 You **must pay back all the money** if the project is not completed.

4 The actress **confessed to having had** Botox injections.

5 He said **he was out of practice at** performing surgery.

6 I **suggest you speak / speaking** to a consultant first.

7 I **wouldn't (not) have invited you if** I thought you didn't want to come.

8 Are you aware that **you are in danger of failing** your exams?

Speaking p.39

Rosa is the better candidate because she does all the things in the list.

Tapescript

E: Do you think we should consider alternative medicine, Stefan?

Stefan: (*said in rather monotonous tone*) Yes, I think so. I think it can be useful for certain illnesses and can help people feel better that they don't have to take loads of medicine. If people feel better then it's good.

E: What about you, Rosa?

Rosa: (*good, lively intonation*) I think it's a *very* good idea. I think people have depended on traditional medicine for too long and it can't cure everything. And there are several possibilities for alternative medicine now. Sometimes traditional medicines can make you ill whereas alternative therapies don't have these problems.

Writing p.39

2 Explain what you thought about the conference
Give your reasons why
Persuade other students to attend

3 Yes it does
para 1: engaging the reader and saying what article is about
paras 2 and 3: good things about the conference with reasons
para 4: criticism of the conference with reasons
para 5: summary and persuading reader to attend

4 b (a is inaccurate and c is boring)

5 It is written in an informal, chatty style (reports and essays should be written in formal or unmarked register).

It gives a very personal view of the speaker and uses emotive language (e.g. *brilliant*). (Reports and essays do need the writer to give a view but in a less personal way.)

UNIT 5

Vocabulary 1 p.40

1 We offer a range of sports all taught by *professionals* /
amateurs who have worked in the sport for several years and
offer expert *instructing* / *coaching*. We offer trial days where we
provide you with the *kit* / *uniform* and you can practise getting
that ball into the back of the *box* / *net*! Come and give it a go!

We're giving our *spectators* / *audience* the opportunity to
umpire / *referee* a football match! All you have to do is control
the game and the players with your *whistle* / *blower*, such as
when you spot a *block* / *foul* and to keep the time. Come along
on Saturday and give it a go, if you think you're brave enough!

2

K	P	B	E	M	O	C	F	A	D	R	E	C	O	R
C	L	O	S	E	M	O	U	L	L	O	S	R	Y	U
M	A	L	A	S	T	M	I	N	U	T	E	A	L	C
O	Y	O	P	E	A	E	W	S	P	E	T	B	C	K
B	E	F	A	T	K	B	A	C	L	A	P	S	E	E
A	L	L	T	O	G	A	S	P	O	M	R	A	N	L
L	S	M	I	N	T	C	M	A	N	P	R	O	S	O
S	E	T	B	A	C	K	I	Y	W	L	A	S	T	M
O	C	G	C	F	A	C	N	E	S	A	L	S	R	A
R	O	R	K	U	T	R	U	C	E	Y	I	W	O	R
A	R	O	A	L	S	E	T	A	R	E	C	O	R	D
N	D	N	P	L	A	Y	E	Y	E	R	K	B	R	E

1	also-ran	3	come-back	5	team-player
2	set-back	4	last-minute	6	set a record

3

1	score / saved / draw	4	race / finishing
2	serve / volleyed	5	caught
3	tackle		

4 circuit: Formula 1
course: golf
court: tennis
pitch: rugby
rink: ice skating
stadium: football

Grammar 1 p.41

1 slightly   absolutely   rather   relatively   fairly
terribly   really   completely   quite   totally
incredibly   unbelievably

gradable, e.g. cold	non-gradable, e.g. freezing	both
slightly	absolutely	really
rather	completely	
relatively	totally	
fairly	really	
terribly		
really		
quite		
incredibly		
unbelievably		

2 a) ii   b) vi   c) iv   d) i   e) iii   f) v

3
1. entirely believable
2. utterly miserable
3. greatly increased
4. highly distinguished
5. significantly different
6. fully booked

4 1 C   2 B   3 C   4 C   5 A   6 B   7 A
8 B   9 C   10 B

Reading p.42

1 1 B   2 D   3 E   4 A   5 C

2 a) vi   b) v   c) vii   d) i   e) iii   f) viii
g) iv   h) ii

3 1 D   2 B   3 A   4 C   5 E   6 A   7 E
8 B   9 C   10 D   11 A   12 E   13 D
14 B   15 C

4

1	figure it out	4	put it in perspective
2	shake it off	5	look up to
3	turn it round	6	get tough

Listening p.44

1

2	reason	5	suggestion
3	reason (why not)	6	purpose
4	reason		

2 1 D   2 B   3 C   4 B   5 D   6 C

Tapescript

I: Good morning. Today I have with me Michael Forbin, who is
a sports correspondent with *The Sporting Herald*. You're here
to talk to us about the amount of money that footballers are
paid – something which upsets a lot of people.

MF: (*laughs*) Yes, that's right. Good morning. Yes, there's been a
lot of heated debate about footballers' pay and the level of
money swilling around in football generally. The sums are
now so huge that that has become a problem in itself.
Television companies pay the clubs handsomely, and justify
their expenditure by saturating viewers with matches. The
accusation is that these are mostly poor performances which
will turn people off – but I think this concern is unfounded.
More valid is the claim that ticket prices, and the replica kits,
are inflated by the cost of footballers' wages and this, in turn,
means fewer spectators. We often hear comments that it's no
longer a working man's game, but I just think that's a sign of
the times as society changes. And it remains to be seen if the
focus on televised matches at national level reduces interest in
international games.

I: But how did we arrive at this point? Where's all this money
come from?

MF: Oooh, a tricky one. Um …… there is no doubt that
footballers have a very real talent in what is today the biggest
sport in the world, so some argue that pay levels are a result
of this. And certainly if, as a club, you wish to keep quality
players, then you have to reward them well to make them
stay. The truth is that millions of people want to watch
football – and they can't all get to matches – so there is a
huge viewing audience. It is this market that has dictated the
economics of the game. Individually the players can earn a
massive amount through advertising contracts, but this is true
in any sport nowadays.

I: But many people feel that footballers' salaries are *not* justified, don't they?

MF: Very true. You can see why it gets people's hackles up. Many people argue that rat catchers and other people who do anti-social work are more useful to society and should be paid more than our so-called celebrities! And it may seem as if footballers are paid a lot for doing very little – a bit of training and turning up to play on Saturday. I think where the argument against them does gain ground is in saying that the clubs at the top don't bother helping those further down the league, so it does look like greed. After all, who can spend £100,000 a week? Others complain that players don't deserve the money when they start behaving badly – getting into fights and so on – when they have so many young fans, but this applies to very few and rather misses the point.

I: So do *you* think their salaries are justified then?

MF: I don't really have a view either way, but I know some people who do feel the sums are justified. They used to present the argument about how footballers only play for five years and the fact that a lot of them start at 15 so have no other qualifications. Today, though, the rationale for that view is that they are under a lot of pressure, facing thousands of fans every week. I mean, it's up to them if they live their lives in the media, but, regardless of that, they are watched carefully for just doing what they do. None of us has a job like that.

I: So do you think there is a solution or will it just go on and on?

MF: Yes, there is a serious debate now about this and proposals include performance-related pay or salaries based on the number of spectators – say, for example, a percentage of the takings on the gate. I would favour something where the money paid to the clubs by the TV companies is proportioned out across the league, but some have suggested we introduce a formalised pay system with a cap on the maximum a player can earn. I'd like to see the figures before I decide on that one.

I: Well, given the huge profits there are at the moment, can they be used more productively, do you think?

MF: Oh, yes, I definitely think this should be addressed and there is much discussion about it at the moment because of the lack of coaching and facilities for children interested in sports. Leisure centres are being closed down and sports fields are lost to building projects, so it's a real issue. I have to say, I think the government has some responsibility there. But there's no reason why players couldn't have reduced wages and the money go towards getting talented players in less developed countries into sports colleges. Another possibility is the excess income of the top clubs being put into the pot to create similar wages for footballers in every country, but I'm less keen on this idea.

I: Right, well now we'll ask callers what they think … *(fade)*

Vocabulary 2 p.44

1
1	illegal	5	disqualified
2	inappropriate	6	outnumbered
3	anti-social	7	immodest
4	unappreciated	8	overpaid

Use of English p.45

1
1	manufacturer	6	prosperous
2	assessment	7	inability
3	unfortunate	8	optimistic
4	occasional	9	action
5	irresponsible	10	sporting

Speaking p.45

1 In my opinion … ✔

Would you go along with that? ✔	I'm not sure I agree … ✔
And what else? ✔	Right, are we agreed then?
What I mean is …	How do you see it? ✔
Is that ok with you? ✔	Shall we say … ✔

2

giving an opinion	asking the other person for their view	coming to a conclusion
In my opinion …	Would you go along with that?	So, have we decided?
What I mean is …	And what else?	Right, are we agreed then?
I'm not sure I agree	How do you see it?	Shall we say …
		Is that OK with you?

Tapescript

M: Ok, let's start with this one, shall we? In my opinion, winning is a huge benefit from sport – it makes you feel good. How do you see it?

F: Yeah, I agree. And team spirit. What I mean is, it gives you a great feeling to be in a team, to be part of something. Would you go along with that?

M: Yeah. Then having someone to look up to I think is really important in your teens and of course making your parents proud – it's something everybody wants to do.

F: I'm not sure I agree with that so much. But I think fitness is a real benefit as it stays with you in your normal life. And what else?

M: Um … well, of course, it's nice to have lots of girls or boys your own age admiring you – it can give you confidence. And one thing sport does give you is concentration and focus and that can help you in exams and at work.

F: Ok, so what do you think are the biggest benefits then? Shall we say fitness and concentration?

M: Er, what about fitness and team spirit? I think that's more important. Is that ok with you?

F: Yeah, ok. So are we agreed then?

M: Yeah.

Grammar 2 p.46

1
1	the most boring	5	far less healthy
2	much fitter	6	as young as
3	nearly as well known as	7	near enough
4	much earlier than		

2 2 Climbers don't earn enough to live on.
3 Fencers earn considerably less than surfers.
4 Riders earn by far the most/the highest salary.

5 Fencers earn too little to get by.
6 The biggest / highest earning sport is riding.
7 Climbers don't earn nearly as much as surfers.
8 The more prestigious the sport, the higher the salary.

Use of English p.46

1 1 in   2 enough   3 not   4 less   5 take
6 every / each   7 more   8 long   9 mean
10 their   11 of   12 Other   13 likes   14 large
15 into

Writing p.47

1 The sports centre you attend is concerned that it is not
attracting enough young people to join in with competitive
sports. You have been asked to write a report for the
management committee <u>detailing why members are not taking
part in competitive sports</u>, and <u>providing suggestions for
encouraging them to do so</u>.

4 sections:
an introduction (stating aims)
a section on why members are not taking part
a section on recommendations
a conclusion

2 c (a is too general; b covers only half of the report contents)

3 a) Current situation
b) Recommendations
c) Conclusion

4 Students want to socialise, so sports competitions should be run
at times when as many as possible can participate and watch.
<u>At present they happen on Saturdays when many students are
reluctant to give up time to attend an event</u> – this should be
changed.
The changing rooms around the swimming pool must be
improved for those who are currently discouraged from using
them <u>because of the state they are in</u>.
The college could run teams for different year groups and offer
a prize annually. <u>This would provide motivation</u> as everyone likes
to be a winner.
Most importantly, <u>students lack information</u> and should be
made more aware of the importance of sport for health and
well-being. I recommend that leaflets should be circulated as
part of an overall fitness awareness campaign.

5 Number 4 is not true

UNIT 6

Listening p.48

1 a iii   b v   c i   d viii   e vii   f ii   g vi   h iv
2 1 F   2 G   3 D   4 C   5 H   6 G
7 E   8 C   9 B   10 F

3 a down ii   e gathering i
b way vii   f hand vi
c knit iii   g there iv
d go v

4 1 hit it off   3 tied up with
2 get together   4 make it up

Tapescript

Speaker One (male)
We're such a huge family, there's hundreds of us – nieces, nephews,
cousins, uncles – but funnily enough we've never really got on that
well. I've had an up and down relationship with my aunt's son, who
I used to be quite close to when I was small. But we live in different
parts of the country and when we do meet up we never hit it off
nowadays. It doesn't particularly bother me, except I suspect it's
because he doesn't have a very good opinion of me and I'd like to
know what that is! I might challenge him on it one day at some
family gathering.

Speaker Two (female)
Oh, we've got a really complicated family. Both my mum's sisters
have married again so there's all the step-families as well! I suppose
I get on best with my sister's husband – he's quite a nice bloke and
very easy to talk to, so we're pretty close. He's helped me with a lot
of things and when I had a big argument with my mum about my
being more independent, he told me how I should tackle it. I didn't
do what he told me and I'm regretting it now as mum seems to be
winning! I'll get my own way in the end though!

Speaker Three (female)
I'd like a big family – mine's very small because my father was an
only child, my mum's parents are no longer alive and my husband's
from a small family too. It does mean that our relationships are
really important to us and we do make the effort to be kind to each
other. My husband's dad has married again so, although we've
always got on well, we don't see much of him because he's tied up
with another family. But he's been ill recently and has been relying
on us a bit more so I want to give him a hand when he comes out
of hospital and see if we can get closer again.

Speaker Four (male)
I'm not a great family person actually. I was close to my aunts and
cousins when I was younger, but I don't see much of them now. I
suppose it's down to how much you rely on your family. My father
was always away a lot on business, so I've always relied more on my
mother. Not that long ago we fell out and it was all my fault, so I
haven't seen much of her since. I wish we could make up but she's
not prepared to listen to me and I miss her wise words and advice.
But I suppose now my friends are more important to me really.

Speaker Five (male)
I think family is important – doesn't matter where you live as long
as you speak to each other regularly. We're quite a close-knit family
– even distant cousins get together for regular family events.
We find it quite funny talking about all the connections. My
grandmother died recently and since then my dad and I have been
really close. I think he fell out with my Gran and regrets it, so now
he says it's important to be kind and caring to all your relatives. I
mean, friends are very important to me, but they come and go,
whereas I know Dad's always there for me and will help if he can.

Vocabulary 1 p.49

1 People have been constantly fascinated by twins – our sense of
self is so strong that we are riveted by the notion that you can
have somebody else who appears exactly the same as you.
Studies *with* / *into* twins and their behaviour have focused on
the role that genes have *in* / *on* determining qualities such as
optimism, religiousity, etc. According *by* / *to* many of these

studies, the environment has a greater impact *with* / *on* behaviour than previously thought and much time has been spent on looking at precisely what behaviour is dictated *on* / *by* our upbringing and what *on* / *by* our genes. Studying twins, brought up separately and apart, allows researchers to decide *about* / *on* the balance in the nature vs nurture debate. Personally, I'm more convinced *by* / *with* the nature argument – but this could lead *to* / *for* families round the country blaming themselves for the faults in their children!

2   A in   B for   C with   D from   E on
    F to   G about

3   1   congratulate me on   5   influence on
    2   confessed to   6   suffers from
    3   apply for   7   worry about
    4   specialise in

4   1 up   2 up   3 with   4 on   5 for   6 by
    7 about (with)   8 for   9 to   10 from

    phrasal verbs:
    1 show up   2 grown up   4 get on

Grammar 1 p.50

1   1 a   2 b   3 b   4 b   5 a
    6 b   7 a   8 b   9 b

2   1   could have   5   hadn't got married
    2   hadn't got   6   started
    3   waited   7   didn't live
    4   would visit   8   had had

3   a)   – feeling sad about an event or action that has happened =
         1, 2, 3, 5, 6
         – a polite formal way to express refusal = 4
    b)   – past 1, 2, 3 (NB: although the wedding is in the future, the
         regret is about 'agreeing', which is in the past), 5, 6
         – present / future 4
    c)   = 4 *regret* + infinitive, because it refers to the present or
         future time
    d)   no, they both mean the same and refer to the same time

4   1   regrets / regretted not being / having been
    2   regret to say
    3   regret telling / having told
    4   regret taking / having taken

5   1   I wish my brother wouldn't borrow / wouldn't keep
         borrowing my clothes.
    2   If only I could travel round the world.
    3   I wish I had a bigger family.
    4   I'd rather we had a big wedding.
    5   It's time my sister got a job!
    6   I wish I had called my dad to apologise.
    7   If only I hadn't worked when the kids were young.
    8   Suppose we buy dad a present together?

Vocabulary 2 p.51

1

2   1 allusion   2 personal   3 proceed   4 seized
    5 confidant   6 suspected   7 accept   8 all ready

Use of English p.51

1   1   She waved until the train **was out of sight.**
    2   I **wish I hadn't spoken** to him like that.
    3   I'm phoning **on behalf of** my son, who is ill.
    4   She **must have gone** to the party.
    5   **It's high time she got him** to do more housework
    6   I was **under the impression** you wanted me to invite him.
    7   We need to know what **role genes play / have in
         determining** behaviour.
    8   I **have nothing in common with** Javier.

Reading p.52

1   2   a disadvantage for   5   to show that
    3   to illustrate   6   mean
    4   Before

2   1 A   2 C   3 C   4 A   5 B   6 C

3   a) ii   b) iii   c) i

4   1   a (a = L; b = M)   3   b (a = L; b = M)
    2   a (a = M; b = L)   4   b (a = L; b = M)

5

colloquial language	academic language
picky	trace
moody	mobility
bossy	corroborating
cheerleaders	verify
check out	

Use of English p.54

1 1 their   2 why   3 not   4 When   5 the
6 who   7 so   8 about   9 however   10 such
11 despite   12 be   13 on   14 case   15 order

2 It is a fact of modern life that in Europe and the USA people are having fewer children than (1) ….. parents and grandparents <u>did</u>. In the States the current birth rate is 2.1 children per woman. In Europe the average is 1.5 children per woman. So (2) ….. is <u>this</u> happening? In a recent poll, many people said that they wanted to have more children but they believe that they could (3) ….. afford <u>to</u>. (4) ….. they were asked how many children they intended to have, some people said one child, though (5) ….. majority said two ^. Of course, some people (6) ….. want to have children are unable to do <u>so</u>. One woman told researchers she was worried (8) ….. not having enough money to pay for their education. Another family said that they had had a lot of children because they were considered a benefit to the farm they lived on. In the city, (9) ….. , children are not (10) ….. an obvious benefit as <u>this</u>. The additional cost ^ means that many young men are not keen to have lots of children (11) ….. the fact that their wives may well <u>be</u>. A further reason is that some young people, in these countries especially, are worried that their families may split up and do not want to inflict <u>this</u> (13) ….. their children. It is also the (14) ….. that, increasingly in Europe and the USA, both halves of the couple have to work in (15) ….. to maintain the lifestyle that they want for their children.

Ellipses:
^ = children   ^ = of having children

Grammar 2 p.54

1 1 So am I.   4 If you can't, I will.
2 So have I.   5 So do I.
3 I'd love to.   6 Neither do I.

2a a) iii   b) iv   c) i   d) vi   e) ii   f) v

2b ii) <u>That</u>'s why I go <u>there</u> so often.
iii) If you want to ^.
iv) I don't know how ^.
v) <u>Such</u> behaviour is unacceptable.
vi) I hope <u>not</u>.

Writing p.54

2 • the name of a person
• a description of the person's character
• information about any connection this person has with children
• why this person would be better than other nominees

4 b

5 & 6 Language of persuasion is underlined. Reasons are in bold (10 reasons).

I would like to nominate Angelina Jolie as an ambassador for children.

Angelina Jolie is a famous Hollywood film star and she would make an excellent ambassador for children for several reasons. First of all, she is **very famous** so wherever she went to talk about children or represent them, people <u>would pay attention</u> because they know her. Secondly, she is **very beautiful** so she

would make people notice her and any children she met <u>would like</u> her a lot. Thirdly, she is **famous for travelling** the world **and adopting children** from all over the world. Not only does **she love children** and have their interests at heart, but also **she is very conscious of the problem** for children in different parts of the world. In addition, she is **very rich** so she <u>could undertake</u> a lot of tasks herself without much need to be funded.

Angelina Jolie <u>should be selected</u> because she <u>would be</u> **better than the alternatives**. A sports person <u>may not be popular</u> with girls and someone who was not famous <u>would not be very good</u> at meeting important people and representing children's interests. Also some people who might be quite good are too old, like Madonna – Angelina **has a very youthful appearance** and <u>could be</u> **more in touch** with young people. Other people are too tied up in their careers to be able to devote enough time to the job.

UNIT 7

Reading p.56

1 1 B is correct.
A & D are hypothetical suggestions in the second sentence of the text about whether it is **likely** to become more popular. C is not mentioned, though there are some similar words in the third sentence. The third sentence expresses the writer's view:
the endless cycle of it being done then wiped away will eventually wear the artists down.

<u>According to the writer</u>, graffiti is <u>unlikely</u> to become more popular because

(The answer must incorporate the writer's view, not simply what he says, and it must explain why he thinks graffiti is <u>unlikely</u> to become more popular.)

2 1 B   2 C   3 C   4 D   5 A   6 D   7 B

3 1 underground   5 dig in
2 fancied   6 dwindling
3 unwittingly   7 cooked up
4 epic

Grammar 1 p.58

1 1 f   2 g   3 e   4 a   5 c   6 b   7 d

2 1 will Reinhart be exhibiting
2 will be studying
3 due to (nb: 'about to' cannot be used with time as it refers to the next moment)
4 are not to be taken
5 will have won
6 is on the point of starting
7 will have sold

3 1 **He's on the point of cancelling**, if they don't agree to give him more publicity.
2 **The programme is due to go** live at 6 o'clock tonight.
3 People arriving late **are to wait** until the interval before entering the theatre.
4 She will be upset not **to have been** asked.
5 I know he **will have taken account of** the problem when he planned the project.

Vocabulary 1 p.59

1

O	T	P	G	O	E	T	K
S	T	H	I	N	K	G	P
E	O	U	T	B	B	S	W
T	E	M	K	R	R	O	O
M	C	O	M	E	I	U	S
W	O	I	N	K	N	G	N
S	G	K	G	N	G	H	O
E	O	G	H	T	O	T	U
G	S	W	O	R	N	I	N

1 think up
2 bring round
3 come to
4 sought out
5 go off
6 set about
7 worn away
8 go away

2
1 turn you on
2 fall out of
3 thought of
4 deal with
5 get out of
6 come across
7 put (money) into
8 go about

Quiz:

all a's – you are not sympathetic to art at all!

all b's – you appreciate and support art

mixed: – you have a fairly typical attitude to art, like most of the population

Listening p.60

1 There are <u>several</u> museums which are interesting to see for the buildings alone. The <u>significant</u> ones are <u>normally</u> vast and located in capital cities. However, the <u>latest</u> designs can more than match these historical buildings. It seems their success <u>depends on</u> the money that is poured into them. But this is recouped through <u>foreign visitors</u> who potentially come and stay in the town.

1 museums
2 significant; vast
3 designs
4 the money
5 foreign

2
1 opposition
2 tourist destination
3 expansion
4 ship
5 weather
6 interior design
7 (river) views

4
1 rundown
2 regenerating
3 backwater
4 knock-on effects
5 head for heights
6 mascot

Tapescript

Speaker (male or female):

I'm fascinated by the way that great architecture can alter the areas that it's built in. It can lift a whole community. An example of this is where I'm standing now, outside the Guggenheim Museum in Bilbao. Bilbao used to be a rather **rundown**, gloomy, industrial town in the north of Spain and it was an extraordinary, far-sighted decision by local councillors, who initially met with significant <u>opposition</u>, to locate the building here. But, faced with the task of **regenerating** the town, they felt the museum would make a statement about what the town wanted to become and it looks as if they have been proved right. It's amazing.

Within the first years of this museum opening, it was a runaway success. Almost overnight Bilbao went from being a **backwater** to a <u>tourist destination</u> of note. Visitors now pour into the city just to see the Guggenheim. Bilbao has changed for ever. This has been as a result of the obvious **knock-on effects** of the growth in visitor numbers. Although retaining the historical core, facilities in the town have been upgraded and there has been an enormous <u>expansion</u>,with more hotels opening, a bigger airport and, significantly, more work.

The Guggenheim was designed by Frank Gehry and opened in 1997. It's hard to come up with new descriptions, but standing by the side of the river, its soft, undulating lines represent, if anything, a <u>ship</u>. The best view of the museum is from a distance. It's clad with hundreds of silvery titanium plates, which are reflective and can change in tone. This means the museum constantly transforms itself, determined by the famously changing <u>weather</u> of northern Spain.

The Guggenheim is just as fascinating inside as out, with walkways suspended from the ceiling linking the galleries over three floors. In fact, I sincerely believe many visitors don't care what's on exhibition as they just go to stare at the breathtaking <u>interior design</u>. You need a good **head for heights**, but you can spend all your time just wandering the walkways between the nineteen galleries, marvelling at the sheer brilliance of the engineering in the building and the use of light, and gazing out at the <u>river views</u>, which are lovely. Outside the front entrance is the Puppy, the giant, floral-coated **mascot** of the museum. It's stunning and just as photographed as the museum itself.

Given the local people's first worried reaction to the museum, which was to wonder why such an enormous sum of money should be spent on one building, they are now extremely proud of it – proving that art and architecture can change communities. It's well worth a visit in my view.

Vocabulary 2 p.60

1 1 C 2 A 3 B 4 D 5 A 6 B

Use of English p.61

1 1 publishing 2 presentation 3 alongside
4 literacy 5 specialists 6 endless 7 competitive
8 openings 9 consultancies 10 aided

Speaking p.61

beneficial	useful / valuable
rewards	outcome / effects / impact / good results
creative	original / imaginative / artistic / inspired
a waste of time	not worth it
it should be	it would be a good idea
because	so, due to, since, owing to

Tapescript

F1: Do you think children should be taught more about art in school?

F2: I think teaching art in school is really <u>beneficial</u> to kids <u>because</u> they learn to look at things in a different way.

M: Yes, I agree. I think <u>it should be</u> taught from age five right through sixteen. <u>It's a good idea</u> to do something different from cramming your head full of facts <u>so</u> you get a break.

F1: Do you think it's important for everybody though?

M: Yes, everybody has something <u>creative</u> inside of them and it's important to bring it out.

F2: I know some people think it's <u>a waste of time</u>, but I think it's actually <u>useful</u> and helps you appreciate modern art.

M: Yes, I don't think at school you need to be especially <u>original</u>; it's just a way of looking at things. If people think <u>it's not worth it</u> then they're not considering its <u>impact</u> carefully enough … (fade)

Grammar 2 p.62

1
1 He encouraged me **to enter** the art competition.
2 Although the design seemed familiar, I couldn't remember **seeing** it before.
3 Something made me stop in front of the strange building. ✓
4 Even though funding for design is very poor in the UK, art students continue to create good designs. ✓
5 I wouldn't risk **asking** him to the opening if I were you.
6 Many people have attempted **to explain** his complex sculptures.
7 The teacher helped her (to) overcome her difficulties with life drawing.
8 I was about to pay for the art books when I realised I'd forgotten **to bring** my wallet.

2 e.g.
1 I sometimes regret not going to university.
2 My parents would let me go into town on Saturdays when I was twelve.
3 My teacher encouraged me to work it out for myself.
4 I don't think I would ever dare be rude to a teacher.
5 I sometimes miss playing tennis as I did it a lot when I was younger.
6 I expect I'll be working in the evenings until I retire.
7 Something I know I should try to cut down on is eating sweets.
8 What I hope to avoid doing is travelling into town on a weekday.

3
1 Breathing slowly **makes you feel** calmer.
2 He **advised me not to argue** about my results.
3 Designers have to **avoid replicating** other people's work.
4 She **threatened not to fund** my art course if I didn't work harder.
5 You **neglected to tell me** that the exhibition was finishing today!

Use of English p.62

1
1 We **set off** at 6 o'clock in the morning.
2 I'm sure **she'll make a success of** her career.
3 I'm going **to attempt to climb** Mount Snowdon.
4 He **is about to blow** the whistle.
5 I**'ve got a bad memory/have no memory for** people's names.
6 I **regretted not taking** the job.
7 Nothing **out of the ordinary** ever happens in my town.
8 He was sacked **on the grounds of his** incompetence.

Writing p.63

2 a) brief details about your chosen building
c) reasons for its importance to the town or region
e) why others should or shouldn't go and see it

3 <u>I suggest</u> you go and visit the stadium – walk round the outside and admire its curves. However, <u>I wouldn't recommend visiting</u> it when it is empty so get yourself a ticket for a match and see what 70,000 people enjoy!

4 <u>Would you bother going to visit a football stadium? No, I thought not. Well, the Millennium Stadium in Cardiff may change your mind!</u>

The Millennium Stadium is a spectacular architectural and engineering triumph. Funded by government money, it was built for the year 2000 to allow the capital of Wales to have a suitable venue for its great passion – rugby. It is built in the heart of the city and has wonderful white arches that reach towards the river and a roof that opens or shuts depending on the weather. Although intended for sport, it is also now a major concert venue and inside has a feeling of intimacy despite its size.

It has proved to be critical to the regeneration of Cardiff as <u>up around it</u> have grown the pubs and clubs that support visitors to the matches. On match days the stadium is the living heart of the city, with spectators being only <u>a stone's throw</u> from all the amenities the city has to offer. It has not only brought extra work to the city but also been an inspiration to the people of the city.

I suggest you go and visit the stadium – walk round the outside and admire its curves. <u>However, I wouldn't recommend visiting it when it is empty, so get yourself a ticket for a match and see what 70,000 people enjoy!</u>

UNIT *8*

Listening p.64

1
1 most useful aspect
2 woman / most concerned
3 opinion / people who are ambitious
4 feel / people who work for him
5 why / decide to leave
6 agree

2 1 A   2 B   3 C   4 A   5 C   6 A

3
1 was put together   4 ended up
2 pick up   5 am / fed up
3 are / on   6 gets on with

Tapescript

Extract One
You hear two people discussing a book on how to do well in an interview.

M: Did you finish that book I gave you on performing well in interviews?

F: Yes, I quite enjoyed it.

M: Mmm, it's a bit hit and miss. And rather strangely put together as it started with an interview and worked backwards. It had some interesting case studies, I thought, which you could learn something from and the advice was clear, but much the same as you'd read in any other book like this.

F: Yeah, I did wonder how successful it would be given I've never heard of the writer – though it's been well marketed – but it doesn't make it clear that you need to bring your own approach to the interview. I think people will just do what it says mechanically and all end up the same. It'll make it difficult for interviewers to choose. Very useful though, especially if you're in the position where you're looking for work and trying to get interviews.

Extract Two

You hear part of an interview with a businessman called Nigel Frame.

F: Nigel, you think ambition in business is a double-edged sword, don't you?

M: Well, there are positive and negative sides to it. Clearly, ambitious people can be a useful resource for a company as they are keen to achieve – and that often translates into successful sales. That is, if they don't end up rushing through things in order to hit targets and then somebody else has to pick up their mistakes. I'm aware this makes it rather frustrating for the people they work with. Which is why sometimes I would prefer to sacrifice sales for efficiency.

F: So do you have lots of highly ambitious people in your company?

M: Only a few. In general, it's more important to me that everyone works well as a team and is really focused on whatever project we're working on. I'm particularly pleased with what they've achieved this year, though I haven't been as hands-on as I would have liked. I'm just glad that they were able to get on with things so successfully without me.

Extract Three

You hear two people talking about their work situations.

M: I heard you'd left your job?

F: Yes, about two weeks ago.

M: Was that for a better job then?

F: Well, luckily I've rather landed on my feet and got something where the benefits, err, like bonuses and whatever, mean I'll be earning more overall. Not that what I was on was bad. It was something I'd been thinking about for a while though. There was an opening – with more responsibility – that may have suited me, but I was never in the running. My boss refused to support my application because we didn't get on, so I was going nowhere. I didn't like him, but it didn't seem to bother the other people I worked with.

M: Ahh, tricky. Actually he's probably done you a favour cos I don't think you should stay in one job too long anyway.

F: Yeah, if you're getting fed up then you should move on.

M: Oh, I meant it looks better to have worked in more places.

F: Depends what sort of job you're in, I think. Perhaps sometimes it's best to let them know when you're getting fed up before moving.

M: Mmm, see if it can be sorted out first. That must apply to all jobs I suppose … (*fade*)

Vocabulary 1 p.64

1

out	in	back	over	down	through	up
outlet	input	drawback	takeover	downfall	breakthrough	setup
layout	inlet	comeback	turnover	breakdown		let-up
outbreak	income	cutback	overlay	comedown		upturn
printout	intake	setback		downturn		upset
outlook	inset			letdown		breakup
outcome	break-in			put-down		uptake
outset						turn-up
breakout						
fallout						
turnout						
lookout						
output						

2 A iii   B i   C iv   D v   E ii

3
A	indepth	iii
B	outgoing	i
C	overloaded	v
D	under / overpaid	ii
E	under / overstaffed	iv

4 up

upgrade	*update*
mobile phone	software
camera	information (e.g. on traffic, weather, etc.)
MP3 player	membership
computer	
components	
insurance cover	

5
1	underpaid	5	outgoing
2	indepth	6	input
3	insight	7	drawback
4	outcome		

6
1 start at the bottom
2 resolve someone's doubts
3 commonplace
4 make an impression on
5 elite

Grammar 1 p.66

1
1 b
2 a or b (this is usually optional e.g. *may* can become *might*, *can* can become *could*)
3 c   4 a   5 a   6 f   7 e   8 e
9 d   10 g   11 d

2
1 Tom asked Alice if she would be able to come to the conference the following week.
2 She asked me if I needed a lift to the airport the following day.
3 The woman asked her who she had spoken to when she phoned the previous week.
4 Sandra explained that she might / may have to leave early that afternoon.
5 The doctor said I should take a few days off.
6 My boss is always asking me where his diary is.
7 Tim asked Lynn if she had seen his report.
8 Simon said he found it very difficult to do presentations.

3
1 I asked him **if he had sent in his** application yet.
2 He told me **that Maria had phoned the previous** day.
3 He **told me that he would help** me with the project.
4 She asked me **if I could come the following** week.
5 He **told me to call him that** afternoon.
6 She asked me **what I wanted her to do** later.

Vocabulary 2 p.66

1 NB: These are suggested answers. Make sure you check the meaning in your dictionary to see if you agree.

positive	neutral	negative
sociable	conformist	pushy
able to work	cautious	aggressive
independently	laid-back	frivolous
has good		indecisive
judgement		
reliable		
willing to follow		
set procedures		
imaginative		
flexible		
trustworthy		
assertive		
has common		
sense		
courteous		
thoughtful		
conscientious		
realistic		

2 1 e   2 a   3 d   4 f   5 b   6 c

3
1 uncommunicative   4 uncreative
2 uncompetitive   5 indecisive
3 uncooperative   6 impractical

4 Possible answers are:
1 2, 4, 6   3 1, 3, 5, 6
2 1, 3, 6   4 2, 5

Speaking p.67

Photo A: serious, isolated
Photo B: happy, enjoying themselves
Photo C: busy, stressed, overworked

List of aspects, e.g.:
colleagues
the office environment
the boss / management
the benefits e.g. bonuses, holidays etc.
the level of responsibility
the amount of training offered
the opportunities for promotion
location

Use of English p.67

1 1 A   2 D   3 C   4 B   5 A   6 D   7 D   8 B
9 C   10 C   11 A   12 B

Reading p.68

1 a 2   b 1   c 3

2 1 F   2 B   3 G   4 C   5 A   6 E

3
1 emerge   5 status
2 nearest and dearest   6 marrying
3 forging   7 thriving
4 take something into account

4
1 let go of   4 move into
2 come to   5 weed out
3 check out   6 light up

Grammar 2 p.70

1
1 **She accused me of** taking the report off her desk.
2 **He complained about** having to work overtime.
3 **She promised to / that she would** finish the report by Friday.
4 **She refused to** work with him.
5 **She warned me not to** take on too much work.
6 **He reminded me** to ask questions in the interview.
7 **He apologised for not coming** to the meeting.
8 **She suggested I made** a list to help organise my time.

2 1 to wear   2 to go   3 for helping   4 to meet
5 on getting   6 to speak   7 to attend
8 forgetting / he forgot

3 1 chance   2 memory   3 demand   4 grounds
5 practice

Writing p.70

2 b) why you are writing
c) why you would be good at the job
d) where you saw the job advertised
f) an outline of your experience
g) why you want the job
h) the qualities of a good sports teacher

4 Yes, it did include all the points relevant from Exercise 2
order: b, d, f, h, c, g

5 a and b

6 a) iii   b) iv   c) i   d) ii

I am writing to apply for the job you advertised in the sports magazine on Saturday for a sports coach for children in the summer.

I am an 18-year-old girl and I have just finished school. I am looking for a job in the summer and I think <u>this job would be ideal for me.</u> (d)

<u>I enjoy working with children and have three younger brothers and sisters so I am used to entertaining children.</u> (c) In addition, <u>I speak good English</u> (c) and <u>have just taken my Cambridge advanced exam.</u> (b) <u>At school I did lots of sports</u> (a) such as basketball, tennis and running and <u>I used to do some training</u> (a) for younger students in the school.

I think a good sports teacher is able to show the technical side but also is patient and calm with the children. I think I have all the skills you need and <u>I would very much enjoy doing this job.</u> (d)

I am able to work the whole summer. I can be contacted at home on 01786 450 876 and am available for interview all next week.

Improve! The sample letter is very short. The letter should use the number of words allowed in the exam (220–260). This flexibility could be used fully to expand on the reasons why you would be good at the job. This would make the letter more persuasive so it would have a better effect on the target reader.

UNIT 9

Vocabulary 1 p.72

2 1 switch off   2 chill out   3 checked out
4 set off   5 soak up   6 held up   7 turn back

3 A vi   B viii   C x   D ix   E v   F iii
G iv   H i   I ii   J vii

4 1 spectacular   6 exotic
2 breathtaking   7 historic
3 unspoilt   8 bustling
4 picturesque   9 romantic
5 dramatic

5 provisional   low   off   confirmed / last-minute
provisional

Listening p.73

1 1 road   2 a qualifier   3 noun   4 noun
5 noun, singular   6 noun, plural   7 noun   8 noun

2 2 (high) volume   3 isolation   4 (mountain) passes
5 flood   6 protests   7 wildlife   8 monopoly

4 **Reasons against**   **Reasons for the bridge**
the bridge   1 income from tourism
1 damage by tourism   2 end community's isolation
2 destroy wildlife   3 easier drive for farmers
3 protect rail company   4 replaces old bridge

Tapescript

I'm reporting today from Machu Picchu, which has stood silently, high up in the Andes, for generations, a preserved town where the Inca tribe lived hundreds of years ago. Since being discovered in 1911, it has had an increasing number of visitors and now the mayor is building a bridge over the Vilcanota river. This means the site can not only be reached by train, as it has been done for years, but also by road, thus vastly increasing visitor numbers. And this has caused a huge row.

[pause]

The problem is a tricky one repeated in tourist sites the world over, where these beautiful sites and regions fall victim to their own success. By walking over the land, demanding services be built so that they can eat and rest, and leaving rubbish, the high volume of visitors begins to damage the very place they have come to see. The Machu Picchu site attracts up to 700,000 visitors each year and the United Nations Cultural Agency wants visitor numbers more than halved because of damage to the site.

At the same time, the local community wanted the bridge to be built in order to end their isolation and improve the local economy, which is mainly farming. Also, in a fairly poor region of the world, many of them depend on tourism for their income. But will the bridge ultimately destroy the site on which they depend for their income? The mayor has defended her decision, saying that instead of a treacherous 15-hour drive over mountain passes, the bridge allows farmers to truck coffee and fruit to the capital in just three hours. She has further defended her decision by reminding critics that the bridge simply replaces one which was washed away in a 1998 flood, which the government refused to rebuild. The mayor claims she begged them to but they refused, so she's gone ahead anyway, using public funds that had been set aside for other projects.

The mayor has taken on the big guns in the capital, who have been making the most noise about the bridge. The central government has launched protests about the bridge, but the mayor is immovable in her belief that it will benefit her community. As it's now almost completed, she knows it'll be difficult to stop it. She also seems impervious to the concerns of conservationists, who have warned that wildlife along the Inca Trail will disappear. These conservationists have been concerned for some years about the stress that visitors are causing to the site. However, the mayor claims that these conservationists are being used, as they are heavily supported by the rail company which wants to protect its monopoly on access to the site. Having spoken to some of the people who live here, a few tourists and the mayor, I'm not sure anyone wins. Only time will tell – and by then it may be too late.

Reading p.74

1 C and D

2 3 A
4 B
5, 6, 7 A, D, E (in any order)
8 A
9 C
10 D
11, 12 A, E (in any order)
13 C
14 B
15 E

3 c

4 1 hectic   2 futuristic   3 noteworthy   4 glitzy
5 intoxicating   6 beguiling   7 celebrated
8 idiosyncratic   9 exhaustive   10 gleaming

Grammar 1 p.76

1 1 B   2 C   3 B   4 C   5 C   6 A   7 C
8 B   9 A   10 C   11 B   12 C

Vocabulary 2 p.76

1
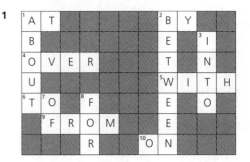

Use of English p.77

1 1 apparently   2 personal   3 unacceptable
4 imaginative   5 instructions   6 attendant
7 disagreement   8 equivalent   9 underestimate
10 frantically

2 fascinated by   separated from   typical of
imaginative in   worried about   equivalent to
restricted by   insisted on   breaking with

Speaking p.77

1 i D   ii A   iii A   iv D   v D   vi A

Tapescript

i You may switch off because you're on your own.
ii You're more likely to meet local people.
iii You could be more in touch with your experiences.
iv On your own you'd be less adventurous.
v You may be too shy to join in with local activities.
vi You'd have plenty of time to read about your destination.

Grammar 2 p.78

1 a 3   b 1   c 5   d 4   e 2

2 1 What they should do is impose restrictions.
2 What I ought to do is try.
3 What we can do is leave a note.
4 What I must do is go to the bank.
5 What we can do is (to) offer you meal vouchers.
6 What I will do is take some photographs.

Use of English p.78

1 1 I'm not **convinced that travel agents always** get the best price for their clients.
2 I need a weekend away, **so what I did was book** something on the Internet.
3 **What I object to is** hanging around in airports.
4 Only after weeks of calling **did I manage** to get my money back.
5 Our train **was delayed due to** a drivers' strike.
6 **What excites me is** travelling/**What I find exciting** is travelling.
7 **What I did was take** an extra suitcase.
8 **What worries me is that** I don't speak another language well.

Writing p.79

2 1, 4 and 6

3 Paragraph 2

Paragraph 1 is not a summary but introduces more reasons. Also it sounds too aggressive.

Paragraph 3 – the persuasion is too personal with not enough solid reasons.

4 e.g.
Introduction
The area and its problems
The solutions / Ways to improve the area
Summary

UNIT 10

Reading p.80

1 main text:
This was worrying news.
As I stepped off the plane …
Mark had spent three fruitless years in Nepal trying to capture one of these increasingly rare animals on film
… there was no sign of the prize animal
When we arrived at the same time the following afternoon
We continued to watch her and take photographs all afternoon as she prowled

missing paragraphs:
A The idea of running a trip to Chitral
B Mark told us encouragingly that with the early snow pushing her lower into the valley, there was a good chance she'd appear
D It also made me proud of myself. …Yet here we were …
E This kind of information
F Luck was with us as only a day later

2 1 C   2 F   3 A   4 G   5 B   6 D

3 1 barren   2 stunning   3 epic   4 prize   5 fruitless
6 towering   7 vicarious   8 agape   9 indolent
10 elusive

Listening p.82

1 1 opinion   2 feeling   3 fact   4 attitude/opinion
5 feeling   6 opinion

2 1 D   2 C   3 A   4 C   5 B   6 B

4 a) iii   b) v   c) i   d) vi   e) ii   f) iv

5 1 came up   4 pitched up
2 jet off to   5 back out
3 went on   6 building up

Tapescript

I: Today we're joined by Mark Latell, who is a volcanologist. This is a scientist who studies volcanoes – things like underground activity and the effects of eruptions. Welcome, Mark.

ML: Thank you and hello.

I: I suppose the inevitable question is, how easy, or even possible, is it to predict when a volcano is likely to erupt?

ML: (laughs) I'm always asked that! The truth is it's a very inexact science. I work with a very experienced team but even with equipment installed, it's hard to say when an eruption will happen or how big it'll be. Also, ideally, governments need to fund staff to watch and measure what's happening 24 hours a day, but the money just isn't available. Each team builds up a knowledge over time of the volcano they work with, so we're more successful at making predictions on that, though we do visit other volcanoes to see the various effects of any differences. We're based in Vancouver, so our area of expertise is the American volcanoes.

I: And have you ever successfully predicted the timing and scale of an eruption?

ML: Yes, it was only a small one on an island, but they heard rumblings and we were called to investigate. In fact, it had come up on the monitoring screens at our base so we knew we were in time to do something. All the people in my team cancelled their weekend leave and we went down there. It was incredible to see how grateful people were when we managed to accurately predict the flow of the lava so they could evacuate the area. Sometimes people can get very cross with you about having to leave their homes. They showered us with gifts – it was quite awkward for us – and I had to remind them we were just doing our job.

I: So when you jet off to other eruptions, do you choose to go or do you wait to be asked?

ML: Well, of course, it's always interesting for us to see other volcanoes and get data from them and usually there are several groups there, so you get to swap ideas with other people in your field. Having said that, we can't just pitch up as and when we want – it has to be a formal request through official sources. But our team is mainly advisors – we aren't equipped to deal with an eruption once it's become a national emergency.

I: Now, I know some people have suggested that volcanologists are cowboys, who live dangerously. Do you think that's a fair picture?

ML: (laughs) Oh, no. We try to be sensible. We have families and we want to do this for several years yet! The danger varies with each situation, but before we go anywhere, we try and minimise what are serious risks by setting objectives and mapping how to achieve those, so that if anyone feels uncomfortable with anything we'll be doing then they can back out. Also, you have to remember that we've got years of experience between us.

I: And have you ever had any close calls?

ML: Oh, yes. A particular one was on Mount St Helens when that erupted in 1980. I was there with my team beforehand. It was erupting on and off and it was restless between eruptions, so we were being very careful and we'd already learned quite a lot about what was going on inside the volcano. Fortunately, we had a helicopter near where we were working ready to leave at a moment's notice. On the day it blew we heard enough warning rumbles to get off in time. In fact, the blast was so big we wouldn't have had time to get away if we'd left it till the last minute. After all my years working on volcanoes, it was certainly very thrilling to be that close to an eruption, though I'm not sure my colleagues agreed!

I: So do you have any predictions about the next big eruption? Where is it likely to be?

ML: Mmm, I'm not sure. Normally you'd expect some smoke or mild eruptions to go on for a while beforehand, though we think this one may be different from that norm. There are recorded cases of volcanoes just blowing unexpectedly, so there is a precedent. What we have to accept is that we are such a dangerous place regarding the planet's ecosystem at the moment that any eruption could contribute to changes in our weather patterns and I don't think there's any way round that.

I: Ok, thanks very much … (fade)

Grammar 1 p.83

1   I don't see **the point in / of going** to see animals locked in a zoo.
2   I had **no idea** how to photograph wild animals.

3   A local myth claims the mountain has **powers to** prolong life.
4   We were prevented from climbing the mountain **by the authorities**.

Vocabulary 1 p.83

1	However	5	In fact
2	This time delay	6	This searching behaviour
3	Alternatively	7	While
4	The controversy	8	this task

Vocabulary 2 p.83

2   1   sanctuary/ies (squirrel and panda texts)
2   roam (panda text)
3   poaching (tiger text)
4   quarantined (parrot text)
5   fat reserves (polar bear text)
6   drought (frog text)

3   1 a and b   2 b   3 a   4 b   5 a   6 a

4   Text A – herald, wooing
Text B – gems
Text C – moved, scratch the surface
Text D – flung open its doors, laboratory

Use of English p.85

1   1 grip   2 crack   3 waste   4 favour   5 accident

Use of English p.86

1   1 no   2 it   3 of   4 on   5 into   6 more
7 who   8 us   9 one   10 its   11 did   12 so
13 never   14 It   15 nor

Grammar 2 p.86

1   1   It's uncomfortable to think how little we are doing to protect our planet.
2   It's extraordinary that the panda has managed to survive.
3   It's incredible to experience watching animals in the wild.
4   It will be too late when we finally try to control the damage we are doing.
5   It's difficult to realise how much we pollute the oceans.
6   It was dangerous to put your hands through that cage at the zoo.

2   a) I can't stand **it** when   iii) people won't even try to recycle things.
b) The politician made **it** clear   v) that global warming was a serious issue.
c) The charity made **it** easy   i) to understand the problem of endangered animals.
d) Most people think   ii) that **it** is not their responsibility to save energy.
e) I wish you wouldn't   iv) leave **it** up to me to walk the dog!

Speaking p.86

So, are we agreed then?
Right, is that ok with you?
Ok, which one(s) shall we choose to …
Right then, let's decide …
So, shall we say …

All the above start with a concluding word, i.e. *so, right* or *ok*.

Tapescript

A: So, are we agreed then? We'll pick the panda as the most endangered animal?

B: We've said we think natural areas are being most damaged by tourism. Right, is that OK with you?

C: OK, which one shall we choose to say is the most affected by tourism?

D: Right then, let's decide which animal we think is the *most* endangered.

E: So, shall we say we think volcanos are more dangerous than earthquakes?

Writing p.87

2 Three points: describing, suggesting and recommending (or not)

4–5 headings: introduction, description, suggestion, recommendation, conclusion (optional as recommendation can serve as conclusion)

3 Example plan:

Section title/paragraph heading:	Include:
Introduction	aims
What the conference did well	interesting handouts – why good
How it could be improved	seminars overbooked – suggest bigger rooms
	no interpreters – employ some next year + reason why
	too little time to speak to representatives – allow fixed time slots
The future	say whether useful to my course
	say whether college should pay for other students to attend + why or why not

4 The best sentences are:
1b, 2a, 3a, 4b

These sentences are better because they use more formal and more objective language.

UNIT *11*

Vocabulary 1 p.88

1

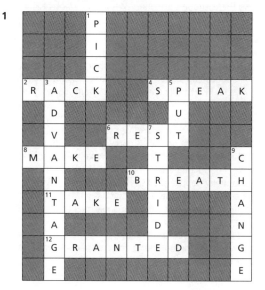

2 1 brain drain
2 brain teaser
3 brain child
4 brainwave

3 1 a piece of my mind
2 walking on air
3 cheer up
4 in the depths of despair
5 At the back of my mind
6 bear in mind
7 down in the dumps
8 on top of the world

Listening p.89

1 2 What is the woman's attitude to people who fear rejection?
3 What made the woman get involved with helping other people?
4 What do the two speakers agree about?
5 The woman decided to do a course to improve her memory in order to
6 How does the man feel about his bad memory?

2 1 A 2 C 3 B 4 C 5 A 6 B

3 Extract One: a, a   Extract Two: b, a   Extract Three: b, b

Tapescript

Extract One

M: So, why do we worry about whether everybody likes us, even people we don't like ourselves?

F: Respecting the opinions of others is part of being a socially functioning adult. But as our social environments have widened and become more competitive, we want to be liked by an ever-growing number of people. Not just close friends and colleagues, but even those we don't like. It's part of our genetic inheritance, to prevent us from being rejected by the group and left to die. But for some, this concern can become all-defining, influencing your decisions, your sense of self-worth and, in extreme cases, your mental health.

M: So are you sympathetic to people who are overly concerned about what others think of them?

F: In order to put the opinions of others into perspective, we need to recognise the intrinsic value of fostering our own happiness. I don't mean by focusing in on ourselves, which is not good for you, but by looking at ways to view life differently, being active in trying to change your thinking rather than doing what most of these people do, which is to say it's their parents' fault for not giving them enough attention. We need to look at ourselves, not others.

Extract Two

F: Oh, I was feeling so down last year I could just feel myself going into this spiral of unhappiness. I talked to a friend about it and she suggested I should try doing some voluntary work helping others. I was really sceptical, but I went along to this unit that helped underprivileged children for a trial day – a very worthy cause, I think – and after that I got completely hooked. The kids were so appreciative and got so much joy out of the attention. Course, they do say you only get back what you put in, but I'm not sure you should do it for what you get out of it.

M: Sounds like a good idea though. It's hard when you feel like that and so many people need someone else, like a therapist, to help them out of it. I can understand why.

F: I can't really – I think it's down to the individual to sort themselves out.

M: Mmm … I think that's hard sometimes.

F: Yeah, but we all go through good and bad periods – it's not the end of the world.

M: I suppose it's just how we deal with it that varies, isn't it?

F: Yeah …

Extract Three

M: I'm so forgetful and you're so organised. How do you do it?

F: Oh, my memory used to be awful and then I did a course to learn how to improve it.

M: Really?

F: Yeah … the thing is, it was really affecting my working life as I was forgetting meetings, orders, where I put things … everything. It was even affecting me at home, though of course that didn't matter so much. And I'd always wanted to be good at presentations, to learn how to do them properly, as it was going to become part of my job, so I decided I had to take action if I was ever going to get to grips with that.

M: I must do something about my memory – maybe I'll take a course too. But I may be a lost cause (*laughs*) – it may take several courses to improve mine! It doesn't really affect me at work – it's more social, just things like meeting people and parties I've been to that I can't remember. It's been like that for years – no change, thank goodness. I'd be worried if it was getting worse!

Grammar 1 p.90

1 1 c   2 f   3 a   4 b   5 d   6 e

2
1 might have
2 wouldn't have
3 could have
4 must have
5 should have
6 can't have
7 may have
8 needn't have

3
1 could have been
2 wouldn't have given
3 shouldn't have
4 may have been
5 couldn't have done
6 can't have
7 must have had

Speaking p.90

2 What the people are doing
What feelings their actions express
What may have just happened

Tapescript

In the second picture the girl looks as if she's upset about something, from her facial expression. I guess she's in her bedroom as she's hugging what looks like a blanket or something similar. She looks a bit depressed, as if her world has fallen apart. She's holding the blanket – or maybe it's a duvet – to comfort her. Maybe she's split up with her boyfriend? Or perhaps she's got bad exam results and doesn't know what to do.

Her situation is very different from the boy holding his hands in the air. He seems very happy, as if he's just won a match. His whole body shows that he feels as if he's achieved something fantastic. He's looking up into the sky and shouting … YES! He must be feeling really pleased with himself and maybe he's looking forward to celebrating.

The boy and the girl look very different in the two pictures – they've got two opposite emotions, but both of them are probably feeling things that will last a long time. The girl's problems don't look as if she'll get over them quickly and the boy's happiness will last as he tells everyone about his victory.

Use of English p.91

multiple-choice cloze (Part 1)

1 A   2 D   3 B   4 A   5 D   6 C   7 B   8 A
9 B   10 D   11 B   12 D

Reading p.92

1
1 summary
2 opinion
3 purpose / reason
4 opinion
5 opinion
6 summary
7 summary

2 1 C   2 B   3 D   4 C   5 A   6 C
7 A (B doesn't capture all of the text; C is untrue of the text; D just repeats the title so doesn't add anything)

3 b

4 1 b   2 a   3 a   4 b   5 b   6 a

5 a 6   b 3   c 4   d 1   e 2   f 5

Grammar 2 p.94

1
1 have I read / had I read
2 did I realise
3 had I witnessed / have I witnessed
4 must you phone / should you phone
5 had I taken
6 did he explain
7 had I apologised
8 did he buy

2
1 **No sooner had she started** working **than** a loud bang broke her concentration.
2 **Never before / Rarely have I been** in greater need of a confidence boost than I am today.
3 **Rarely / Never before had he met** such a fascinating and intelligent person as Madeleine.
4 **Not only does he forget** people's names, he also finds it difficult to remember the words for common objects.
5 **Under no circumstances should you let** anyone disturb you unless it is an emergency.
6 **Hardly had** she started work **when** the phones started ringing.

7 **Only after she had** posted the letter **did she realise that** she had forgotten to post the cheque.

8 **At no time did she** doubt that he would make her happy.

Use of English p.94

1
1 **Never have I seen** such a fantastic performance before.
2 **No sooner had I arrived than** he insisted on going out again.
3 **Hardly has she ever been** in greater need of a friend.
4 **Only when they split up** did they realise that they loved each other.
5 **Under no circumstances must you** disturb someone when they are sleepwalking.
6 **Barely had I got** on the train, when it left.
7 **At no time did she doubt** that she would be able to meet the challenge.
8 **Seldom have I come across** such a strange man.

Writing p.95

3 b, c   **4** b, c

Improve! The last paragraph repeats the same point about making yourself feel better and not relying on others. This could have been expanded by giving examples or suggesting consequences.

UNIT *12*

Vocabulary 1 p.96

1
1 kill time	3 pressed for time
2 waste of time	4 on time

2 1 c   2 a   3 d   4 b

3

happening soon: the ... future	a positive outlook – a ... future	a negative outlook – a ... future
foreseeable, immediate, near, not-too-distant	bright, great, promising, rosy, secure	bleak, grim, uncertain, gloomy

4
1 vision of the future
2 immediate future
3 secure future
4 question mark over your future
5 foreseeable future
6 uncertain future

5 1 shape   2 face   3 determine   4 invest in
5 forecast

Listening p.97

2 1 H   2 E   3 B   4 F   5 D   6 G   7 H
8 E   9 A   10 B

4
1 passing through		4 taken round
2 wiped out		5 were holed up
3 wander off		6 head for

Tapescript

One
Oh, it was fascinating – it's a huge site, which we didn't have time to visit as we were just passing through, but we did stop off later on and look at the king's burial chamber. There were some really interesting artefacts in there – nothing particularly precious, just everyday things such as mirrors and whatever. And drawings of their pets – loads of them. Clearly this was something that was very important to them, much more so than today. Things have clearly changed since then. It was so many hundreds of years ago and it must have been a very harsh world, so these creatures provided some form of comfort, I suspect.

Two
Well, originally we went at that time of year to see the famous carnival, but we just missed it. Anyway, while we were there we were taken around the old town, which is right on the river banks around the harbour, and looked at all the original houses – really interesting. I think people living there then had fairly simple lives that just revolved around servicing all the big ships. I don't think it was a very rich community. What you could see though was that all the furniture was smaller and doorways were lower, so they obviously weren't as tall as us. Plus they probably didn't have a very good diet.

Three
It's a very, very famous area because of all the battles that took place there in the past. If you wanted to you could walk round the site. We headed for the exhibition though. It was in part of a mansion, where the generals used to meet and plan campaigns. The exhibition wasn't that great so I wandered off and looked round the building. Riveting. I mean, you could see how these generals, who were all lords or whatever, clearly had lots of people working for them and never had to lift a finger! The staff had special quarters, which were really unpleasant, poor things.

Four
Have you ever been? We went last weekend. We walked round the City of London first and you can see the boat from the embankment, so the kids wanted to go on it. Brilliant – all guns and torpedoes. You can still have a go on some of them. Much more interesting than a museum for them. And you got a real sense of what it must be like to be holed up in there for months. I mean, really restricted living quarters – I just can't imagine how awful it must have been to be living on top of each other like that and then getting up to fight a war every day.

Five
I've always been interested in ancient life so I decided to visit this old Roman site over the summer. I never made it as en route I found out about this festival that's held every five years where they give thanks for the grape harvest and they have exhibitions showing all the gadgets that have been used over the years to make wine. And they have lots of information such as what type of jobs everyone did through the years and medical records. In some years the community was almost wiped out by plague and things that don't affect us now. It's amazing to think how devastating that would have been.

Reading p.98

1   Text A: paragraph 1 = a; paragraph 2 = b
Text B: paragraph 1 = b; paragraph 2 = a
Text C: paragraph 1 = b; paragraph 2 = b

2   1 B   2 C   3 A   4 D   5 B   6 A

3 a)
passive structure text = A
e.g.
much astrological theory is unproven.
It cannot be judged
it is **putting the cart before the horse**.
if astrology cannot be explained

rhetorical questions = C
e.g.
Why is so little known about this?
What about the facts?
Why would aliens need to abduct millions of people?
Why have implants inside abductees eluded X-ray examination?

idioms and colloquial expressions text = B
e.g.
turned into a movie
the answer to the sci-fi fan's primal need to see lots and lots of **cool stuff**.
Whisked off the planet
goofy **jaunt**
getting a laugh

b)
a review = text B
an academic argument = text A
a sensational story = text C

c)
magazine = text C
newspaper = text A
website = text B

4 Text A
a) plausible
b) putting the cart before the horse
c) sideswipe
d) scoff

Text B
a) left in the dust
b) stumbles
c) cool stuff
d) jaunt

Text C
a) probed
b) implanted
c) prodded
d) scanned

Grammar 1 p.100

1 1 a   2 b   3 b   4 c   5 a   6 c

2 1 He wanted to be employed by the museum (agent must be mentioned).
2 I'd like to be shown round the exhibits (agent not important or not known so no need to mention)
3 I'm not keen on being asked questions by tourists (agent must be mentioned)
4 I'm pleased to have been asked to help with the project (by the director) (agent may be mentioned or not)
5 The exhibits were displayed in new glass cases (agent not necessary)
6 The pictures will be put up (by him) later today (agent may be mentioned or not)
7 The entrance prices have been reduced (agent not necessary)

Use of English p.100

1 1 a   2 how   3 by   4 own   5 when   6 my
7 so   8 it   9 which   10 few / couple   11 at
12 me   13 with   14 or   15 what

Vocabulary 2 p.101

1 1 the benefit of hindsight   4 catch a glimpse
2 highly dubious   5 in due course
3 give weight to   6 free will

2 1 take responsibility for
2 negative impact on
3 make of
4 acting in our own best interests

Speaking p.101

Tapescript

F: I think vaccinations had a very important effect on the future because they've saved so many lives and prevented disease which could have wiped out whole populations.

M: Yeah, and TV of course has affected us cos we all just sit and watch it now – it's made us lazy.

F: Education is very important because it can change how rich a country is.

M: Yes, and electricity meant we could all work longer hours and there'd be no computers without electricity! Weapons seem like a bad thing, but they changed which countries were the most dominant and I don't think we would have such terrible wars without them.

F: Mmm, I think things like vacuum cleaners are important because they gave women more time so they could go out and work.

M: Yes, and space, I suppose, means not just what we know about it. A lot of new inventions, like foil and plastics, came from space exploration.

F: So which two do we think are the most important? I'd say vaccinations and education because they've changed our lives so much.

M: I think weapons and vaccinations as weapons have altered the history of so many countries.

F: Ok, well, let's agree to differ then!

Grammar 2 p.102

1 a I'm speaking to you now but haven't had time until now; *was going to* refers to time up until phone call started
b both clauses in the past; *was going to* refers to up until time speaker got exam results
c I'm cancelling my plans because of how I feel now; *was going to* refers to time up until now

```
            b                    a      c
past ———x— past ———x— present ——— future
```

2 1 d   2 c   3 b   4 e   5 a

3 I never imagined that achieving my dream _would be_ / _was about to be_ so difficult. I had it all mapped out and my horoscope predicted my success. I thought I _were to_ / _was going to_ be a pop star by the time I was twenty-five. I actually envisaged how I _would get_ / _would have got_ there – I imagined writing songs in my room, finding a band and finally recording a disk to send to a music entrepreneur who _would make_ / *was to make* my dreams come true. According to my master plan, I _was to have_ / *will have* a top ten hit at age twenty-one and then make it big in the USA. My dream however, was cut short when I was only sixteen. As I listened to my idols and started trying to imitate them, I _was pleased_ / *was to be pleased* with my progress and offered to play at a school gig. I was excited. But I _had forgotten_ / *would have forgotten* one crucial thing about performing – I had never sung in front of an audience before. Just as I _was about to_ / *would* open my mouth, I went into a kind of shock and nothing came out – I had no voice. I _would have given_ / *was to give* anything at that moment for the floor to swallow me up. Now my friends _joke_ / *will joke* about my thwarted dream.

4 A Thomas Watson, chairman of IBM (computer company)

B Western Union internal memo (USA communications company)

C H.M. Warner, Warner Brothers (film)

D Decca Recording Company (music)

E The President of the Royal Society (an organisation of scientists)

F Drillers who were being enlisted to work for an oil company

G Charles Duell at the U.S. Office of Patents (which registers inventions)

H Pierre Pachet, Professor of Physiology at Toulouse

Writing p.103

2 A 1 introduction
      2 reasons for
      3 reasons against
      4 conclusion with own opinion

B paragraph 1: 30
   paragraph 2: 80–90
   paragraph 3: 80–90
   paragraph 4: 50

C probably no more than three in each set of 80–90 words if each point is to be developed properly

3

reasons for	reasons against
1 no face-to-face contact – e.g. no conversation as all online; staying at home	1 people will use newly available time to socialise more, e.g. in the daytime
2 will encourage further uses of computer, e.g. to book holidays, to contact friends so more isolation	2 prices will be reduced as shops won't have to have stores so people will have more money to socialise and e.g. use their purchases
3 streets etc. will become empty and no community so more dangerous	3 Not everybody will shop online – for some things, e.g. clothes, the senses are important and you still need to try on, feel the material and see the colour

4 On the one hand / At first, online shopping will save time and money as we won't have to travel to and from the shops. According to me / It seems to me that this will be better both for the planet and for our stress levels. Furthermore / On the other hand, traditional shops may go out of business and communities may die. The streets may be deserted and become dangerous.

For this reason / And so, we should approach the growth of computer shopping cautiously. Personally / It seems to me that, although people like going on the internet, they also still enjoy contact with the rest of their community. For this reason / It is the case that, I think traditional shops will survive. Also / But many people like to see and touch what they are buying, especially with food.

Improve!
From my point of view … (2)
I believe that … (2) or (5)
In addition … (7)
This means that …(4)

UNIT *13*

Listening p.104

1 A opinion immediately successful beautiful enormous talented dramatically extremely variety

B talked talks talk
   related relation
   exciting excitement
   secret secrets
   prize price

C polite (you don't need extremely as 'very' is on the page)
   version (you don't need most recent as 'latest' is on the page
   in private (you must include the preposition for the sentence to be grammatically correct; you cannot change the word to 'privately').

2 1 social status   5 listen
   2 in secret   6 eye contact / eye-contact
   3 isolated   7 negotiating
   4 concentrating   8 apologise

4 1 b   2 b   3 a   4 b   5 a

Tapescript

F: I know many adults feel that young people are always on their mobile phones and that some rely on this far too heavily as a way to communicate with their friends. So, I've been doing some research, looking into the way technology has begun to affect communication etiquette. In other words, what are the new 'polite' rules for communicating when you are mainly doing this by text or phone?

Now, all my research was focused on young people. One of the things that's come to light is that the number of calls and text messages these young people make and receive represents something. Obviously having a high mobile phone bill requires a certain degree of wealth, although it's the social status it confers that matters as how busy your phone is as is an indication of how popular you are. On the other hand, mobiles have an enormous appeal for youngsters as, although they use them constantly, the texting facility means that all your communications can be in secret. This is much more critical for youngsters than for adults.

However, it's not all pluses. Yes, mobiles do give young people a certain degree of independence, as they can always check in with their parents, but at the same time it can leave them <u>isolated</u> as they are less dependent on friends to be physically with them. And of course, when they do finally meet up with their friends, they all keep their mobiles on. This provides a slightly superficial form of engagement that, rather than stopping them from noticing things as we suspect, in fact keeps them from <u>concentrating</u> on what's going on at the time. Interestingly, we did an experiment where we took some of their phones away from them. They really struggled and, although we hoped they would talk one to one more, an unexpected result was that their families said they noticed that they did <u>listen</u> whereas when they had their phones they never did!

Now the point about mobile communication, and especially texting, is that new ways round certain communicative strategies have to be found. What we might call conversation, which is effectively what a text exchange is, ends up being very tricky without the clues provided by <u>eye contact</u>, for example. And so this technology is enabling young people to build their own new politeness rules to allow for this and they are starting to create new possibilities and methods of <u>negotiating</u>. And don't believe they are as dependent on their phones as much as you think, or that their manners have gone out the window. In our survey the majority said that they didn't rely on their phones to make arrangements and 54 percent of young people will still <u>apologise</u> in person. Interestingly, they more likely to do so than any other age group.

Vocabulary 1 p.105

1

B	A	S	F	R	A	C	L	Y	C	L	E	L	L	Y
A	C	T	U	A	L	L	Y	I	V	T	R	I	O	B
S	L	E	N	P	V	N	O	L	E	Y	S	T	B	A
I	E	R	M	P	F	R	A	N	K	L	Y	E	A	R
C	A	Y	T	A	L	L	F	R	O	C	L	Y	S	Y
A	R	P	E	R	S	O	N	A	L	L	Y	F	C	E
L	L	R	S	E	I	O	B	Q	U	E	P	S	I	L
L	Y	E	D	N	A	C	I	V	A	L	Y	O	L	A
Y	I	S	O	T	M	P	R	T	I	C	K	L	Y	T
O	P	L	A	L	Y	S	U	R	P	O	B	A	R	C
A	N	Y	D	V	K	A	T	I	E	U	K	M	U	
S	F	U	L	T	G	S	E	S	T	L	Y	S	O	L
C	L	E	L	Y	C	L	R	L	S	A	X	S	L	L
E	L	D	Y	S	E	Y	T	Y	V	E	W	E	K	Y

2

expected	surprising	important	fortunate / unfortunate
unsurprisingly inevitably predictably typically	amazingly interestingly remarkably strangely	significantly	thankfully luckily regrettably disappointingly

3
1 strangely 1
2 regrettably 2
3 typically 1
4 unsurprisingly 2
5 thankfully 1
6 interestingly 2

4
1 we were talking at cross purposes
2 I got a real talking to
3 she had got hold of the wrong end of the stick
4 I couldn't make head nor tail of
5 I couldn't get a word in edgeways!
6 she always speaks her mind

Reading p.106

2 1 C 2 E 3 B 4 C 5 A } 6 C} in any order
7 A 8 E 9 B } 10 E } in any order
11 D 12 B 13 C 14 D 15 E

3 1 B 2 A 3 C 4 D 5 E

4 a) the underlying message
b) endemic
c) frictions
d) array
e) boasting
f) falling short of
g) nag
h) ventilation
i) banter
j) dynamic

Grammar 1 p.108

1 1 b 2 a 3 a 4 b

2 1 People choosing to study medicine are very committed.
2 Having applied early, I was disappointed not to be accepted.
3 It being so good, I read the book quickly.
4 Courses running this term start on Tuesday.
5 Having got the students to be silent, the lecturer started to speak.
6 Anyone wishing to join the book club should come along on Wednesday.

3 1 Their car having crashed, they couldn't get home.
2 People learning languages are offered more jobs.
3 Having lost his job, he went travelling abroad.
4 The library closing early, she had to leave.
5 Having completed her course, she decided to get a job.

Vocabulary 2 p.108

1 a) cool
b) busy
c) light
d) strong
e) quick
f) cold
g) free
h) white

2 1 like a tin of sardines
2 like a fish out of water
3 like a bullet
4 like a log
5 like a red rag to a bull
6 like cotton candy

3 1 C 2 A 3 B 4 D 5 C 6 C 7 A
8 B 9 C 10 B 11 A 12 D

Speaking p.109

I agree up to a point, but …
I completely disagree. ✓
I'm not sure if I agree. ✓
Actually, as a matter of fact. I think … ✓
You could be right, but … ✓
I'm afraid I don't agree.
That's an interesting idea, but …

Strongest
I completely disagree.

Weakest
You could be right, but …
I agree up to a point, but …

Tapescript

E: Do you think people communicate more nowadays or less?

F: I think more – before we just had the telephone at home and had to wait to see someone. Or even write a letter!

M: I'm not sure I agree. We still speak the same amount in a day. Maybe now we just talk to friends more.

F: You could be right, but before maybe we read or watched TV more – now we're talking and texting all day.

M: Actually as a matter of fact I think texting is not proper communication – it feels like it, but it's not really communicating. Normally you're just telling somebody something.

F: Oh, I completely disagree! It's all a connection with someone … (*fade*)

Grammar 2 p.110

1 ii) b   iii) a/d   iv) c   v) d   vi) a   vii) a/c
It is text type a because of the many uses of the passive.

2 1 **I am frequently asked** if parapsychology is recognised by universities.
2 **I had been warned** that revisiting the past may bring back some painful memories.
3 **References must be listed** at the end of an essay.
4 His sources **were questioned**.
5 **It is often said** that things were better in the 'good old days'.
6 **It has been thought** for some time that life on other planets is possible.

Use of English p.110

1 1 It has been decided **that the book will be published** this summer.
2 The principal **was said to be resigning** in the summer.
3 The **students were given an insight into** modern history by the lectures.
4 **A leaflet was issued by** the school telling students how to apply.
5 The exams **are being set by the school** in June.
6 Bilingual children **are thought to have been disadvantaged** in the past.
7 No **attention is paid to** children who fail at school.
8 A second language **should be taught to** everybody.

Writing p.111

2 1 a   2 b   3 b   4 a

3 The aim of this proposal is to suggest (d) a charity organisation which would benefit from having free mobile phones.

A very worthy charity organisation is KidsHelp. This is an organisation in my local school which looks after and helps kids who do not have the opportunity to do many things. It may be that (f) their parents do not have much money or maybe they have a lot of other children in their family. KidsHelp provides (a) them with time in the gymnasium where they can practise sports or get together to do other activities and it also takes the children out for the day during the holidays to local museums or beaches.

If we had some mobile phones this would help us enormously as we have no official office we can use on the school premises. We could use the phones to check up on children in their own homes and to find out where they are if they miss a session. Additionally, the phones would be very important when we are travelling for the day both to stay (e) in touch with the whole group and to allow children to speak to their parents while they are away, for example if we are delayed getting back.

I would strongly recommend that our organisation be given (c) the free phones as (b) it would improve our safety and security and make the parents feel more confident about letting the children come to us for activities and so on. Also it would allow us to make a range of calls seeking sponsorship for our charity, without having (g) to use our private numbers for this.

UNIT *14*

Reading p.112

1 a) action books
b) by asking them / a questionnaire / survey

2 1 C   2 G   3 A   4 F   5 D   6 E

3

1	A	B	<u>C</u>	D	E	F	G H
2	A	B	C	D	E	F	<u>G</u> H
3	<u>A</u>	B	C	D	E	F	G H
4	A	B	C	D	E	<u>F</u>	G H
5	A	B	C	<u>D</u>	E	F	G H
6	A	B	C	<u>D</u>	E	F	G H

Vocabulary 1 p.114

1

2 1 iii   2 vii   3 v   4 i   5 vi   6 viii   7 ii   8 iv

3 1 paints a picture   5 cliches
2 opens with   6 brims with
3 flashbacks   7 convincing
4 densely written   8 derivative

Speaking p.114

DO	DON'T
use a range of vocabulary and structures	speak as quickly as possible
listen to your partner	go back and correct yourself if you make a mistake
ask the examiner to repeat anything you don't understand	repeat your points
disagree with something said if you have a different view	

Listening p.115

1   1 A   2 B   3 C   4 A   5 B   6 C

2

Part 1			
1	**A**	B	C
2	A	**B**	C
3	A	B	**C**
4	**A**	B	C
5	A	**B**	C
6	A	B	**C**

3   1   throws up   4   mores
        2   put me off   5   hung out
        3   prolific

Tapescript

Extract One

M: John Grisham is a very prolific author – he seems to get a book out every year. And they are all set in the legal world. But I think *The Pelican Brief* is more enjoyable than his other novels.

F: In what way?

M: Well, in overlapping the legal world with politics I think he creates a momentum that draws the reader in. You can barely keep up but, nevertheless, you're dying to get to the denouement.

F: Yes, I enjoyed it and I do think it's different, as you say. Many of his stories do seem far-fetched – unless you like conspiracy theories – and I don't think this one is any exception. But there's something very appealing about Darcy, the female lawyer, and Gray, her partner, that makes you root for them – you want them to win. And also that theme of who you trust and how trust is established is, I think, one of Grisham's trademarks but is core to this novel.

M: Yes, it's certainly very enjoyable.

Extract Two

F: I'm quite happy to buy more books for you but I'm not going to spend money on endless computer games. You need to read more, especially if you want to do well in your exams.

M: Look, I just don't like reading that much. Anyway, I read magazines.

F: Oh (*exasperated*), boys always say that! I don't understand why teenage boys always have to hang out together all the time. The problem is, you all start doing sport and playing computer games with each other – you seem to be able to concentrate on those without any problem – and then you don't get any time on your own.

M: The thing is, I'm used to reading magazines now – I like the way they're laid out. Books always put me off because there's so much to wade through. Then, if you come across a new word, you have to go and look it up and I never remember them anyway cos it's not usually a word I'd use! Anyway, I do read textbooks at school …

Extract Three

M: Your paper has a whole separate section for book reviews, doesn't it? Do you not feel that books are a dying form?

F: (*laughs*) I think that's what a lot of people think now, and I'm sure they're right. Certainly no one can deny that the rise of the Internet and its possibilities have created problems for publishers. There's no doubt that the next generation will read in a different way and this has altered the view of publishers, who are looking at limited profits from traditional sales. They'll be looking more and more at publishing online and how they can make money there. We then have to ask ourselves what the role of the bookshop will be. Who knows?

M: But this won't affect the type of books published, will it?

F: I don't think so. Writing is affected by the social and cultural mores of the time, not how it is delivered.

M: I guess so, and each generation throws up its own writers, who I suppose may adapt their writing to new media?

F: There's only so far you can go down that route. Readers will still process information in the same way, so the need for a good plot won't change!

Grammar 1 p.116

1   a 2   b 5   c 1   d 4   e 3

2   1   'm getting / having / will get / have my hair cut
        2   get the letter written
        3   get your room tidied
        4   get / have my watch repaired
        5   get him to do
        6   get / have our house painted
        7   get my father to pay

Use of English p.116

1   1 packed   2 thrown   3 birth   4 kick   5 name

2

1	PACKED	1 0 u
2	THROWN	1 0 u
3	BIRTH	1 0 u
4	KICK	1 0 u
5	NAME	1 0 u

Vocabulary 2 p.116

1
1 boost c   increase a   maximise b
2 far-fetched b   unlikely a   inconceivable c
3 typically a   generally b   normally c
4 countless a   numerous b
5 coincidence b   luck a   chance c

2
1 boost   4 countless
2 far-fetched / inconceivable   5 coincidence
3 generally / typically

Use of English p.117

1
1 intellectual   2 specialist   3 rewardingly
4 beliefs   5 masterly   6 literary   7 perseverance
8 likelihood   9 unreadable   10 purposely

2
1 INTELLECTUAL
2 SPECIALIST
3 REWARDINGLY
4 BELIEFS
5 MASTERLY
6 LITERARY
7 PERSEVERANCE
8 LIKELIHOOD
9 UNREADABLE
10 PURPOSELY

Grammar 2 p.118

1
whether   necessary   receive   disappointing
choice   interesting   recommendation   believe
comfortable (correct)   require

2
The story in this book is a lot darker than the previous ones and opens up more possibilities for the storyline. Relationships are made so we understand the characters more, there are a few surprises and we learn a few things about Voldemorte. We also learn more about the characters' feelings towards each other; not that these weren't fairly clear through the previous few books.

However, the story isn't quite as enjoyable as the others, the humour seems to be a little darker and there is less action in this but this doesn't affect the book much overall. I loved it, although it seems to be orientated more towards older readers this time. I can't wait for the next book to come out next year. The questions and possibilities for the next book at the end of this one leave you waiting for more. Overall this is well worth reading.

3a Writing: Part 1 and Part 2
Use of English: Part 2, Part 3, Part 4, Part 5
Listening: Part 2

3b Writing: Part 1 and Part 2

Writing 1 p.118

2 Choosing a Part 2 question:

	topic vocabulary	grammar	functional language	task type
Question 2	Chosen collection, e.g. stamps	Past and present tenses, range of adjectives, modals	Describing, explaining, persuading/ justifying	Article: title, probably informal, rhetorical questions
Question 3	Shopping, buildings	Past and present tenses	Evaluating Giving opinion	Essay: clear logical thread, summary at conclusion, formal or unmarked
Question 4	Sports and fitness	Past tenses, conditionals, modals	Describing, suggesting, recommending	Report: headings, formal register

3 You must be able to do the grammar and vocabulary required by a question. If you include features of the genre or a good range of functional language you may get extra marks but you will not be able to pass if your answer does not demonstrate the appropriate grammar and vocabulary. Don't, for example, do the article or letter just because you think it is the genre you are most familiar with – you must be able to show a range of language relevant to the topic as well.

Practice exam

Paper 1 Reading

PART 1 1 D   2 B   3 C   4 B   5 C   6 A

PART 2 7 C   8 F   9 A   10 G   11 B   12 E

PART 3 13 D   14 A   15 C   16 A   17 B
18 D   19 B

PART 4 20 B   21 B   22 C   23 E   24 A   25 E   26 D
27 A   28 B   29 C   30 D   31 D   32 C   33 E
34 A

Paper 3 Use of English

PART 1 1 D   2 B   3 C   4 A   5 B   6 B   7 C   8 D
9 D   10 A   11 B   12 C

PART 2

13 been	18 once / when	23 how
14 your	19 which / that	24 if / though
15 about	20 them	25 not
16 it	21 into	26 will
17 thanks	22 by	27 could

PART 3

28 daily	32 encouraging	35 warmth
29 rejection	33 posture	36 powerful
30 unhelpful	34 proud	37 strengthen
31 ideally		

PART 4

38 terms	40 corner	42 race
39 step	41 ice	

PART 5

43 I realised **after I had broken up with** him that I missed him.
44 **Never before had I seen** such a wonderful painting.
45 I **regret to say that** we are unable to help.
46 I **wouldn't have been late if** I hadn't lost my keys.
47 She was **having second thoughts about taking** the job.
48 I**'m / am not to blame for** the problem.
49 He **was thought to have been living** in Canada.
50 His wallet **must have been stolen.**

Paper 4 Listening

PART 1 1 B   2 C   3 A   4 C   5 C   6 A

PART 2

7 sponsor	11	musicians
8 brochure	12	metals
9 projects	13	rainwater / rain water
10 (local) experts	14	cabinets

PART 3 15 C   16 D   17 A   18 B   19 A   20 D

PART 4 21 D   22 B   23 F   24 E   25 H   26 C   27 F
28 H   29 E   30 G

Paper 4 Listening

PART 1

Extract One

You will hear part of an interview with a biologist who has just returned from Chile.

F: You've done research in other desert areas, so did you find any aspects of the Atacama Desert surprising?

M: Yes, actually, I did. Death Valley had accustomed me to the fact that although we think of desert as sand, in fact it has mountains and valleys and different colour rocks in it so, although this variety was much more apparent in Atacama, I was prepared for it. Unlike the weather, which only differed by about ten degrees between morning and night when I was there. In fact, some people find it amazing that such a variety of plants can grow in that.

F: And do you plan to go back?

M: I'd love to – but I don't see it happening in the near future, as I have to write up the papers from my research. But they're struggling to maintain plant growth at the higher levels in the desert and I'd be interested to know why, so that might take me back. The problem is there are always new deserts and new plants to look at in other regions, so it's a question of fitting it in.

Extract Two

You will hear two people talking about a problem with a bank.

M: I've decided to close my savings account at my old bank and I'm going to invest the money instead.

F: Are you sure that's a good idea?

M: Yeah. I'm fed up with them – they've got so few branches you'd think they'd be able to keep an eye on things, but they always seem to mess up. I'm always having to correct things. I know their interest rates are fairly competitive, but I'm not sure it's worth it for the hassle. I can make the same on the stock market.

F: Well, I think you should think again. I'm not sure I really understand why you're doing it. It's no good just getting cross – you should go in and see them. You may be making a mistake and you could lose a lot of money – but I guess that's your concern. But I don't really see how closing down your account is going to be to your advantage.

Extract Three

You will hear part of an interview with a champion tennis player called Mark Bevan.

F: Mark, hi. Thank you for talking to us today – and congratulations on your win. Did you ever think you'd get this far in tennis?

M: (*laughs*) No, I never used to take it that seriously. In fact, if I hadn't been offered the chance to go to college all expenses paid, I don't think I'd be here. I had to play for the team, so it gave me the opportunity to hone my competition skills, which is a very important aspect of the game. I know a lot of my fellow players have gone to specialist schools, but I'm glad I got here the hard way.

F: So you don't approve of very young children being trained for the game?

M: Look, club tennis is fine, but these days kids get involved in being seriously competitive far too young. They're pushed by their parents who oversee their training but don't bother controlling any other aspect of their lives. And they have to study as they're playing – it's no way to live. I was happy to see more rules governing children's competitions come in, but the tennis organisations can't do the parents' job.

PART 2

You will hear a photojournalist called Angus MacDonald talking about a trip he made recently. For questions 7–14, complete the sentences.

Presenter: Today we are going to hear from Angus MacDonald, a photojournalist who recently went on a fabulous assignment along the Silk Road across central Asia. Angus.

Angus: Thank you. Yes, today I'm going to tell you about my recent trip to some of the most remote areas of the world. It was the kind of assignment every photographer dreams of. Last September, completely unexpectedly, I was contacted by this charity and asked if I would be interested in travelling to virtually every country in South and Central Asia. Normally, as a reporter, the newspaper paid for my trips, but in this case the charity said they had a sponsor who would fund the whole thing. I was delighted. Obviously the trip had an objective – the charity gives money to support the preservation of art all around the world, normally in areas that don't really have the spare finance to do this. My work was to create a brochure to highlight the charity's work and encourage people to apply for grants to preserve important artistic works.

So, between October and December I travelled to eleven countries – a fantastic trip. What I was doing during this eight-week period was visiting organisations which were already receiving funding from the charity and documenting twenty-four projects. The money had been used for a wide variety of things and this range was what the charity wanted to advertise. It was a fascinating trip. And I was very well looked after – I didn't have to travel alone but was instead accompanied in each region by local experts. Their job was to fill me in on each of the important works being preserved.

Often we were miles off the beaten track in very remote areas that had been key posts in the past, hence all the art that was there. And there were some amazing highlights – it wasn't all about visiting dusty museums. For example, one highlight was when we witnessed a wonderful moonlit show given by a group of wandering musicians who played on ancient instruments – a real lost art. And of course, I got to photograph some incredible pieces of art. I think the experience that sticks most in my mind was taking photographs of all the metals in the state museum in Kyrgyzstan. In the basement there was also a series of wonderful gold objects and then upstairs were some previously uncovered murals, which were badly affected by rainwater. This is exactly the sort of thing the charity is trying to help preserve, so the work has been very successful there. When the restoration work the museum is doing at the moment is completed, all these objects will be put into custom-built cabinets, which are secure and climate controlled in order to preserve the objects, and then the Kyrgyz people will be able to see them for the first time.

PART 3

You will hear part of a radio interview in which John Tulsa, a lecturer in business studies, is talking about motivation. For questions 15–20, choose the answer (A, B, C or D) which fits best according to what you hear.

I: Have you ever started out with great enthusiasm on the road to achieve an important goal and, after several months or even years, found that you are not much closer to your goal? Well, our expert in the studio today to talk about this is John Tulsa. John, isn't it true that most of us are distracted by something and this is why we don't achieve our goals?

J: Yes, distraction is probably the cause, but we need to look at why – in other words, what are the effects of this distraction. All kinds of distractions are thrown at the person who is trying to concentrate on their main priorities in life. For example, when I was at school, I worked hard at every subject except two or three where I was too easily distracted by talkative friends. In other words, I should've had the wisdom to concentrate or focus my mind on what we were supposed to be studying. However, most of the issues of distraction can be resolved if we take control of ourselves and take steps to avoid paying attention to things that don't matter and are not part of the task in hand.

I: And of course we have to motivate ourselves to work hard as well, don't we, to achieve our goals.

J: In fact, hard work itself leads to greater motivation because the more you work at something, the better you get and becoming good at doing something is a great motivator. You may, of course, have to primarily focus on the activity or skill in question for half a year or more. But hopefully, you will eventually begin to enjoy the increasing level of skill you're achieving and this will motivate you to put in even more concentrated effort and to focus on developing your abilities further. You'll always reach a time when you have to force yourself to work at what you're not that good at and this is not easy. But you have to keep going.

I: And are people who are successful – the so-called experts – keen to pass on their tips on motivation?

J: Yes. Unfortunately, most of us actually have to work very hard to achieve our goals. But this is not something which is usually mentioned by the so-called motivational 'experts'! I notice that these gurus, who make millions and then tell you how easy it all was, do seem to forget about what a struggle it was. Perhaps they're so used to working hard that they start believing that the work involved in their success was minimal and so not worth mentioning. Or, possibly, the pleasure of the rewards which have followed their hard work has made them forget the hard grind which they endured before the rewards started to arrive.

I: So, is it really all one long, hard grind – no relaxation?

J: No, once you have put in the focus, time and effort needed to develop the skills you desire, you will no longer need as much motivation as before. Your own skill, self-confidence and new self-image will create a self-renewing fountain of motivation. This means you'll be able to relax more and relaxed effort is usually more productive than tense effort. You'll have an image of yourself as a hard-working expert who's able to resist all manner of distractions and overcome all manner of problems and obstacles.

I: And is it important to develop that positive image of yourself?

J: Yes – if you can focus on one project until it is completed, you'll feel a sense of achievement and develop the kind of confidence and determination which will help you to focus on your next project and complete that as well. This will create a clear distinction between your old self-image and your new victorious self-image. Aim high so that your new image of yourself will be that of a winner who is top of the class in everything you do. Get up early or stay late if necessary and do more than you are asked to do instead of complaining about how much you have to do.

I: So, do you need more or less motivation as you become more successful?

J: Once you believe in yourself and have a new self-image, you'll be able to work harder and with greater intelligence. You'll start to enjoy the respect and admiration of others. Once you have that respect, you'll be motivated to work even harder to keep it. You'll no longer need as much motivation because you'll know what it feels like to be a success and you won't want to lose that. The memory of that feeling may be enough to motivate you for years to come. Add focus and hard work to that strong self-image and you will have a recipe for success and for the motivation that usually accompanies success.

I: John, thank you … *(fade)*

PART 4

Part 4 consists of two tasks. You'll hear five short extracts in which people are talking about their work in a museum. Look at Task 1. For questions 21–25, choose the person who is speaking from the list A–H. Now look at Task 2. For questions 26–30, choose the opinion each speaker expresses from the list A–H. While you listen you must complete both tasks.

Speaker 1

I find doing all the physically hard bits, like unloading things and putting stuff on shelves, wearing, but generally I enjoy my job because I like being with people. And there are busy and quiet times so we're not always rushed off our feet – people generally go round the museum first, then come here. In fact, I wouldn't mind running things myself, so if the manager leaves I'll put myself forward as I can't do this for ever. It would probably give me a more flexible work schedule, but I think I can handle that. I would definitely enjoy having more input.

Speaker 2

My job can be quite tiring at times because you have to answer so many questions and to be honest some of them are a bit daft. If people don't know where they're going or they lose something, then they come to me and we give out information on the other museums nearby. You might think the work's a bit boring but we're usually rushed off our feet, but at least that makes the time pass quickly. I'm not sure I could do a routine nine-to-five job now because every day is different. I love my work because it's about solving problems for our visitors, so you generally get a lot of job satisfaction.

Speaker 3

I'm responsible for making sure nothing breaks down so that the kids can get the most out of the museum – but I don't actually have much contact with the children. The guides let us know when something has gone wrong and often I'm working night shifts when the museum is closed to get it sorted, but you just get into a pattern. We're supposed to keep a record of everything we do and file it before we leave, but I'm hopeless. It's not what I joined the museum to do – I'm a very hands-on person and I think they should have an administrator to do that.

Speaker 4

I've done this sort of work for years and the museum is better than some places that I have worked. The visitors are usually quite nice and don't expect you to clear up after them and I think our prices are quite reasonable. We have children's stuff as well so that's popular. Thing is, they're trying to cut costs so we're running on a skeleton staff and we can never get everything ready in time so in that sense it's rather stressful as I feel we can only do our job properly if we work over our set hours and I don't like doing that.

Speaker 5

I've worked in the museum for about two years now and I think I've been successful as our visitor numbers have gone up. Mind you, I have a very good boss – he's always out there showing people around and drumming up business. And it's a rather cushy job – we don't work to a set timetable as sometimes we have evening events, especially if we have a big promotion. And it's a very sociable job – in fact, I get really fed up if things calm down and nothing's happening. It's a bad sign as we should be on the go the whole time if we're doing our job properly.

Paper 5 Speaking

PART 1

First of all, we'd like to know something about you.
Where are you from? [*bleep*]

How long have you lived here? [*bleep*]
What do you like about studying English? [*bleep*]
Do you enjoy playing sport? Why or why not? [*bleep*]
Do you prefer learning in a group or on your own? [*bleep*]
What are you hoping to do in the future? [*bleep*]
Can you tell us what kind of holidays you enjoy? [*bleep*]
What do you like doing at weekends? [*bleep*]

PART 2

In this part of the test, I'm going to give you each three pictures. I'd like you to talk about two of them on your own for about a minute and also to answer a question briefly about your partner's pictures.
Candidate A, it's your turn first. Here are your pictures. They show people in the natural world. I'd like you to compare two of the pictures and say what different aspects of seeing wild animals they show and how the people might be feeling.

All right?
[*bleep*] [*bleep*]
Thank you.
Candidate A, which picture do you think shows the best way of seeing wild animals?
[*bleep*]
Thank you.
Now, candidate B, here are your pictures. They show people watching sports. I'd like you to compare two of the pictures and say what different aspects of watching sports they show and how the people might be feeling.

All right?
[*bleep*] [*bleep*]
Thank you.
Candidate A, which picture do you think shows the best way of watching sports?
[*bleep*]
Thank you.

PARTS 3 AND 4

Now I'd like you to talk about something together for about three minutes. Here are some pictures showing the different ways that people live. First, talk to each other about the different ways of living these pictures show. Then, decide which picture best shows the most difficult way to live.

All right?
[*bleep*]
Thank you.

Do you think that where we live is important to us? Why or why not? [*bleep*]
What are the advantages of living with very few possessions? [*bleep*]
How do you think the way we live will change in the future? [*bleep*]
Would you prefer to live with lots of people or on your own? Why? [*bleep*]
Do you think that governments should build houses for people who can't afford them? [*bleep*]